WOMEN AND THE PAMPHLET CULTURE
OF REVOLUTIONARY ENGLAND,
1640–1660

Women and Gender in the Early Modern World

Series Editors: Allyson Poska and Abby Zanger

In the past decade, the study of women and gender has offered some of the most vital and innovative challenges to scholarship on the early modern period. Ashgate's new series of interdisciplinary and comparative studies, 'Women and Gender in the Early Modern World', takes up this challenge, reaching beyond geographical limitations to explore the experiences of early modern women and the nature of gender in Europe, the Americas, Asia, and Africa. Submissions of single-author studies and edited collections will be considered.

Titles in this series include:

Women and the Pamphlet Culture of Revolutionary England, 1640–1660

MARCUS NEVITT
University of Sheffield

ASHGATE

Published by
Ashgate Publishing Limited
Gower House
Croft Road
Aldershot
Hampshire GU11 3HR
England

Ashgate Publishing Company
Suite 420
101 Cherry Street
Burlington, VT 05401-4405
USA

Ashgate website: http://www.ashgate.com

British Library Cataloguing in Publication Data
Nevitt, Marcus.
Women and the pamphlet culture of revolutionary England, 1640-1660. - (Women and gender in the early modern world)
    1.English literature – Early modern, 1500-1700 – History and criticism 2.Women political activists – England – History – 17th century 3.Politics and literature – England – History – 17th century 4.English literature – Early modern, 1500-1700 – Women authors 5.Women – England – Intellectual life – 17th century 6.Women and religion – England – History – 17th century 7.Women in literature 8.Great Britain – History – Commonwealth and Protectorate, 1649-1660 – Pamphlets 9.Great Britain – History – Charles I, 1625-1649 – Pamphlets
    I.Title
    828.4'08099287

Library of Congress Cataloging-in-Publication Data
Nevitt, Marcus.
  Women and the pamphlet culture of revolutionary England, 1640-1660 / by Marcus Nevitt.
    p. cm. — (Women and gender in the early modern world)
  Includes bibliographical references and index.
  ISBN 0-7546-4115-5 (alk. paper)
    1. Great Britain—History—Puritan Revolution, 1642-1660—Historiography. 2. English prose literature—Early modern, 1500-1700—History and criticism. 3. English prose literature—Women authors—History and criticism. 4. Politics and literature—Great Britain—History—17th century. 5. Pamphlets—Publishing—Great Britain—History—17th century. 6. Women and literature—Great Britain— History—17th century. 7. Women in politics—Great Britain—History—17th century. 8. Political science—Great Britain—History—17th century. 9. Women—Great Britain—Intellectual life— 17th century. 10. Pamphleteers—Great Britain—History—17th century. 11. Pamphlets—Authorship— History—17th century. I. Title. II. Series.

DA403.N48 2006
941.06'2082—dc22

ISBN-10: 0 7546 4115 5

2005026512

Printed and bound in Great Britain by MPG Books Ltd, Bodmin, Cornwall

Contents

List of Figures

List of Abbreviations

Bod	Bodleian Library, Oxford
BL	British Library, London
CPW	*Complete Prose Works of John Milton*, 8 vols., gen. ed. Don M. Wolfe (New Haven, CN, 1953–83)
CSPD	*Calendar of State Papers, Domestic*
DNB	*Dictionary of National Biography*
Harl. MS	Harleian Manuscripts
OED	*Oxford English Dictionary*
PMLA	*Publications of the Modern Language Association*
PRO	Public Record Office, London
SEL	*Studies in English Literature*
SP	State Papers
Wing	Donald Wing, *Short-Title Catalogue of Books Printed in England, Scotland, Ireland, Wales and British America and of English Books printed in Other Countries 1641–1700*, 3 vols (New York, 1972–94)

Acknowledgements

It seems entirely appropriate in a project about multiple and concealed agencies that I begin by writing about the other people lurking behind this work. It was my great good fortune, as an undergraduate, to be taught by David Norbrook. The field of early modern studies would be much poorer without his presence and I know that without his encouragement and honesty, this book (along with countless others) would never have been ventured. My doctoral supervisor, Rachel Falconer, was the model of everything a supervisor should be.

Over the past few years numerous others have also signposted me in the right direction. Frances Babbage, Mike Braddick, Eliane Glaser, Mark Greengrass, Lorna Hutson, Robert Jones, Claire Jowitt, Hamish Mathison, Michael Mendle, Anthony Milton, Sue Owen, Joad Raymond, Andrew Rettman and Sue Wiseman have all read and commented on sections of the arguments in the book. Conversations with Sarah Barber, Andy Gordon, Laura Gowing, Paul Hammond, Tom Lockwood, Erica Sheen, Brendan Stone and Malcolm Thomas have done much to reshape my thoughts about this material. Any errors that remain have nothing to do with them. Erika Gaffney at Ashgate was patience itself and the anonymous reader did much to ensure that what follows is better than it otherwise might have been.

The task of research has been made inestimably easier by the kind assistance of the staff at the following libraries and archives: the Angus Library, the Bodleian Library, the British Library, the Brotherton Library, Cambridge University Library, Friends House Library, the John Rylands Library, the Public Record Office, the University of Sheffield Library, and the University of Minnesota Library.

Different versions of some of the arguments in these pages appear elsewhere as 'John Selden Among the Quakers' in Lorna Hutson and Erica Sheen (eds.), *Literature, Politics and Law in Renaissance England* (Basingtoke: Palgrave Macmillan, 2005), pp. 189–208; 'Elizabeth Poole Writes the Regicide', *Women's Writing* 9:1 (2002), pp. 233–248; 'Women in the Business of Revolutionary News: Elizabeth Alkin, "Parliament Joan", and the Commonwealth Newsbook', in Joad Raymond (ed.), *News, Newspapers and Early Modern Britain* (London: Frank Cass, 1999), pp. 84–108; <http://www.tandf.co.uk>. I am grateful to the publishers for permissions.

The debts I've amassed over the course of the project aren't simply academic. Thanks also, therefore, to Asif Boda, Steve Harmston, Rowland Hughes, Tarek

Iskander, Sam Leith, Ian McCarthy, Andrew Nevitt, Luke Perry, Ivan Stein, Matthew Turner, Conal Walsh and Sarah Wood for their friendship and spare beds. At earlier stages, the doctoral research was funded by the Centre for Early Modern Studies at the University of Sheffield and the generosity of my grandparents Mary and Gerard Lymer. Without the support of Frances Babbage, I doubt that the book would have appeared at all.

Finally, an inexpressible amount of gratitude is due to my parents David and Janet Nevitt. They have spent the bulk of their working lives striving to give me chances they never had. No number of words can convey my thanks; eighty-odd thousand isn't even close.

Introduction

Women's Agency and Early Modern Pamphlet Culture

Women and the Pamphlet Culture of Revolutionary England is a study of agency. More specifically, it offers a series of case studies of the ways in which groups of non-aristocratic women responded to an assortment of assumptions about (and interdictions or prohibitions against) female participation in the pamphlet culture of revolutionary England. This may seem a curious enterprise since pamphlets, and pamphlet culture more generally, have frequently been located amongst the most inclusive or democratic aspects of early modern English society. Milton's vision of a freeborn English people was famously based upon an emancipated readership, citizens whose inalienable democratic rights were best expressed through the ability to read pamphlets freed from the tyranny of pre-publication licensing. In a passage that pledges a belief in the potential of the popular political imagination he maintains:

> Nor is it to the common people lesse than a reproach; for if we be so jealous over them, as that we dare not trust them with an English pamphlet, what doe we but censure them for a giddy, vitious, and ungrounded people; in such a sick and weak estate of faith and discretion as to be able to take nothing down but through the pipe of a licenser.[1]

More recent readers have shed light on the ways in which these short, unbound books were read and penned by artisans and aristocrats, republicans and royalists, radicals and conservatives alike.[2] The first pamphlet historian, Myles Davies,

---

[1] John Milton, *Areopagitica*, in *CPW*, vol. 2, pp. 536–7.

[2] In the early modern period the term 'pamphlet' was as pejorative word rather than precise bibliographical category. 'Pamphleteer' could be a term of abuse for the sixteenth- or seventeenth-century writer seeking to assert the respectability of himself and his text alongside the meanness and triviality of his opponent. Similarly, a writer could refer to her own lengthy text as a mere 'pamphlet' in order to perform a familiar humility *topos*. In referring above to pamphlets as 'short unbound books', I follow Joad Raymond's useful working definition of them as short, stitched (rather than bound) quarto books of no more than 96 pages – 96 pages representing the maximum that the Stationers' Company, in an attempt to protect the interests of bookbinders, allowed for books which could be sold. See

writing at the start of the eighteenth century, reflected on their ubiquity and the manner in which their inexpensiveness had led to the cultivation of opinion at all points on the social scale:

> From pamphlets may be learned the Genius of the Age, the Debates of the Learned, the Follies of the Ignorant, ... the Oversights of Statesmen, the Mistakes of Courtiers; ... in *Pamphlets*, Merchants may read their Profit and Loss, Shopkeepers their Bills of Parcels, Country-men their Seasons, ... Sailors their Longitude, Soldiers their Camps and Enemies; thence School-boys may improve their Lessons, Scholars their Studies, Ministers their Sermons, and Zealots their Devisions. *Pamphlets* furnish Beau's [sic] with their Airs, Coquets with their Charms: Pamphlets are as Modish Ornaments to Gentlewomen's Toylets as to Gentleman's Pockets: Pamphlets carry reputation of Wit and Learning to all that make them their companions: The Poor find their account in Stalling, and in hawking them: The Rich find in them their Shortest Way to the Secrets of Church and State. In fine, there's scarce any degree of people but may think themselves interested enough to be concerned with what is published in Pamphlets ... Pamphlets are too often over familiar and free.[3]

Davies's reading of the early pamphlet's promiscuity, its shameless tendency to traffic intelligence, apparent sophistication and rumour, whilst breaching all manner of social and generic boundaries, has been developed by modern commentators who have analyzed the ways in which it 'dissolv[ed] ... systems of classification or opposition'.[4] Sharon Achinstein has argued that 'the literature of the civil wars was new in that pamphleteers fused the techniques of pre-existing low genres with openly political argument' with the effect that they 'brought political debates from behind the closed doors of parliamentary chambers into the

---

Joad Raymond, *Pamphlets and Pamphleteering in Early Modern Britain* (Cambridge, 2003), p. 82.

[3]   Myles Davies, *Eikon mikro-biblike: sive, Icon libellorum, or; A Critical History of Pamphlets* (London, 1715), pp. 2–3.

[4]   Alexandra Halasz, *The Marketplace of Print: Pamphlets and the Public Sphere in Early Modern England* (Cambridge, 1997), p. 7. Other recent discussions of the pamphlet culture of seventeenth-century England are Raymond, *Pamphlets and Pamphleteering*; James Holstun, *Ehud's Dagger: Class Struggle in the English Revolution* (New York, 2000); Dagmar Freist, *Governed By Opinion: Politics, Religion, and the Dynamics of Communication in Stuart London, 1637–1645* (London, 1997); Joad Raymond, *The Invention of the Newspaper: English Newsbooks 1641–1649*, (Oxford, 1996); Sharon Achinstein, *Milton and the Revolutionary Reader* (Princeton, 1994); Nigel Smith, *Literature and Revolution in England 1640–1660* (New Haven and London, 1994); James Holstun (ed.), *Pamphlet Wars: Prose in the English Revolution* (London and Portland, 1992); Elizabeth Skerpan, *The Rhetoric of Politics in the English Revolution 1642–1660* (Columbia, MI, 1992); Thomas Corns, *Uncloistered Virtue: English Political Literature, 1640–1660* (Oxford, 1992); Sandra Clark, *The Elizabethan Pamphleteers: Popular Moralistic Pamphlets 1580–1640* (London, 1983).

noisy, dusty, crowded street'.[5] Achinstein's readings of revolutionary pamphlet culture have been extremely influential in siting the emergence of the public sphere in a mid-seventeenth-century rather than an eighteenth-century context. If 'the swell of pamphlets in the press indicates that many ordinary citizens were willing [and able] ... to participate in the political life of the nation', then the classic Habermasian model of the 'structural transformation of the public sphere' clearly needs some modification.[6] A number of early modernists have joined Achinstein in this move. Alexandra Halasz, too, has looked at the ways in which pamphlets relocated participatory politics onto more inclusive, 'crowded' street levels. She usefully accounts for pamphlets' democratizing force by theorizing that:

> pamphlets are – in the abstract – ubiquitous and polymorphous, they imply a generalized access to the circulation of printed discourse and thus open up the social space that will come to be conceptualized as the public sphere. At the same time, they imbue that nascent sphere with ambivalence about the loss of social distinction that generalized access suggests.[7]

With pamphlets instrumental in robbing social spaces of their distinction, it should come as no surprise, therefore, to discover their importance to seventeenth-century revolutionary politics. Nigel Smith uncovers this in his seminal study of the interdependence of political and generic revolution in the seventeenth century. In demonstrating how times of civil war were also times of pamphlet war he maintains:

---

[5]   Achinstein, *Milton and the Revolutionary Reader*, p. 11.
[6]   Sharon Achinstein, 'Women on Top in the Pamphlet Literature of Revolutionary England', *Women's Studies* 24 (1994), pp. 131–63, p. 154. Throughout this study I follow Achinstein's Habermasian definition of the public sphere as the place 'in which participatory political processes and the media, along with social and cultural institutions coalesced to make it possible for the public to become the basis for politics'; ibid., p. 155. For other studies of pamphlet culture which shift Habermas's eighteenth-century bourgeois public sphere into earlier periods see David Zaret, *Origins of Democratic Culture: Printing, Petitions, and the Public Sphere in Early Modern England* (Princeton, 2000); Joad Raymond, 'The Newspaper, Public Opinion, and the Public Sphere in the Seventeenth Century' in idem., *News, Newspapers and Society in Early Modern Britain* (London and Portland, 1999), pp. 109–40; Susan Wiseman, *Drama and Politics in the English Civil War* (Cambridge, 1998), pp. 35–8; Steve Pincus, '"Coffee Politicians Does Create": Coffeehouses and Restoration Political Culture', *Journal of Modern History* 67 (1995), pp. 807–34; David Norbrook, ' *Areopagitica*, Censorship, and the Early Modern Public Sphere', in Richard Burt (ed.), *The Administration of Aesthetics: Censorship, Political Criticism and the Public Sphere* (Minneapolis and London, 1994), pp. 3–33; David Zaret, 'Religion, Science, and Printing in the Public Spheres of Seventeenth-Century England', in Craig Calhoun (ed.), *Habermas and the Public Sphere* (Cambridge, MA, 1992), pp. 212–35.
[7]   Halasz, *The Marketplace of Print*, p. 4.

In that all but the poorest now had the possibility of authorship, we can say that the
English Revolution was more thorough going in the extension of the possession and
use of words than it was in property distribution.[8]

Pamphlets have thus been placed centrally in the vanguard of a cultural and textual
egalitarianism.

The riches unearthed by these pioneering critics cannot be overestimated.
What follows, however, is an attempt to construct a more gender-sensitive picture.
Two related arguments are implied throughout. First, that the rhetoric of inclusivity
and democratization which has characterized most writing about the pamphlet
frequently conceals the material and rhetorical barriers that women encountered
when participating in revolutionary pamphlet culture. Second, that the academic
disciplinary divides which lurk behind many of the more modern studies of
women's writing in mid-seventeenth-century Britain have also tended to produce
only partial, blurred, or anachronistic pictures of female agency. Whereas the vast
majority of literary approaches to cheaply printed women's writing have offered
vital, illuminating readings of pamphlets' verbal strategies and rhetorical qualities,
it has too frequently been left to the historian of early modern print culture to
adumbrate the material circumstances which enabled the transformation of
women's rhetoric into cheaply printed text.[9] For example, in a recent and insightful
literary study Katharine Gillespie urges us to take 'stock of *the rhetorical devices*
these writers used to open up and structure new, potentially antipatriarchal
conceptualisations of political and religious authority'.[10] Before her, Hilary Hinds
scrutinized the verbal styles of women's pamphlet writing in minute detail in order
to sound a feminist counterblast to traditional definitions of English literature.[11]
Women and the Pamphlet Culture of Revolutionary England, however, maintains
that reading stylistic or verbal features in isolation risks transforming agency into a
privilege of the rhetorically gifted or prophetically inspired and denies it to those
innumerable other women who were engaged in different varieties of goal-oriented
action but have been effaced (or effaced themselves) from the historical record.
Therefore in what follows I aim to pay attention to women's involvement in
revolutionary pamphlet culture at the levels of both practice and utterance, doing

---

[8]   Smith, *Literature and Revolution*, p. 6.

[9]   For some authoritative accounts of women's material involvement in early modern print
culture see Freist, *Governed By Opinion*; Maureen Bell 'Hannah Allen and the Development
of a Puritan Publishing Business 1646–1651', *Publishing History* 26 (1989), pp. 5–66;
idem., 'Mary Westwood, Quaker Publisher', *Publishing History* 23 (1988), pp. 5–66; idem.,
'Women Publishers of Puritan Literature in the Mid-Seventeenth Century: Three Case
Studies', unpublished Ph.D. thesis (Loughborough, 1987). See also Raymond, *Pamphlets
and Pamphleteering*, pp. 276-322.

[10]   Katharine Gillespie, *Domesticity and Dissent in the Seventeenth Century: English
Women Writers and the Public Sphere* (Cambridge, 2004), p. 12; emphasis added.

[11]   Hilary Hinds, *God's Englishwomen: Seventeenth-Century Radical Sectarian Writing
and Feminist Criticism* (Manchester and New York, 1996), p. 17.

and speaking, work and text. If, as I will demonstrate, this interdisciplinary approach is concordant with many early modern women's senses of their own agency, it also follows the lead set by a number of current accounts of Quaker women's writing which endeavour just such a bridging of the disciplinary divide.[12] Crucially, however, the different backgrounds and affiliations of the non-aristocratic women in the coming chapters ought to indicate that I do not associate female agency with a particular political position; it *can* but need not always be the site of resistance to and contestation of hegemonic discourse.

There has, however, been a general tendency in some important analyses of early modern women's writing to conflate agency with either radical action or a specific political programme. For instance, Gillespie's account of the rhetoric of some of the sectarian women who feature later in this study presents them as strident matriarchs of liberalism who 'began the process of building a "feminist theory of the state" which, in order to recognise a woman's right to preach and prophesy, rested on a necessary separation of a private sphere of individual and group-based self-determination from a public government sphere of patriarchal domination.'[13] These very same women have, elsewhere, been presented as the mothers of modern feminism. In a trailblazing account of Quaker women pamphleteers, Phyllis Mack contends that 'we can trace a direct line from the earliest Quaker women leaders to the nineteenth-century movements of abolition and women's suffrage and to twentieth-century feminism and peace activism'.[14] From this perspective it would seem that women's agency is absolutely reliant on a transhistorical narrative of feminist solidarity. A similar alliance is pressed in Hilary Hinds's *God's Englishwomen: Seventeenth-Century Radical Sectarian Writing and Feminist Criticism*. Through her provocative interleaving of early modern radical women's pamphlets and twentieth-century feminist texts, Hinds alerted her readers to the ways in which both the sectarians and theorists she studied engaged in 'radical transformation'.[15] Her book thus brings the different work of 'women [who] challenged existing authority and questioned long-standing beliefs' into productive dialogue with each other.[16] Once again, individual, historically specific moments of agency are put into the service of a longstanding, collective feminist solidarity.

To equate agency with radical action, however, potentially marginalizes or ignores the activity of those innumerable women who worked towards less spectacular, all-consuming goals such as sustaining businesses, households and families. This book, in contrast, maintains that agency can be traced in the

---

[12] See, for instance, Kate Peters, *Print Culture and the Early Quakers* (Cambridge, 2005); Catie Gill, *Women in the Seventeenth-Century Quaker Community* (Aldershot, 2005).

[13] Gillespie, *Domesticity and Dissent*, p. 66.

[14] Phyllis Mack, *Visionary Women: Ecstatic Prophecy in Seventeenth-Century England* (Berkeley and Los Angeles, 1992), p. 9.

[15] Hinds, *God's Englishwomen*, p. 1.

[16] Ibid.

quotidian struggle for bread as much as in more spectacularly public or radical female acts. In doing so it chimes with those post-Foucauldian theories of agency that have demonstrated the inability of dominant Western feminist models – structured around a familiar opposition of oppression and resistance – to account for social change.[17] Judith Butler, for instance, has recently scrutinized the ways in which 'the subject might yet be thought as deriving its agency from precisely the power it opposes, as awkward and embarrassing as [this] might be, especially for those who believe that complicity and ambivalence could be rooted out once and for all'.[18] In a very different context Arlene Elowe MacLeod has reminded us that:

> women always play an active part that goes beyond the dichotomy of victimization/ acceptance, a dichotomy that flattens out a complex and ambiguous agency in which women accept, accommodate, ignore, resist, or protest – sometimes all at the same time ... [We must] think beyond the dichotomies of victim/actor and passive/powerful toward the more complicated ways that consciousness is structured and agency embodied in power relations.[19]

The following case studies each respond to this imperative. By dealing with both rhetoric (in chapters 1, 2 and 4) and material culture (in chapters 3 and 5) this study attends to the ways in which revolutionary pamphlet culture was dependent upon multiple and frequently concealed agencies; it proceeds through the analysis of the writings and milieus of a number of seventeenth-century women who worked for particular ends with moveable type. It begins, however, with a woman talking in bed in a Whitehall tavern.

Trancing It at Whitehall: The Performances and Prophecies of Anna Trapnel

Early in January 1654, less than a month after Oliver Cromwell was pronounced England's Lord Protector, the Council of State spent the day examining the Welsh radical and notorious millenarian preacher Vavasor Powell. Powell, aghast at the

---

[17] See, for example, Terry Lovell, 'Resisting With Authority: Historical Specificity, Agency and the Performative Self', *Theory, Culture and Society* 20:1 (2003), pp. 1–17. For an encyclopaedic account of the ways in which modern theorists have constructed agency see Lois McNay, *Gender and Agency: Reconfiguring the Subject in Feminist and Social Theory* (Cambridge, 2000); Judith Kegan Gardiner (ed.), *Provoking Agents: Gender and Agency in Theory and Practice* (Urbana and Chicago, 1995).

[18] Judith Butler, *The Psychic Life of Power: Theories in Subjection* (Stanford, 1997), p. 17. For a critique of Butler's theories of agency see Lois McNay, 'Agency, Anticipation and Indeterminacy in Feminist Theory', *Feminist Theory* 4:2 (2003), pp. 139–48; idem., 'Subject, Psyche and Agency: The Work of Judith Butler', in V. Bell (ed.), *Performativity and Belonging* (London, 1999), pp. 175–94.

[19] Arlene Elowe MacLeod, 'Hegemonic Relations and Gender Resistance: The New Veiling as Accommodating Protest in Cairo', *Signs* 17:3 (1992), pp. 533–57 (pp. 534, 557).

chain of events that had led to the dismissal of the Nominated Assembly (or Barebone's Parliament) and the constitution of the Protectorate in the previous December, had spent much the intervening period publicly denouncing Cromwell and his regime as tyrannous backsliders.[20] The inauguration of the new regime had spelled the end of any hope that Powell and a group of like-minded theocratic republicans, known as Fifth Monarchists, might have ever had of seeing the English state ruled along radical sectarian lines.[21] When news reached the authorities that Powell was continuing to inflame his Christ Church congregation against the government some three weeks after Cromwell was proclaimed Lord Protector, he was summoned for questioning. Fearing, no doubt, that the minister was likely to be imprisoned for his seditious activities (he never was, since he escaped to Wales), a sympathetic member of a neighbouring congregation took herself to Whitehall, waiting and praying for Powell in a small heated room adjacent to the Council chamber. Anna Trapnel herself now takes up her own narrative:

> She was beyond and besides her thoughts or intentions, having much trouble in her heart, and being seized upon by the Lord: She was carried forth in a spirit of Prayer and Singing, from noon till midnight, and went down into Mr Roberts lodging, who keeps the Ordinary [inn] in Whitehall; And finding her natural strength going from her, she took her bed at eleven a clock in the night.[22]

She did not leave for another 12 days, during which time she scarcely ate and extemporized countless prayers, songs and prophecies. If the manner of her delivery varied, the tenor of her utterances remained very much the same in that they were consistent, scathing critiques of Cromwell and his regime. Trapnel continually repeated what was becoming the standard Fifth Monarchist message in late 1653 and early 1654: that the Protector who in his opening address to Barebone's had sounded so fervently milleniarian had subsequently betrayed the trust of his sectarian friends by dismissing a nominated assembly (containing at

---

[20] Powell's radical activities, along with those of other millenarian preachers, such as Christopher Feake and John Simpson, were monitored and recorded throughout this period by the authorities. See, for instance, *A Collection of the State Papers of John Thurloe*, 7 vols (London, 1742), vol. 1, p. 641; vol. 2, p. 93.

[21] The definitive account of Fifth Monarchism in the period is still Bernard Capp, *The Fifth Monarchy Men: A Study in Seventeenth-Century English Millenarianism* (London, 1972). For an authoritative assessment of this transitional historical period see Austin Woolrych, *Britain in Revolution, 1625–1660* (Oxford, 2002), pp. 537–615; idem., *Commonwealth to Protectorate* (Oxford, 1982). The term 'theocratic republicans' is from Holstun's *Ehud's Dagger*, p. 277.

[22] Anna Trapnel, *The Cry of a Stone* (London, 1654), p. 1. Trapnel remained loyal to Powell throughout her career.

least a dozen Fifth Monarchists) in order to arrogate to himself the title of Lord Protector.[23]

Thus in one rapture she prayed for Cromwell to be released from pomp and poor advice:

> Must thy Servant that now is upon the Throne, must he now die and go out like a candel? ... Oh that he might be recovered out of that vainglorious Counsel, out of their Traps and Gins! Oh his soul is in bondage ... He is in Chains by reason of that outward glory and pomp that is round about him.[24]

Such glory and ostentation, many Fifth Monarchists contended, made the Protectorate court appear every inch a royal one. From his prison cell in Windsor castle, one of the movement's leaders, Christopher Feake, lamented that 'my name be cast out, as vile, and I am separated by the new-fashioned King, and his council from the society of saints'.[25] Similarly, John Rogers pondered 'how like this present Government looks to that which the Lord ... hath so eminently ingaged against, laid in the dust, and stamped upon with disdain'. Just like Cromwell, 'the former K[ing] (cut off) had his Courts, Councels, State, Pride, Idleness, and vanity in persons around him, rich beds, hangings, Coaches and Attendants, evill Councellors'.[26] Trapnel, too, lyricized this sentiment when she switched from prayer to song in one session:

---

[23]   According to Cromwell in his opening speech to the Nominated Assembly 'it pleased God, much about the middle of this war, to winnow ... the forces of this nation'. He reminded the assembly 'of those very great appearances of God, in crossing and thwarting the purposes of men, that he might raise up a poor and contemptible company of men' and offered an eschatological reading of recent history as 'so many insurrections, invasions, secret designs, open and public attempts, quashed in so short a time ... by the very signal appearance of God himself'. See W. C. Abbott (ed.), *Writing and Speeches of Oliver Cromwell*, 4 vols (Cambridge, MA, 1937–47), vol. 3, pp. 53–4 . For studies of millenarian rhetoric in the period see James E. Force and Richard H. Popkin (eds.), *The Millenarian Turn: Millenarian Contexts of Science, Politics and Everyday Anglo-American Life in the Seventeenth and Eighteenth Centuries* (London, 2001); Christopher Hill, *Antichrist in Seventeenth-Century England* (Oxford, 1971); Peter Toon (ed.), *Puritans, the Millenium and the Future of Israel: Puritan Eschatology, 1600–1660* (Cambridge, 1970); William Lamont, *Godly Rule: Politics and Religion 1603–1660* (London, 1969); Michael Walzer, *The Revolution of the Saints: A Study in the Origin of Radical Politics* (London, 1966). See also J. P. Laydon, ' "The Kingdom of Christ and the Powers of the Earth": The Political Uses of Apocalyptic and Millenarian Ideas in England, 1648–1653', unpublished Ph.D. thesis (Cambridge University, 1976).

[24]   Trapnel, *Cry of a Stone*, p. 22.

[25]   Christopher Feake, *The Oppressed Close Prisoner in Windsor Castle His Defiance* (London, 1654), p. 116.

[26]   John Rogers, *Mene, Tekel, Perez, Or A little Appearance of the Handwriting (In a Glance of Light) Against the Powers and Apostates of the Times. By a letter Written To and lamenting over Oliver Lord Cromwell* (London, 1654), p. 8.

That thou shouldst not assume to thee
Higher Power than Christ doth give:
But thou shouldst say unto all Saints,
O come let us here live ...

O do not thou aspire, for to
So high a title have;
As King or Protector: But oh
Vnto Christ that do leave.[27]

Even as the tension between expected syntactic pauses and the tetrameter and trimeter alternations of the ballad rhythm threatened to pull this song apart, lines like these exerted a tremendous hold on contemporary inhabitants of London. During her two week confinement at Roberts's tavern, no fewer than eight of the dismissed members of the Nominated Assembly came to visit her.[28] The government were also notified about her activities; indeed Cromwell's informant at the inn, the pamphleteer Marchamont Nedham, was berated by one Cornish contributor to the official newspaper he edited for the fact that he had 'not inquired better into her business when she tranced it at Whitehall'.[29] Journalists more inclined to a radical sectarian viewpoint were also present. Henry Walker, editor of *Severall Proceedings of State Affaires*, preferred Trapnel's prayers to her songs, estimating 'many hundreds do daily come to see and hear' her.[30] Whether or not, as one critic has speculated, Walker is massaging the figures here, Trapnel's fame was such during this period that it even provoked suspicion amongst fellow radicals.[31] When the royalist sectarian, Arise Evans, published a pamphlet account of the trances and spiritual outpourings of another woman, Elinor Channel, he reassured his readers that the latter was:

very sensible and profound in what she spake to me, but as she said, when she is dumb, all her senses are taken up, and then the matter which troubles her mind, is dictated and made plain to her by the Spirit of God ... And though [this pamphlet] be but short, yet you shall find more truth and substance in it, than in all Hanna Trampnels [sic] songs, whom some account of as the Diana of the English.[32]

---

27 Trapnel, *Cry of a Stone*, pp. 28–9.
28 Ibid., p. 2, where Trapnel names each of her eminent visitors.
29 *Mercurius Politicus* 201, 13–20 Jan. 1654, p. 3430.
30 'She is heard and understood very plainly by all when she prayes, but when shee sings, very little is to be understood what she saith ... Her prayers are in exceeding good method and order, good language and such as indeed all that come doe much admire what they hear from her, excellent words, and well placed; such as are not ordinary'; *Severall Proceedings of State Affaires* 225, 12–19 Jan. 1653{4}, p. 3563.
31 Holstun, *Ehud's Dagger*, p. 283.
32 Elinor Channel, *A Message from God, but a dumb woman to his Highnes the Lord Protector, together with a word of advice to the Commons of England and Wales, for the*

Trapnel had clearly attained sufficient celebrity that some thought that she was worshipped as a false god by an idolatrous people; hostile, opportunistic publishers, on the other hand, could also use her fame to publicize their own pamphlets. Her reputation endured to such an extent that in his retrospective account of the tumults of the revolutionary decades Thomas Hobbes paused to recollect that Trapnel was 'much famed for her dreams and visions, and hearkened to by many'.[33]

Trapnel's renown later in the seventeenth century is in part the result of a well-judged Fifth Monarchist publication campaign in the wake of her spectacularly disorderly journey to Cornwall in mid-1654 (during which she continued to declaim against the new regime, and from which she was sent back for a period of imprisonment in Bridewell). However, it was her appearance at the Whitehall ordinary not long after the inauguration of the Protectorate that did much to secure her image in the minds of the English people.[34] In fact, it was the visual aspect as much as the rhetorical qualities of her protest, the sight of her prone frame confined to a bed, which so fascinated contemporaries. Newsbooks pored over every aspect of the spectacle recording the patterns of her breathing, the number of times she tossed and turned, even detailing the arrangement of her bedclothes.[35] The precise scrutiny given to the setting, Trapnel's gestural vocabulary and the way in which she modulated her delivery in both poetry and prose suggest that seventeenth-century commentators regarded the occasion as supremely theatrical. As both serials and intelligence reports put it, Trapnel 'acted a part' or 'played a part at the ordinary'.[36] Much modern analysis of her protest has consolidated this view. A brilliant recent reading of the incident has presented it as a carefully choreographed piece of political theatre through which Trapnel transforms the

---

electing of a Parliament. By Elinor Channel. Published according to her desire, by Arise Evans. (London, 1653), p. 8.

[33] Thomas Hobbes, *Behemoth Or the Long Parliament*, ed. Ferdinand Tönnies (Chicago and London, 1990), pp. 187–8.

[34] One contemporary newsbook reported news from Cornwall: 'That Hannah Trapnel is come into these parts, and three young fellows with her ... These fellows with her having ... a sword, were met by an honest Trooper; To this they replyed thy: *Thy Lord Protector we own not; thou art the Army of the Beast*'; *The Publick Intelligencer* 13, 24–31 Dec. 1655, pp. 193–4. For firsthand accounts of Trapnel's journey see Anna Trapnel, *Anna Trapnel's Report and Plea, Or a Narrative Of her Journey from London into Cornwal, the occasion of it, the Lord's encouragements to it, and signal presence with her in it* (London, 1654); idem., *A Legacy for Saints* (London, 1654). There have been numerous studies of Trapnel's career. See Gillespie, *Domesticity and Dissent*, pp. 92–106; Hostun, *Ehud's Dagger*, pp. 257–304; Anna Trapnel, *The Cry of a Stone*, ed. Hilary Hinds (Tempe, 2000), pp. xiii–xlvii; Hinds, *God's Englishwomen*, pp. 164–70; Stevie Davies, *Unbridled Spirits: Women of the English Revolution* (London, 1998), pp. 150–80, 246–8; Champlin Burrage, 'Anna Trapnel's Prophecies', *English Historical Review*, 26 (1911) pp. 526–35.

[35] *Severall Proceedings of State Affaires* 225, p. 3563.

[36] *Mercurius Politicus* 201, p. 3430; *CSPD* 1653/4, p. 393.

social space of tavern bedroom into a birthing room, parliament, meeting house and stage.[37] Less supple interpretations refer to the 'histrionic ostentation' of the scene 'which had something of the pull of a raree-show'.[38] However, those responses which merely foreground either the theatrical or the visual aspects of Trapnel's protest, tell at best half truths or, worse, travesty the complex agency structuring her work. Tellingly, therefore, the only engraving of Trapnel to survive from the seventeenth century – by Richard Gaywood – takes considerable imaginative license in depicting her as a Quaker taking her cue from the devil (see figure 1).

Throughout her prophetic career, though, Trapnel was at great pains to distinguish her public activities from mere spectacle. She lamented the way in which her journey to Cornwall had transformed her into 'a gazing stock for all the people'. She joined her London congregation in a condemnation of the ways in which 'all sorts of people' had made her 'a spectacle to the whole land', and in an attack on the Protectorate authorities derided those 'Rulers and Clergy who have brought me upon the world's stage'.[39] This is partly the result of a Puritan distrust of theatrical display coupled with a prophetic imperative which dictated that a divine message was always more important than its medium. Trapnel expressed the latter belief with characteristic force:

> I came not into the country to be seen ... I desired Christ and the beauty of holiness might be taken notice of, so that others might be taken with Christ; and that I might be onely a voyce, and Christ the sound.[40]

However, if Trapnel here promotes the auditory or verbal (as opposed to visual) nature of vatic intervention, she presents her earlier Whitehall protest as something that exceeds the merely rhetorical. In her pamphlet account of that event, *The Cry of a Stone*, she reveals instead a much fuller sense of the multiple and concealed agencies that facilitated her work and words in Roberts's tavern and beyond. This involves more than an awareness that she was divinely inspired. She demonstrates, as I will go on to show, a sense of her own agency as being informed by the material (as well as verbal) dimensions of revolutionary pamphlet culture.

---

[37] Holston, *Ehud's Dagger*, pp. 282–6.

[38] Woolrych, *Britain in Revolution*, p. 550.

[39] Trapnel, *Report and Plea*, pp. 24, 47; Trapnel, *Legacy*, sig. A2v.

[40] Trapnel, *Report and Plea*, pp. 28–9. On women's use of prophetic discourse in the period see Susan Wiseman, 'Unsilent Instruments and the Devil's Cushions: Authority in Seventeenth-Century Women's Prophetic Discourse', in Isobel Armstrong (ed.), *New Feminist Discourses: Essays in Literature, Criticism and Theory* (London, 1992), pp. 176–96; Diane Purkiss, 'Producing the Voice, Consuming the Body' in Isobel Grundy and Susan Wiseman (eds.), *Women, Writing, History: 1640–1740* (London, 1992), pp. 139–58; Mack, *Visionary Women*, Elaine Hobby, *Virtue of Necessity: English Women's Writing, 1649–1688* (London, 1988).

HANNAH TRAPNEL,

a Quaker and pretended Prophetess.

(From a scarce Print by Gaywood)

For an account of this extraordinary woman, see Heath's Chronicle, Cromwelliana & the High Court of Justice.

Figure 1: Anna Trapnel, *The Cry of a Stone* (1654)

A rare, imaginative engraving of Trapnel by Richard Gaywood (fl. 1650–80), which is pasted into the first edition in Cambridge University Library. Since there is no evidence to link Trapnel with the Quakers, this is perhaps the starkest example of the way in which an emphasis on the merely visual misrepresents her agency.

From Prophecy to Pamphlet: Anna Trapnel's *The Cry of a Stone*

Towards the end of the 76-page pamphlet account of her Whitehall trances, prayers and songs, Trapnel records another of her invective prophecies against the Lord Protector. In the midst of a labyrinthine series of rhetorical questions she continues her critique of the pomp of the Protectorate court with a reflection on the economic effects of Cromwellian militarism: 'Art thou a rational man, a wise and valiant souldier? How can the Commonalty be relieved, and thou hast great things for thy Table? Wars shall come out against other Nations, and what will you do then for pay [for your soldiers]?'[41] As the questioning reaches its climax, Trapnel inveighs against the abuses of the established clergy and describes her own critique in striking terms:

> Those of the Clergy that are about you, they do not speak plainly, and faithfully against you; therefore the Lord hath sent a poor handmaid into the Pallace, and there she shall declare it, and though you will not come yourselves, yet your Servants shall declare it to you, and it shall be left on the beams and walls of this very house against you: I have brought my word into thy place, thy very Pallace and it shall enter the very walls and hangings thereof against thee.[42]

The clerical abuse here is standard enough – the anticlericalism of the Fifth Monarchists had become more pronounced with the resignation of Barebone's parliament and Cromwell's repeated procrastination on the subject of tithe reform – but Trapnel's brand of materialism, her radical anti-Cromwellian rhetoric, is unprecedented. By criticizing the conspicuous refinements of the 'Pallace' of Whitehall, with its opulent 'hangings' and adornment, Trapnel reveals her decision to prophesy from a modest rented room in the immediate vicinity to be no accident. Furthermore, paying attention to the imposing 'beams' and 'walls' of the Protector's accommodation subtly invokes the splendour of Solomon's temple since the 'beams, posts and walls thereof' were, according to Chronicles, gilded with gold.[43] Unlike Solomon, however, who with David built anew for the spiritual well-being of a chosen nation's future generations, Cromwell has occupied a former royal palace with altogether baser, self-aggrandizing motives. Trapnel then ends this compressed materialist account of Protectoral statecraft with a forceful reminder of the location of her protest and the materiality of her own words.[44]

---

[41] Trapnel, *Cry of a Stone*, p. 68.
[42] Ibid., p. 70.
[43] See 2 Chronicles 3, v. 7: 'He overlaid the house, the beams, the posts, and the walls thereof, and the doors thereof with gold; and graved cherubims on the wall'.
[44] In the year before Trapnel appeared at the Whitehall ordinary another Fifth Monarchist woman writer, Mary Cary, sought to remind the Nominated Assembly of the material importance of words. In a reformist pamphlet she proposed a system of poor relief which was based upon a three pence levy 'fixed on the portage of all inland letters', the profits of

Having situated herself in the 'place', or immediate environs, of Cromwell's Whitehall 'Pallace', she informs him that her intrusion has been more successful than anyone could possibly have imagined; her very words have 'enter[ed]' the building fabric too. At one level, by speaking a truth so pointed that it penetrates the very bricks and mortar of Whitehall's walls, Trapnel distinguishes her discourse from the lies of the false prophet and the hot air of the sycophantic churchman. At another, she draws on shared memories of the divine graffiti witnessed at Belshazzar's feast and predicts the downfall of the Protectorate regime in much the same way that the mysterious inscription of 'Mene, Mene, Tekel, Upharzin' foretold the end of the Babylonian empire in Daniel 5.[45]

Arresting as this suggestion is, her insistence on the material as well as rhetorical dimensions of discourse is perfectly concordant with the way in which the authorities noted Trapnel's appeal early in 1654. Marchamont Nedham, for instance, wrote a letter to Cromwell in which he alerted him to 'a two-fold design about the prophetess Hannah; one to print her discourses and hymns which are desperate against your person, family, children, friends and the government; the other to send her all over England to proclaim them *viva vôce.*'[46] Indeed this nervous attention to the double impact of Trapnel's words as both printed page and verbal proclamation is strikingly reminiscent of the manner in which she presents the agency which has brought her pamphlet into existence from its start. In a daring series of self-referential motifs, Trapnel represents the current crisis of historical transition as a symbolic counterpart to the genesis of the material text itself. She reflects upon political turmoil at the same time as she alerts her readers to the fact that her own pamphlet is embroiled in a crisis of transmission. Just as there is a danger that the radical energies of Cromwellian reform might dissipate, might turn out to look rather like tyranny, there is also a real risk that her utterance might not realize itself as material text.

It is precisely for this reason, then, that *The Cry of a Stone* is punctuated by myriad reminders that it is an incomplete or corrupted narrative. This contributes to a sense that Trapnel's prophetic utterances are transitional, situated on the threshold between spoken and written word. Thus, before a single Whitehall prophecy is recorded, her readers are twice told, either side of a page break, of the

---

which were 'to come in for the use of the poor'; Mary Cary, *Twelve Modest Proposals to the Supreme Governours of the three Nations* (London, 1653), p. 9.

[45] The inscription in Daniel means 'God hath numbered thy kindom, and finished it ... Thou art weighed in the balances and found wanting ... Thy kingdom is divided'; Daniel 15 vv. 25–28. Trapnel's use of Belshassar's feast as an analogy for the dissolution of the Protectorate was appropriated in a later Fifth Monarchist work. In 1654 John Rogers wrote an anti-Cromwellian pamphlet in which he pleaded for Trapnel's release from Bridewell following her return to London from Cornwall. See *Mene, Tekel, Perez, Or A little Appearance of the Handwriting (In a Glance of Light) Against the Powers and Apostates of the Times. By a letter Written To and lamenting over Oliver Lord Cromwell*, p. 12.

[46] *CSPD* 7 Feb. 1654, p. 393.

presence of a nameless, status-less male 'Relator' who is transcribing her words in the cramped tavern bedroom. We are immediately informed, however, of his unfitness for the difficult task in hand: 'Now followes the Relation of so much or her Prayers and Songs, as by a very slow hand could be taken for eight days'.[47] This in itself is a radical departure from the way in which some women's prophetic work was published in pamphlets in the period. Frequently, prophetic texts by women bear the authorizing stamp of approval from an approving male friend, relative, fellow saint or acquaintance. Elinor Channel's prophecies were only 'published' by Arise Evans once he had deemed them 'very sensible and profound'.[48] Similarly, during the late 1640s and 1650s some seven editions of the prayers and pious sayings of a young Baptist woman, Sarah Wight, were presented to public view in pamphlet form by Henry Jessey, eminent Independent and sometime millenarian leader of London's earliest Baptist congregations.[49] Jessey's heavy editorial hand can be felt throughout the pamphlet; he affixes a precise date to each of Wight's utterances which only he reprints after his own substantial 'Relator's Epistle', several copious indexes and numerous letters which he sent to and received from notable radical Puritans in London and Oxford. The length of this paratextual material (some 39 pages) and Jessey's guiding influence on Wight as spiritual leader, amanuensis, and editor of the pamphlet are such that John Saltmarsh wrote approvingly to Jessey declaring that 'I find in this spiritual Treatise *of yours* ... things very experimental [exemplary]'.[50] Even though Trapnel knew Wight, having visited her sometime in 1647, *The Cry of a Stone* refuses to imitate the publication model provided by Jessey's and Wight's extremely popular *Exceeding Riches*.[51] Whilst Jessey emerges from the earlier work as a well-connected amanuensis-editor with a good memory, a sharp eye for the repetitious phrase and considerable skill in transcription, the man who notes Trapnel's words

---

[47] Trapnel, *Cry of a Stone*, p. 15.

[48] Channel, *A Message from God*, p. 8.

[49] Henry Jessey, *The Exceeding Riches of Grace Advanced By the Spirit of Grace, In an Empty Nothing Creature, (viz) Mrs Sarah Wight, Lately Hopeless and Restless* (London, 1647). This pamphlet was reissued or 'perfected' a further six times until 1658. It was reprinted twice in the eighteenth century. See Carola Scott-Luckens, 'Propaganda or Marks of Grace? The Impact of the Reported Ordeals of Sarah Wight in Revolutionary London, 1647–52', *Women's Writing* 9:2 (2002), pp. 215–52; Nigel Smith, *Perfection Proclaimed: Language and Literature in English Radical Religion 1640–1660* (Oxford, 1989), pp. 45–51.

[50] Jessey, *Exceeding Riches* (3rd edn, 1652), sig. a2r; emphasis added.

[51] 'Hanna Trapnel' is named as one of Wight's visitors in all editions from the 1640s. Her name – along with that of one foreign visitor, 'Dinah, the Blackamore' – is absent, however, from editions reprinted in the 1650s and later. This is presumably because Jessey was acutely aware of Trapnel's increasing celebrity and notoriety during this period and sought, like Arise Evans, to distance himself and his protégée from potentially harmful association with her. For evidence of Trapnel's presence at Wight's bedside see Jessey, *Exceeding Riches* (1st ed.), sig. av.

is entirely deprived of status, religious affiliation or worldly accomplishment. The pamphlet asks us to believe instead that this anonymized individual records her utterances rather badly:

> The Relator coming into the Chamber where she lay, heard her first making melody and spiritual Song, which he could not take but in part, and that too with such imperfection, as he cannot present any account of it to the understanding of others.[52]

Even if we allow that the missing words revealed at this moment are symptomatic of the kind of interpretive difficulty that Henry Walker experienced when listening to Trapnel's songs, there is the unmistakable impression throughout the pamphlet that this helping hand is peculiarly error-prone. Such slips and gaps, though, should not be used to adduce a sense of *The Cry of a Stone* as sloppily composed or, more moralistically, in need of strict correction in the manner of a 'bad' quarto edition of a seventeenth-century play text. On the contrary, they ought to be read together as one of the pamphlet's principal counter-narratives, one which recounts its own prehistory as a series of heroic if faltering steps towards the effective transcription of speech and song into text.

On numerous occasions, therefore, we are told the Relator cannot transcribe because 'of the press of People in the chamber'; at others, Trapnel's delivery is such that it exceeds the skill and speed of his pen.[53] Sometimes the noise of the assembled throng drowns out the prophetess's song and in one instance, it is the 'lownesse' of Trapnel's voice itself which inhibits an accurate record.[54] At certain key stages, the interventions of the Relator are more prominent as when he inquires after her health or arrives late at the tavern one Sunday to find Trapnel mid-prophecy.[55] His contribution in the following passage is more striking still:

> They shall look on the Sun so bright,
>   and on its beames of grace,
> Which doth appeare, and cometh forth,
>   and on them casts its rayes.

> The foure last words of the last Verse are added by the Relator, who could not take the Maids owne words, her voyce as it were dying, and sinking into her breast.[56]

The drama of this scene stems from its multiple sites of suspense. Trapnel apparently hovers between life and death, just as the text is precariously balanced between conclusion and incompletion. 'Words' themselves are poised uncertainly on the cusp of speech and text, caught between God, his prophetess and an

---

[52] Trapnel, *Cry of a Stone*, pp. 15–6.
[53] Ibid., pp. 21, 31, 39, 45, 49, 53.
[54] Ibid., pp. 19, 58.
[55] Ibid., pp. 50, 61.
[56] Ibid., p. 45.

amanuensis who can ventriloquize prophetic discourse so convincingly that he captures it and fails to record it simultaneously.

This anxiety surrounding the transcription of word into text, the urgent sense that prophetic speech must be accompanied by its written cypher, is as evident in Trapnel's prayers and songs themselves as in this fascinating account of the Relator as heroic failure. In yet another prayer-ballad which her amanuensis 'because of the press of people in the Chamber, could not take', Trapnel sings of the relationship between a communicative company of saintly believers and a God who has a conflicted response to the sound of faithful voices:

> For they know that thou dost delight
> To hear their panting soul;
> They do rejoyce in thy Marrow,
> And esteem it more than gold.
>
> Therefore thou hearing their hearts cry,
> Thou sayest, Oh wait a while!
> And suddainly thou wilt draw near,
> The worlds glory to spoile.[57]

The deity to whom this is addressed is only partly pleased by songs of praise; if he is delighted by them in the first line of the extract, they urge him towards violent, vengeful rage by its close. We, perhaps like (or perhaps because of) the Relator, are thrown by the disjunction concealed by the connective 'therefore', dreadfully uncertain whether singing or silence will avert divine wrath. Neither of these, it soon appears, will suffice; salvation resides in the material facts of paper, writing instruments and continuous acts of transcription. Thus the very next lines of the ballad run:

> Oh you shal have great Rols of writ
> Concerning Babylons fall,
> And the destruction of the whore,
> Which now seems spiritual
> Come write down how that Anti-Christ,
> That is so rigid here,
> Shall fall down quite, when Christ comes forth,
> Who suddenly will appear...
>
> Write how that Protectors shall go,
> And into graves there lye:
> Let pens make known what is said that
> They shall expire and die.
>
> Oh write also that Colonels

---

[57] Ibid., p. 19.

And Captains they shall down,
Be not afraid to pen also,
That Christ will them cast down.[58]

Reference has become confused and Christ, the conventional object of the prayer at its start, drifts out of focus as the rapture gathers momentum. The bibliophilic deity of the first stanza is replaced by a series of indeterminate addressees who struggle to respond to the speaker's repeated imperatives to render the auditory graphic. Furthermore, the prophetic account of historical change in which a dictatorial Cromwell and his army grandees are consigned to obscurity and oblivion is prefigured in the transitional moment of dictation; a political elite will be brought 'down' through the non-violent interventions of an unidentifiable group of holy scribes (comprising both the 'Relator' and a nameless company of believers) hurriedly taking 'down' words. This is not the delusion of one who, conflating world and text, believes that the machinery of state can be brought grinding to a halt through giddying acts of interpretation; it is rather the optimism of the pacifist who saw in the union of both spoken and written forms of communication the most effective means of changing the world.[59]

One of the many appeals that *The Cry of a Stone* makes, therefore, is that agency ought not to be equated simply with the radical verbal performance of an individual engaging in prophetic utterance. Every thrilling prophetic syllable is accompanied by the sound of hands and pen on paper; accordingly, this noisy pamphlet produces a distinct sense that transformative action does not arise from a single source but is always mediated and preceded by other actions. It resides in prayer and song, but it must be traced back, too, to the less spectacular material operations involved in making a text. If agency can be resistance (to an authoritarian administration or individuals hostile to women's public expression) it can also be co-operation, unseen association and dialogue; it has, then, perhaps less to do with self-assertion than self-effacement (be it in a community, behind a nameless male 'Relator', with God or before an enemy). In what follows I offer five readings of non-aristocratic women's agency in revolutionary pamphlet culture at the level of both rhetoric and material culture. These case studies might be read alongside those recent analyses of power which have seen early modern

---

58 Ibid., pp. 19–20.

59 Throughout her career Trapnel continued to advocate regime change through non-violent means. She repeatedly distanced herself from those other Fifth Monarchists, most notably those congregating around the radical sectarian John Venner, who sought in the late 1650s to overthrow the Protectorate through militaristic insurrection. Trapnel styled the Fifth Monarchist insurgents as 'rash brains' who 'causeth the Name of God to be blasphemed'; Anna Trapnel, *Poetical Addresses* (London, 1659), pp. 273–4. On Fifth Monarchist militarism see Capp, *Fifth Monarchy Men*, pp. 117–120, 199–200; Champlin Burrage, 'The Fifth Monarchy Insurrections', *English Historical Review* 5 (1910), pp. 722–47.

historians, following a lead provided by Jonathan C. Scott, seeking to replace the dyad of domination and subordination with a complex (often ineffable) network of negotiation. As the editors of one collection of essays have written:

> negotiation operated continuously, being inscribed in the everyday politics of relationships of domination and subordination. The relatively weak had available to them means of affecting the terms of their subordination that were both less dramatic and more continuous than riot. Some of these might be so casual as to escape the historical, if not the sociological record.[60]

The following chapters eschew a theoretical perspective in favour of a series of close-analyses of the historical conditions of some of the casual (and indeed less casual) negotiations of non-aristocratic women in the mid-seventeenth century. They take the form of five chronologically arranged studies of women's involvement in the pamphlet culture of revolutionary England. The first two of these focus on the rhetorical or discursive strategies which a number of women chose to deploy in the texts they produced. Chapter 1 explores the writings of the sometime Leveller Katherine Chidley and considers them within the controversy surrounding religious toleration in the 1640s, a controversy that shaped so many of the physical and polemical encounters throughout the revolutionary decades. In particular I delimit some of the antifeminist, masculinist parameters of that arena and its chief literary or generic form, animadversion, and demonstrate how Chidley manages to write and thrive in this hostile environment by manipulating a complex rhetoric of self-effacement. In chapter 2, attention shifts to the related and most intensely sustained controversy of the revolutionary (and subsequent) decades, the regicide. I examine the pamphlet texts of two women writers who wrote most extensively on the subject in the immediate context of the trial and execution of Charles I. Mary Pope and Elizabeth Poole were both conservative defenders of monarchy and presented their messages before less-than receptive audiences, in Poole's case at the General Council of the Army itself. Chapter 3 offers less textual close-readings than an extended exploration of the material culture which produced many of the types of pamphlet texts under discussion. In it I give sustained attention to the roles that women played in making and shaping the pamphlet newsbooks which flooded the streets of London in the 1640s and 1650s. Drawing on manuscript as well as pamphlet sources, this chapter uncovers the life and work of Elizabeth Alkin (or 'Parliament Joan' as she was more frequently dubbed by her contemporaries), a woman who engaged in the frequently unremunerative work of spy, newsbook publisher, private petitioner and nurse. In chapter 4 I scrutinise how one woman's protest (at a Church not far from the tavern which Trapnel made famous for nearly two weeks) was written about by contemporary male

---

[60] Michael J. Braddick and John Walter (eds), *Negotiating Power in Early Modern Society: Order, Hierarchy and Subordination in Britain and Ireland* (Cambridge, 2001), p. 8.

pamphleteers. Although this nameless, naked woman wrote no text of her own, an examination of the pamphlet exchange that erupted in the wake of her particular brand of dissent encourages us to temper the democratic and inclusive rhetoric that has characterized much historiography of the pamphlet. With chapter 5 I arrive at the eve of the Restoration and investigate the tithe controversy of 1659, another ultra-masculinist controversy which had been raging throughout the revolutionary decades. This year however saw the culmination of the Quakers' radical campaign against tithes and in particular the publication of a number of massive petitions made by Quaker women to the Rump parliament. Here I interrogate the material culture of collective petitioning and show how the collection and printing of a series of proper nouns, actually the names of some 7,000 Quaker women, could be used to counteract the broad disapproval of female participation in the discourse of tithe dispute.

Attending to both the rhetorical and material dimensions of revolutionary pamphlet culture in this way, this book aims to be of use to both literary scholars and historians of the pamphlet culture of the mid-seventeenth century. Like Anna Trapnel, prophesying, singing and whispering from her crowded bedroom in Whitehall, the women in the following pages provide insistent reminders that agency is both manner and matter, speech and deed, practice and utterance.

Chapter 1

'Justification Cannot Be Self-Justification': Katherine Chidley and the Discourses of Religious Toleration [1]

At another time an Anabaptist and great Sectary came to Mr Greenhill, and said he might as lawfully baptise a dog as a beleevers childe. *Katherine Chidley* about *August* last came to *Stepney* ... and was with Mr Greenhill, where shee with a great deale of violence and bitternesse spake against all Ministers and people that meet in our Churches, and in places where any idolatrous services have been performed: Mr *Greenhill* answered her by Scripture, and laboured to reduce to a short head all that she had spoke, asking her if this were not the sum [of her position], namely, that it was unlawfull to worship God in a place which had been used or set apart to idolatry under the Names of Saints and Angels ... but instead of being satisfied and giving any answer, shee was so talkative and clamorous, wearying him with her words, that he was glad to goe away, and so left her.[2]

When Katherine Chidley, sometime Leveller and seamstress, confronted William Greenhill, the leader of one of London's burgeoning nonconformist congregations, to dispute the theological bases of religious separatism in August 1645 only a political and religious adversary recorded the incident in any detail.[3] Thomas Edwards, the notorious Presbyterian lecturer, pamphleteer and enemy to all things Independent included the confrontation in the first part of his compendious catalogue of some 180 sectarian 'errors' as yet further evidence of the misguided

---

[1] The quotation is taken from Mikhail Bakhtin, *Problems of Dostoevsky's Poetics*, trans. Caryl Emerson, (Manchester, 1984), p. 287.
[2] Thomas Edwards, *Gangraena or A Catalogue and Discovery of many of the Errors, Heresies, Blasphemies and pernicious practices of the Sectaries of this time, vented and acted in England in these last four yeers,* (London, 1646), vol. 1, pp. 79–80.
[3] Thomas Alle alludes briefly to the confrontation when he writes: 'Another thing in Master Edwards his booke is about Mistresse Chidley who had some discourse with Master Greenhill, and he used arguments towards her which is true'; *A Breif [sic] Narration of the Truth of Some Particulars in Mr Edwards His Booke Called Gangraena* (London, 1646), p. 4.

and heretical nature of congregational worship.[4] For Edwards, who made the extirpation of sectarianism and separatism his life's work, the anarchy that Independency threatens to loose on the world is perfectly exemplified by the sight of a woman publicly disputing matters of religion with a man.[5] According to a logic of adjacency, this sight is deemed as absurd and blasphemous as that of a dog in a baptismal font. Edwards's insinuation is that such an equation is but a small logical step for anyone who hears the restraint, reason and decorum of masculine discourse, which he validates and echoes stylistically through free indirect speech, being jarred by the passion, 'bitternesse' and 'violence' of Chidley's pointedly unrecorded public words. If those words are indeed 'wearying' they are certainly disturbing as they enforce male silence and disappearance from the arena of dispute. The full implications of Edwards's report are actually only revealed once we realize that his argument is dependent upon the conflation of partisan anti-tolerationist arguments of 'high' Presbyterianism with a more broadly consensual and cross-party point concerning the necessary deference and silence of women in the early modern period. If you thought the voluble or garrulous woman intolerable, as did any number of early modern commentators, then, according to Edwards, the toleration of religious separatism and sectarianism becomes logically untenable.[6]

---

[4]   The most recent account of Edwards's *Gangraena* and the role it played in the anti-tolerationist Presbyterian campaigns of 1645–1647 is Ann Hughes, '"Popular" Presbyterianism in the 1640s and 1650s: The case of Thomas Edwards and Thomas Hall', in N. Tyacke (ed.), *England's Long Reformation 1500–1800* (London and Bristol, 1998), pp. 235–59. See also, I. Gentles, *The New Model Army in England, Ireland and Scotland, 1645–1653* (Oxford, 1992), p. 191; M. Mahoney, 'Presbyterianism in the City of London, 1645–1647', *Historical Journal* 22 (1979), pp. 93–114; Tolmie, *The Triumph of the Saints*, pp. 130–34; V. Pearl, 'London's counter-revolution', in G. E. Aylmer (ed.), *The Interregnum: The quest for settlement* (London, 1972), pp. 29–56; Leslie Stephen (ed.), *Dictionary of National Biography* 17 (London, 1889), pp. 127–8.

[5]   For sectarian proliferation and responses to it during the civil war see John Morrill and John Walter, 'Order and Disorder in the English Revolution', in Richard Cust and Ann Hughes (eds.), *The English Civil War* (London, 1997), pp. 310–40; Nigel Smith, *Literature and Revolution*; idem., *Perfection Proclaimed: Language and literature in English Radical Religion 1640–1660* (Oxford, 1989); O. P. Grell, J. I. Israel and Nicholas Tyacke (eds.), *From Persecution to Toleration: The Glorious Revolution and Religion in England* (Oxford, 1991); Christopher Hill, *The World Turned Upside Down;* Michael Walzer, *The Revolution of the Saints: A Study in the Origins of Radical Politics* (London, 1966).

[6]   On the issue of religious toleration in this period see Grell, *From Persecution to Toleration;* pp. 17–76; Avihu Zakai, 'Religious Toleration and Its Enemies: The Independent Divines and the Issue of Toleration During the English Civil War', *Albion* 21:1 (1989), pp. 1–33; Blair Worden, 'Toleration and the Cromwellian Protectorate', in W. J. Sheils (ed.), *Persecution and Toleration: Papers Read at the Twenty-Second Summer Meeting and the Twenty-Third Winter Meeting of the Ecclesiastical History Society* (Oxford, 1984), pp. 199–235; Jay Newman, *Foundations of Religious Tolerance* (Toronto, 1982); W. K. Jordan, *The Development of Religious Toleration*, 4 vols (London, 1932–1940).

In this chapter I will interrogate how one female pamphleteer created and manipulated rhetoric in order to negotiate the antifeminist limits placed upon women in the masculinist environment of the toleration debates. Before undertaking this, we must remember that the view of Edwards, just discussed, is but the misogynistic, seventeenth-century version of the current, credible arguments of contemporary feminist historians and literary scholars who have demonstrated the relatively favourable conditions that civil war sectarianism fostered for female agency. In theological contexts, which posited the equality of all souls before God, there was clearly some room for those women writers and activists who desired more direct forms of action and expression.[7] However, viewed in a fuller historical context, Edwards's own version of this narrative appears curiously selective. The passage that opened this chapter is the first occasion in which Chidley is catalogued as evidence of the 'gangrene' of heresy currently afflicting and corrupting the body of the English nation. It certainly was not, however, the first time that she had disputed religious matters with men. Nor, more pertinently, would Edwards have been unaware that she had publicly and eloquently contested theological issues with him well before 1646.

This is because ever since the first appearance of his anti-tolerationist writings some five years earlier, Chidley had been the foremost of Edwards's pamphlet-respondents. His *Reasons Against the Independent Government of Particular Congregations* was published early in 1641 in the vanguard of the Presbyterian campaigns against the nonconformist reaction to the Laudian scheme of episcopal polity. It received no printed rebuttal whatsoever until (or indeed after) Chidley published her lengthy *Justification of the Independent Churches of Christ* later that

---

[7]   The wealth of literature on this topic is considerable. See Sara Mendelson and Patricia Crawford, *Women in Early Modern England 1550–1720* (Oxford, 1998), pp. 394–418; Hilary Hinds, *God's Englishwomen*; Elaine Hobby, *Virtue of Necessity: English Women's Writing 1649–1688*, (London, 1988); Ann Hughes, 'Gender and Politics in Leveller Literature' in S. D. Asmussen and M. A. Kishlansky (eds.), *Political Culture and Cultural Politics in Early Modern England: Essays Presented to David Underdown* (London, 1995), pp. 162–88; Patricia Crawford, *Women and Religion in England 1500–1720* (London, 1993); idem., 'The Challenges to Patriarchalism: How Did the Revolution Affect Women?' in John Morrill (ed.), *Revolution and Restoration: England in the 1650s* (London, 1992), pp. 112–28; Phyllis Mack, *Visionary Women*; Susan Wiseman, 'Unsilent Instruments and the Devil's Cushions: Authority in Seventeenth-Century Women's Prophetic Discourse', in Isobel Armstrong (ed.), *New Feminist Discourses: Essays in Literature, Criticism and Theory*, (London, 1992), pp. 176–96; Dorothy P. Ludlow, 'Shaking Patriarchy's Foundations: Sectarian Women in England, 1641–1700', in R. L. Greaves (ed.), *Triumph Over Silence: Women in Protestant History* (Westport, CT, 1985), pp. 93–123; Patricia Higgins, 'The Reaction of Women', in Brian Manning (ed.), *Politics, Religion and the English Civil War* (New York, 1973), pp. 179-222; Claire Cross, '"He-Goats Before the Flocks": A Note on the Part Played by Women in the Founding of Some Civil War Churches', *Studies in Church History* 8 (1972), pp. 195–202; Keith Thomas, 'Women and the Civil War Sects', *Past and Present* 13 (1958), pp. 42–62.

year.[8] Similarly, when Edwards's *Antapologia* (1644) took its place in the pamphlet war which engulfed London in the wake of the Thomas Goodwin et al.'s *Apologeticall Narration*, Chidley's *New Yeares Gift* was one of only a handful of texts to maintain the congregational position of the Apologists and explicitly refute the basic tenets of Edwards's text.[9] His refusal to acknowledge Chidley's public interventions in religious controversy until 1646 is made more explicit elsewhere in the first part of *Ganraena*. Surveying the range of his printed writings he reminds his readers that:

> In the last week of June, or the first of July 1644 ... came forth my Answer (entituled *Antapologia*) to the *Apologeticall Narration*: Ever since which time I have forborne the Presse, out of an expectation of a Reply ... with much patience passing by the many reproachfull scornfull speeches, and railings both in publike Sermons and printed Pamphlets, and many other ways cast upon me and my *Antapologie*: I was not willing to be provoked by the barking of every dogge ... but rather resolved to reserve my time and strength, for some learned and solid reply from the Apologists, or any other for them, to which I might have given a *Rejoynder*. But now 18 Moneths being almost expired since the *Antapologie* came abroad into the World ... I shall waite no longer, but am resolved to appear again in publike against the errours of the time.[10]

Amongst those 'printed Pamphlets' and 'barking dogges' that he disdains to engage with are Hezekiah Woodward's *A Short Letter* and Richard Overton's *The Arraignment of Mr Persecvtion* (1645), and only the first of these contends with Edwards's text in anything like the detail of Chidley's *New Yeares Gift*. Given Edwards's voracious reading habits, his obsessive concern with the public reception of his work, and the tireless predilection for compendious source compilation in his writing, it is extremely unlikely that he could have missed a

---

[8]   Katherine Chidley, *The Justification of the Independent Churches of Christ. Being an Answer to Mr Edwards his Booke, which he hath written against the Government of Christ's Chvrch, and Toleration of Christs Publike Worship* (London, 1641). For a sense of the politico-religious context see John Adair, *Puritans: Religion and Politics in Seventeenth-Century England and America* (Stroud, 1998); Hughes, '"Popular" Presbyterianism', pp. 239–40; Pearl, 'London's Counter Revolution'.

[9]   Katherine Chidley, *A New Yeares Gift or A Brief Exhortation to Mr Thomas Edwards, That he may break off his old sins in the old yeare, and begin the New yeare with new fruits of Love* (London, 1645). Chidley's pamphlet and Hezekiah Woodward's *A Short Letter Modestly Intreating A Friends Judgment upon Mr Edwards His Book* (London, 1644) are the only two works to deal extensively with Edwards's text in late 1644–45. The most systematic refutation of *Antapologia* only appears two years later. See John Goodwin, *Anapologesiates Antapologias. Or the Inexcsuableness of that Grand Accusation of Brethren called Antapologia* (London, 1646).

[10]   Edwards, *Gangraena*, vol. 1, sig. Br.

pamphlet written by a woman that engaged with his own writing directly.[11] He was also, as one contemporary alleged, at the centre of an extremely active Presbyterian intelligence network who sent 'forth ... Emissaries ... to discover and report unto him the slips and weaknesses of the servants of God ... drinking in with so much greediness all and all manner of reports that are brought into him, whether with ground or without'.[12] It seems rather, then, that Edwards chose to ignore Chidley's pamphlet work until he published the third part of *Gangraena* in December 1646 when, besieged by hostile critical reaction to the first two sections, he endeavoured to engage the sympathies of his readers with a confession of the ignominy he felt at having to contend with a female respondent:

> The sectaries by writing and speaking have set themselves to disparage me, to cast scorns of all kinds upon me, such as hardly were upon any man in any age, and all to weaken my esteem, credit and authority with the people, that being looked upon so weak a woman can answer my writings.[13]

This mysterious woman is almost certainly Katherine Chidley, and Edwards's reluctance to acknowledge her written word fully is riddling. Why should female discursivity denote male weakness in this context? What follows is an attempt to answer this question by reading Chidley's pamphlets in the masculinist milieu of early modern religious controversy. If Edwards was indeed, as Ann Hughes has shrewdly suggested, the 'hard man' or 'rough-houser' of English Presbyterianism at this time, I will show that this was a reputation in part secured by the antifeminist underpinnings of the dominant humanist rhetorical mode (and set of typographical conventions) which structured pamphlet exchange in mid-seventeenth-century religious dispute.[14] As we will see, in her productive

---

[11] An anonymous pamphlet alluded to his insatiable appetite for information in its very title: *A Letter to Mr Thomas Edwards. The Dedication of the Letter to our much suspected friend, Mr T Edwards, Scavenger Generall, throughout Great Britaine, New England and the united Provinces* (London, 1646). Edwards was undoubtedly sensitive to public responses to his work. Four or five days before the appearance of *Antapologia,* one of the Apologists, Sidrach Simpson, published *The Anatomist Anatomised* in response to Alexander Forbes's *Anatomy of Independency.* In it he briefly alludes to the fact that 'there is an Antapology in Presse or a Collection of such faults as either mens mistakes and malice or perhaps mens own infirmities have made, either beyond the Seas or here. The Anatomist is a forerunner to that, as some few great drops before a shower.' Edwards was incensed by the remark and complained that Simpson's tract was 'printed, rather to prepossesse the reader against the Antapologie, then to Answer the Anatomy of Independencie (as all may see)'; Sidrach Simpson, *The Anatomist Anatomised or A Short Answer to some things in the Book Intituled An Anatomy of Independencie* (London, 1644); Edwards, *Antapologia,* sig. Ar.

[12] John Goodwin, *Cretensis: Or A Brief Answer to an Ulcerous Treatise Lately Published by Mr Thomas Edwards intituled Gangraena* (London, 1646), p. 18.

[13] Edwards, *Gangraena,* vol. 3, no sig.

[14] Hughes, '"Popular" Presbyterianism', p. 240.

encounter with a number of genre-specific, misogynistic prohibitions, Chidley's writings exhibit complex patterns of self-effacement which are at once complicit in her erasure from the historical record by men like Edwards and at the same time are the means and form through which her texts participate in dialogue with that record.

'A spetting in his face': The Contemporary Reception of Chidley's Pamphlets

Until fairly recent developments in feminist literary and historical scholarship paved the way for the recovery and research of texts by non-aristocratic women in the early modern period, the writings and political activities of Katherine Chidley were significantly overlooked. With notable exceptions, historians and literary critics were, like Edwards, reluctant to admit the full significance of the work of this sectarian businesswoman in the pamphlet controversies of the 1640s.[15] The pamphlets themselves make interrogative appeals for the religious toleration of a number of doctrines and faiths and at their most compelling filter anti-episcopal sentiment through images of the empowered housewife:

> The power of the Keyes is absolutely the Churches, which is Christ's wife, as the power of the Keyes of the Family are the Mistresses, to whom the Husband giveth full power; and I think no reasonable man will affirme (if her husband give her sole power in his absence) that she is subordinate to any of her servants. Now the Scripture is cleere, that Christ (who is ascended up on high) hath delivered the power to his Church, therefore it is also against the light and law of nature, to conceive the Church to be thus subordinate to her servants; but rather ... that her servants are subordinate to her. And it is a dishonour unto Christ for them to usurp ecclesiastical authority over her.[16]

If Chidley is keen here to recuperate the agency of women confined to subordinate subject positions for tolerationist ends, she offers trenchant critique elsewhere when it comes to highlighting the economic oppressions of women under prelacy. She is particularly sensitive, for instance, to the material exigencies and demands

---

[15]   The foremost of these earlier exceptions are Ian Gentles, 'London Levellers in the English Revolution: The Chidleys and Their Circle', *Journal of Ecclesiastical History* 29:3 (1978), pp. 281–309; Higgins, 'The Reactions of Women', pp. 207–11; Joseph Fletcher, *The History of Independency,* 4 vols (London, 1847), vol. 3, pp. 244–9; Benjamin Hanbury, *Historical Memorials Relating to the Independents of Congregationalists: From Their Rise to the Restoration of the Monarchy,* 3 vols (London, 1841), vol. 2, pp. 108–17. For more recent treatment see Gillespie, *Domesticity and Dissent,* pp. 62–92; Patricia Crawford and Sara Mendelson, *Women in Early Modern England, 1550–1720* (Oxford, 1999), pp. 332, 393, 405–12; Hinds, *God's Englishwomen,* pp. 71, 90, 159–61; Patricia Crawford, *Women and Religion in England, 1500–1720,* (London, 1993), pp. 55, 129, 132–5.

[16]   Chidley, *A New Yeares Gift,* sig. Cv.

of motherhood, exposing the dangers of childbirth whilst thoroughly deriding those ministers who 'will have a share of him that is borne [sic] without life ... for if a dead child shall be borne into the world, they will be paid for reading a dirge over it, before it shall be laid in the earth'.[17] Those same ministers are also attacked on the issue of churching (the public appearance of women at church to return thanks after childbirth), which Chidley argues consigns women to positions of ignorance and superstition. In a wryly understated passage she reminds her readers that ministers 'must have another patrimony for the birth of [a] childe, for before the mother dare go abroad, shee must have their blessing, that the Sun shall not smite her by day nor the Moone by night'.[18] The compelling logic and insightful materialist analysis of this argument become even more distinct when we recall that the most radical Leveller calls for social reform were notoriously deaf to the voices of those women who were so active and voluble in support of the party.

The reasoned, perspicuous anti-clericalism of Chidley's work meant that there were other contemporary readers of her pamphlets who were, for a variety of politico-religious interests, slightly less inclined than Edwards to mute their distinctive sound.[19] For instance, John Goodwin's 1646 refutation of Edwards's *Antapologia* delighted in the fact that 'this piece of his hath [already] been convicted, and baffled by the pen of a woman, and was never yet relieved by him with any REJOYNDER'.[20] Goodwin here envisages the textual dynamics of pamphlet exchange as commensurable with those of aristocratic violence ('baffled' being a chivalric term for the public disgrace of a knight) in order to manufacture a sense of the superiority of his own adversaria. This was a common tactic (the implications of which will be discussed in due course), but Goodwin's criticism of Edwards soon became more focused. Referring to the heresiographer's complaint of the general lack of rebuttals to his pamphlets, and more specifically of the Apologists' silence in response to his earlier *Reasons Against the Independent Government of Particular Congregations*, Goodwin ridiculed the fact that:

> He [Edwards] tells them that by their silence (in not answering) they seem to give consent to what was written against them. And ... that if they answer not this Antapologie, he shall be like enough to interpret their silence, that either they are ashamed of some of their opinions, or able to say little for them. I marvailed that

---

17 Chidley, *Justification*, p. 57.

18 Ibid.

19 That said, some contemporaries preferred to see her work as the result of collaborations with her son Samuel. For instance, a reference to Chidley in a seventeenth-century manuscript compilation conflated allegations of collaborative authorship with those of sexual immorality: 'O Kate, O Kate, thou art uncleane I heare/ A man doth lie between thy sheets I feare'. Thomas Edwards did much to ensure this reputation when he claimed that 'Katherine Chidley and her sons books (for the mother and son made them together, one inditing and the other writing) are highly magnified'. See BL Harl. MS 4931 f.9; Edwards, *Gangraena*, vol. 3, p. 170.

20 John Goodwin, *Anapologesiates Antapologias*, p. 12.

upon this ground, he doth not wipe off from himselfe the *seemingnesse* of his giving consent to Mris [sic] Chidley in what she hath written against him; yea and answer all the books in the world, that are written in opposition to any opinion which he holds.[21]

We should be wary of taking Goodwin's witty riposte as that of a proto-feminist member of a supportive, seventeenth-century, Chidley-reading community since the specific terms in which he acknowledges the presence of her *Justification of the Independent Churches of Christ* are problematic. Nowhere in his encyclopaedic and compendiously referenced tome does Goodwin direct the reader to the title of Chidley's work, nor does he offer a single quotation from her pamphlet, as he does repeatedly with the wealth of contemporary and classical male authorities that glut his rebuttal. Instead he offers merely the briefest and vaguest of allusions, preferring to dwell on the 'seemingness' or implications of the pamphlet's existence for Edwards himself. The *Justification* is thus less a text, Chidley less an author, than a symbolic sleight, a slur, something Edwards must, pointedly, 'wipe off'.[22] If Edwards, the polemicist-errant, is ultimately 'baffled', his defeat is inflicted by a strange opponent indeed.

This rendition of Chidley's work, which converts its material effects from the textual to the bodily, and effects its reception at a physical, rather than an intellectual, level is also performed by another of her mid-seventeenth-century readers. In the August immediately following the appearance of *Antapologia*, Samuel Hartlib wrote to his friend, the nonconformist divine Hezekiah Woodward, requesting his opinion on Edwards's monumental controversial text. Ever the irenicist in pursuit of unity in the Protestant cause, he deplores 'these differences of Religion, which are fallen out amongst Brethren' and requests Woodward's advice 'that we may be instruments by the grace of God of healing those breaches'.[23] Hartlib was soon granted the authoritative and instructive reading he requested, but if he had anticipated that Woodward would provide him with an irenic, moderate and dispassionate interpretation of Edwards's text he was mistaken.[24] Woodward's

---

[21]   Ibid., pp. 168–9. The passage Goodwin is mocking is 'you [the Apologists] should have done well (either any one of you, or all of you) to have answered it, and had you shewed those Reasons to have been weake and unjust, then there had been some colour for you to have made that a Provocation to have acted for your selves and way, but by your silence you seem to give consent to what was written against you.'; *Antapologia*, p. 228.

[22]   A Presbyterian participant in a contemporaneous, all-male pamphlet exchange sought to preserve the decorum of religious dispute in a similar fashion: 'Reader, though I were neither a Prophet, nor son of a Prophet, nor the friend of a Prophet; I could not indure to see so much dirt throwne in the face of all Authority, & not pull out my handkerchife [sic] ... to wipe it off'; *An Hue-And-Cry after Vox Populi* (London, 1646), sig. A2r.

[23]   Woodward, *A Short Letter*, sig. Av.

[24]   Woodward's tract caused such 'great Offence' that John Dury, another key member of the Hartlib circle wrote to Hartlib in April 1645 advising him to distance himself from

nonconformist beliefs led him to take offence at Edwards's virulently anti-tolerationist tract and he began his attack with a reading of the stylistic development of Edwards's prose in the four years between the appearance of *Reasons Against the Independent Government of Particular Congregations* and *Antapologia*:

> he hath improved his growth not a little within these foure yeares; for then he was matched by, *he knoweth whom*: (surely the Lord would have had him accounted that as a spetting in his face) and now hath attained to that height in the eyes of all the learned, that he is too tall a match for a woman. God man! (indeed the best have their failings).[25]

According to Woodward, the achievement of *Antapologia* is not a matter of doctrine or theology, but the manner in which it implies its addressee: Edwards's latest publication is written 'for the eyes of all the learned' and in such a way as to preclude any possible confutation by a female respondent. His earlier *Reasons* represents an inferior work because, tellingly, 'it was matched by, *he knoweth whom* ... a woman'. Despite the fact that the grounds for Woodward's encomium proved to be unsound when Chidley's *A New Yeares Gift* appeared in the following January, it seems incontrovertible that this mysterious 'woman' is, again, Katherine Chidley. The case for Chidley is made even stronger when we recognize that the way in which Woodward alludes to the text of this female respondent and the terms in which John Goodwin refers (however obliquely) to Chidley's *Justification of the Independent Churches of Christ* are strikingly similar. As we have seen, the latter confirms that Edwards has had to 'wipe off' the implications of a printed response by a female disputant – her texts are sensed rather than read. Woodward joins Goodwin in presenting women's pamphlet production in religious controversy as a male 'failing', but figures female authorship in a much more disturbingly graphic way. In a reading that is, apparently, divinely sanctioned ('the Lord would have had him' interpret it this way) he sensationally renders the woman's textual confrontation with Edwards as 'a spetting in his face'. The antifeminist aspects of this image are numerous. Most obvious is that move that denies the female disputant access to and knowledge of the lexis of religious controversy; she can only encounter her principal addressee with the indecorousness of a barbaric, pre-verbal code. Furthermore, set in its fullest misogynistic light, Woodward's pamphlet is perhaps more subtly irenic than other members of the Hartlib circle realized since the broadest spectrum of Protestant belief is appealed to at the precise moment that gender solidarity is invoked. Thus the religious breach can be healed when, according to the dictates of antifeminism and an ecumenical Christian brotherhood, this particular image of a confuted,

---

Woodward's partisan, inflammatory pamphlet; 3/2/109B, *The Hartlib Papers* (Sheffield, 1996).
[25] Woodward, *A Short Letter*, p. 5.

beleagured Edwards assumes the pathos of stock representations of the persecuted, spat upon Christ.[26]

If it is indeed Chidley who features as the contesting woman in all of these works then, as we shall see, insinuations of the bilious and violent nature of her writings are wide of the mark. The significance of such remarks, however, lies not in the acuity of their reflection upon Chidley's texts, but rather in the weight of connotative cultural assumption they bear. The image of spitting in someone's face registers as a shocking symbol for the wilful transgression or violation of societal prohibition. At such moments the relationship between language and authority is intensified; the radical resort to this violent non-verbal gesture is an attempt to flout and place oneself beyond the structures of power; as an authoritarian act it denotes the capacity of the powerful to signify and vilify as they choose. In this instance, Chidley's text is presented as a wilful violation of the language and authority of religious dispute, an unwarrantable female intrusion into an exclusively masculine domain.

Slingshots and Scolds: Gendering the Polemical Contexts of Religious Toleration

What are the assumptions governing Goodwin and Woodwards's peculiar rendition of this discursive encounter? Why must a woman's writing be rendered violent and non-verbal? We can only answer such questions by exploring some of the registers that structured early modern religious controversy. When Woodward was forced to publish a printed defence of his contentious reading of Edwards in the following year, he confirmed the centrality of authoritarian masculinism in religious controversy by justifying his arguments on gender rather than theological grounds. His pamphlet opens with the brash assertion that 'I shall speak in matters where no man ought to be silent' and proceeds to account for and validate the disruptive influence of his previous text by placing it within a scheme of Protestant history which is also a history of disruptive, argumentative men running from Calvin to Thomas Edwards:

> Brethren have troubled the Churches peace, and have broken the rule of charity, all throughout their writings ... Calvin speaks of a rough mouthed fellow; *Strides non loquitur*. And this which is visible too, and in every man's eye, That the sonnes of the Church have shown themselves to be the sonnes of the Cole, they have blown a

---

[26]   In a very different context, Edward Hyde, Earl of Clarendon, sought to evoke the pathos of being spat upon when reconstructing the heroism of Charles I at his trial. The perfect equanimity of the king when faced with 'barbarous and brutal behaviour' was best exemplified when 'one spit in his face, which his majesty without expressing any trouble wiped off with his handkerchief'; Edward Hyde, Earl of Clarendon, *History of the Rebellion and Civil Wars in England,* ed. W. Dunn Macray, 6 vols (Oxford, 1888), vol. 4, p. 487.

spark so long, that it is become a cole ... I thought it a matter greatly conducing to peace of the Church, to marke those and their writings, which have troubled the peace thereof; And here I noted Mr Edwards book ... so crosse is his manner of proceeding there ... And then also I shall not retract [my pamphlet], or repent of what I have done, touching that matter.[27]

For Woodward, it is no surprise or accident that amid this succession of incendiary pamphlets, his own should be deemed so inflammatory. Moreover, it is only through the recognition and acceptance of this unified system of disunity, an awareness that the history of Protestantism itself is one of *concordia discors*, that a Church of 'sonnes', 'men' and 'brethren' can be united in 'peace.' Such points were echoed by Presbyterian divines like Samuel Rutherford, who also saw that the diachronic way to God was composed of a series of synchronic disputes and disorders amongst men. In a pamphlet which appeared in the same year as Edwards's *Antapologia* he informs his readers: 'We strive as we are carnall, we dispute as we are men ... We often argue and dispute as we sail'.[28] Religious controversy thus rendered becomes homosocial engagement.

The masculinism of such positions was inevitably heightened by the fact that in other literature of the period the mutually constitutive quests for truth and the extirpation of all brands of religious error (whether Roman Catholic, Jewish, atheistical or wildly sectarian), had long been tied to images of Christian heroism. When bishop Tunstall wrote to Sir Thomas More requesting his assistance in writing the first vernacular refutation of William Tyndale and other Reformist heretics in 1528, he described the discursive and theological task in hand as a 'championship', predicting that More would find himself beset on all sides not by learned controversialists but by 'Andabatae', or visored gladiators.[29] Later in the century this figure of the solitary Christian champion was extensively interrogated and problematized by Spenser in *The Faerie Queene* with its need to frame the possibilities for female heroism in patriarchal Elizabethan contexts. Milton scrutinized the issue further in *Paradise Lost* wherein the respective merits of Christian and Satanic valour are frequently and complexly indeterminate. These monumental texts aside, it was common for more overtly polemical seventeenth-century writers to co-opt the image of the Christian hero as an unambiguously masculine trope.[30] Accordingly the valorous Christian writer would engage in

---

[27] Hezekiah Woodward, *Soft Answers Unto Hard Censures* (London, 1645), sig. Ar, p. 10.
[28] Samuel Rutherford, *The Due Right of Presbyteries* (London, 1644), sig. A3v–A4r.
[29] See 'Tunstal's Licence to More to Keep and Read Heretical Books' reprinted in C. Sturge, *Cuthbert Tunstall* (London, 1938), pp. 363–4. By styling controversialists as 'Andabatae' Tunstall was re-appropriating and re-energizing a term which had first been introduced to Reformist polemic by Luther in his *De Servo Arbitrio* (1525); Gordon Rupp et al., *Luther and Erasmus: Free Will and Salvation* (London, 1969), p. 170.
[30] See Michael West, 'Spenser and the Renaissance Ideal of Christian Heroism', *PMLA* 88:5 (1973), pp. 1013–32; Stanley Fish, 'Standing Only: Christian Heroism in *Paradise Lost*', *Critical Quarterly* 9:2 (1967), pp. 162–78.

pamphlet wars, duel with an adversary in print to defend the honour of the true Protestant religion. Edwards and his respondents are no exception here in that they, too, imagine the textual dynamics of religious controversy as highly rhetoricized instances of chilvalric gage exchange. John Goodwin, who, as we saw earlier, rejoiced in Edwards's bafflement at the hands of a female opponent, opens his response to *Gangraena* as if it were the prelude to ritualized aristocratic violence:

> I here cast the glove to him, that if he will accept of the challenge I will ... discover and find out as many errors and heresies ... as those he pretends ... to be at this day extant among those who by the authoritie of his pen are voted Sectaries in a far lesser number of his Classique party.[31]

In casting this particular material 'glove', Goodwin allows himself and his opponent access to those codes of honour and refinement which Woodward denied Chidley when he typed her textual engagement with Edwards as a 'spetting'. Gender and class imperatives coalesce here; Chidley lacks the vocabulary to articulate an honourable challenge to Edwards not only because she is a woman, but because she is a seamstress who – with a very different sense of the affinities between fabric and text, the material and the metaphorical – composed her pamphlets in distinctly non-elite contexts. Goodwin, a university-educated republican divine, attempts to use his sense of the decorum of aristocratic ceremony to his advantage elsewhere in his encounter with the younger Edwards. Goodwin mocks the heresiographer's appropriation of the rhetoric of adversarial combat on the grounds that it betrays his ignorance of the reciprocal form of the aristocratic challenge. He reminds his readers of:

> Those frequent *challenges* (if some of them for that height of spirit which breaths in them, be not defiances rather) made by him, not to a single adversary, nor to two or three onely but to halfe the number of perfection, to five at once, yea and those no babies neither, ... nay sometimes to all comers, to as many as have any mind to try their strength by dint of argument with him ... But for the Apologists ... he challengeth them over and over, at ease. *I professe myselfe of the judgement, and cast the glove to any of you five or to you all* ... p. 53. He hath the other glove yet to cast, and casts it (p. 98), after this manner *And I challenge you in all your reading to name me one Divine &c.* A third glove he casts to them (p. 117), with somewhat more indulgent reflection upon his own sufficiency.[32]

Whereas Goodwin presents himself as intimately acquainted with the etiquette of such trial-by-argument, Edwards seems absurdly unaware of the fact that for every challenge there must be a counter-challenge, for every text a rebuttal, and that in the world of religious controversy, as in that of the duel, you cannot issue material challenges, whether they be texts or gloves, indefinitely. Goodwin's sense of the

---

[31] Goodwin, *Cretensis*, p. 3.
[32] Idem., *Anapologesiates Antapologias*, p. 3.

absurdity of Edwards's position in this encounter is strikingly reminiscent, then, of the memorably satirical scene in Shakespeare's *Richard II* where Aumerle, Bagot, Fitzwater, Percy, Surrey and the enigmatic 'another Lord' exchange gage after gage in fits of hyperbolic, histrionic chivalry.[33] Viewed from another angle, though, Goodwin paints the strange picture of a heresiographer who revels in masculinist, socially elevated varieties of controversial rhetoric, only to be trapped by them.

It is telling, then, that Chidley's first pamphlet, *The Justification of the Independent Churches of Christ*, should seek to disrupt the martial thrust and rhetoric of religious controversy from its very title page (see figure 2). She begins with a biblical gloss from David's struggle with Goliath in the first Book of Samuel: 'Thou commest unto me with a Sword, and with a Speare, and with a Shield, but I come to thee in the name of the Lord of Hoasts'. This is a judiciously chosen text for a Separatist pamphlet since it records that period of Israelite history where local congregational rule was replacing more absolutist forms of civil government.[34] Whilst this gloss undoubtedly gestures towards the case for religious freedom which her pamphlet later argues so persuasively, it also reflects upon the adversarial arena of early modern religious controversy. If that arena was, as John Goodwin contended, littered with Edwards's misplaced gloves or pamphlet challenges, it was also filled by any number of other polemicists' textualized swords, spears and shields. Chidley, however, was sensitively attuned to the pseudo or mock aristocratic tenor of much religious controversy and therefore styled her own text in a radically different manner, rendering it as a rescripting of the David and Goliath encounter.

This was by no means an entirely original move. Countless Davids and Goliaths had been fronting the polemical skirmishes of male writers throughout the early modern period. Gabriel Harvey, for example, regarded his own pamphlet exchanges with Thomas Nashe as rhetorically violent episodes and mocked his opponent's famed corpulence by imagining him as a rather inferior, down-at-heel Goliath who, somewhat heavy around the middle, was more given to drinking than hand-to-hand combat.[35] So too when Rachel Speght's *Mouzell for Melastomus*

---

[33] See William Shakespeare, *King Richard II,* ed. Andrew Gurr (Cambridge, 1984), IV, i.

[34] See Gillespie, 'A Hammer in Her Hand', p. 218.

[35] 'Though I neuer phansied Tautologies, yet I cannot repeat it enough: I looked for a treaty of pacification: or imagined thou wouldest arme thy quill, like a stowt champion, with the compleat harnesse of Wit and Art: nay I feared the brasen shield, and the brasen bootes of Goliah, and that same hideous speare, like a weauers beame: but it is onely thy fell stomacke, that blustereth like a Northern winde: alas thy witt is as tame, as a duck; thy art as fresh as sower ale in summer; they brazen shield in thy forehead; thy brasen bootes in thy hart; they weauers beame in they tongue.'; Gabriel Harvey, *Pierces Supererogation or A new prayse of the olde asse* (London, 1593), pp. 184–5. For later examples which conceive of pamphlet exchange as the David and Goliath encounter see William Prynne, *The Church of Englands old antithesis to new Arminianism* (London, 1629), sig. ¶ 2r; Thomas Hall, *The*

appeared in 1617 as a confutation of Joseph Swetnam's infamous misogynstic tract *The Arraignment of Lewde, idle, froward and unconstant women*, it began in outraged, combative mood. The first pamphlet printed bearing a woman's name proclaimed 'The ... reason why I have adventured to fling this stone at vaunting *Goliah* is, to comfort the minds of all *Hevahs* sex'.[36] Crucially, though, at least one reader took offence at Speght's appropriation of such adversarial rhetoric and scrawled 'What, throwinge stones? Give me her arse' in the margin of their copy.[37] Arresting as this comment is (the desire for degradation rather than refutation is oddly situated in an interpretive context), it is also reminiscent of those later readings of Chidley's pamphlets which seek to 'wipe off' the effects of her words. The readers and writers of women's pamphlets must always, it would seem, be diverted by bodily matters with the result that correction of a female pamphleteer is construed as something to be administered physically rather than argued persuasively. Acutely aware of this, perhaps, Chidley adds a second biblical quotation to her title page, from the fourth book of Judges, and forces a space for the non-aristocratic female pamphleteer amid the rhetoricized male violence of a pamphlet war. Surrounded by male controversialists, she reminds her readers of Jael 'who tooke a naile of the tent, and tooke an hammer in her hand, and went softly unto him, and smote the naile into his temples and fastened it to the ground'. By provoking memories of the biblical heroine who pierces the temples of the Canaanite chief Sisera with a tent-peg, she acknowledges that her public religious discourse is bound to be styled as aggressively intrusive, a 'spetting' in the face as Woodward would have it. Chidley prefers from the outset, however, to stress the penetrating nature of her argument and the audacious, distinctly gendered nature of her intervention.[38]

Pulpit Guarded (London, 1651), p. 13. For a more extended deployment of the motif see *Goliah's Head Cut Off With His Own Sword* (London, 1655).

[36] Rachel Speght, *A Mouzell for Melastomus*, repr. in Barbara Keifer Lewalski (ed.), *The Polemics and Poems of Rachel Speght* (Oxford, 1996), p. 4.

[37] Rachel Speght, *A Mouzell for Melastomus* (London, 1617), sig. B4r; copy held Beinecke Library, Yale University, Ih Sp 33617M.

[38] This title page was remembered by sympathetic and hostile contemporaries alike. Edwards dismisses Chidley sorties into pamphlet controversy as inappropriate and aggressive when he labels Chidley 'a brazen-faced audacious old woman resembled unto Jael'. This image is also recalled by her staunchest seventeenth-century defender, John Lanseter. He views her print encounter with Edwards as a piece of divinely retributive Old Testament violence: 'when the woman came and strook the naile of Independency into the head of their Sisera, with the hammer of God's holy word; then their sport was spoiled and quasht'. The heroic actions of Jael were also remembered in the Leveller women's petitions of 1649; Chidley may have been instrumental in framing these texts. See Edwards, *Gangraena*, vol. 3, p. 170; John Lanseter, *Lanseter's Lance for Edwards's Gangrene* (London, 1646), sig. A2r; *The Humble Petition of Divers Wel-Affected Women* (London, 1649), p. 5; Gillespie 'A Hammer in Her Hand', pp. 223–9.

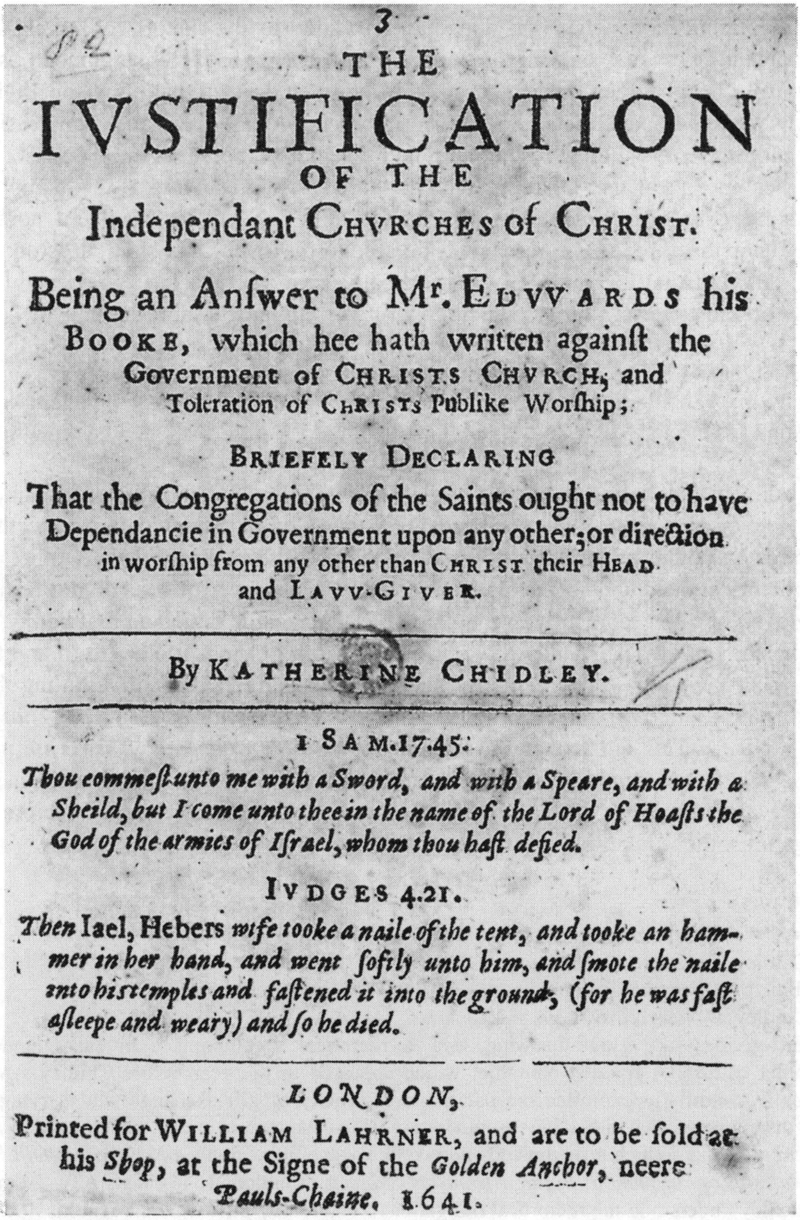

3

THE
IVSTIFICATION
OF THE
Independant CHVRCHES of CHRIST.

Being an Anſwer to Mr. EDVVARDS his BOOKE, which hee hath written againſt the Government of CHRISTS CHVRCH, and Toleration of CHRISTS Publike Worſhip;

BRIEFELY DECLARING

That the Congregations of the Saints ought not to have Dependancie in Government upon any other; or direction in worſhip from any other than CHRIST their HEAD and LAVV·GIVER.

By KATHERINE CHIDLEY.

1 SAM. 17.45.

Thou commeſt unto me with a Sword, and with a Speare, and with a Sheild, but I come unto thee in the name of the Lord of Hoaſts the God of the armies of Iſrael, whom thou haſt defied.

IVDGES 4.21.

Then Iael, Hebers wife tooke a naile of the tent, and tooke an hammer in her hand, and went ſoftly unto him, and ſmote the naile into his temples and faſtened it into the ground, (for he was faſt aſleepe and weary) and ſo he died.

LONDON,

Printed for WILLIAM LAHRNER, and are to be ſold at his *Shop,* at the Signe of the *Golden Anchor,* neere *Pauls-Chaine,* 1641.

Figure 2: Katherine Chidley, *The Justification of the Independent Churches of Christ* (1641) Chidley disrupts the aristocratic tenor of religious controversy from her title page.

In a similar fashion, when she does have recourse to the rhetoric of adversarial combat in her work (reading Edwards's construction of his argument as a 'mustering up of forces' and the process of confutation as a 'battering' or driving back), Chidley constructs her own intervention as distinctly amateurish. 'Concerning Armies', she says at one stage, 'I be very ignorant in these things'.[39] It soon becomes clear that Chidley reads the militaristic metaphors of this pamphlet war as Edwards's imposition when she informs him that 'neither this Scout, nor the joined, nor the subjoined forces, shall be able to discover what strength is on my side, although they be formed *by you* in battle array'.[40] She then goes on, in an archly literalistic turn, to mock the hollow ring of Edwards's sabre-rattling:

> If you intend to make your rejoinders, and large tractates ... of such stuffe as you have made this ... it were better for you to put on a buffe coat, & to go fight in the Army against your enemies, then to sit at home.[41]

This comically deflating moment reveals Chidley's desire to develop a much more finely nuanced view of the reciprocal dynamics of pamphlet controversy than Edwards and other polemicists of the period; she eschews the annihilative rhetoric and rhetorical dead ends of textualized violence. Thus her own texts do not feature as 'gloves' thrown scornfully in the face of an implacable opponent, but betray, as will be shown, a pacifistically dialogical perception of the pamphlet form and the agency involved in early modern pamphlet exchange. Thus in entitling her response to *Antapologia* as *A New Yeares Gift ... To Mr Thomas Edwards; That he may breake off his old sins in the old yeare, and begin the New yeare, with new fruits of Love* she binds herself not to a masculinist rhetorical system of incisive printed assertion and its counter, but to a very different series of reciprocal obligations, those inherent in gift exchange.[42]

---

[39] Chidley, *Justification*, p. 11.

[40] Ibid., p. 20; emphasis added.

[41] Chidley, *A New-Yeares-Gift*, p. 21.

[42] Gift-giving, like glove-throwing, was a rhetorical commonplace in early modern pamphlet culture. A royalist pamphlet which appeared in the year before Chidley's *New Yeares Gift* similarly exploited the pacifistic reciprocity of gift exchange whilst trying to press its message that the King should return to parliament in order to halt civil war's 'stream of blood/ Which now runs down even like a swelling flood'; *A New-yeares-Gift For his Majesty, or an humble Petition from his Subjects* (London, 1644), sig., A2v. Gerrard Winstanley understood the reciprocal obligations triggered by gifts when he sent his *A New-Yeers Gift* (1650) 'to the parliament and armie'. He expected the authorities in return to make English Common Land available to all: 'make restitution of the Lands which the Kingly power holds from us: *Set the oppressed free*; and come in, and honour Christ'; G. H. Sabine (ed.), *The Works of Gerrard Winstanley* (New York, 1941), p. 374. Pamphlet 'gifts' could also, however, be hostile as in the case of a sixteenth-century anti-Catholic pamphlet which opposed the generosity of gift giving with the mean-spirited ingratitude and civil

That said, Chidley's attempt to find a place for herself in this realm of aristocratic Christian champions, her endeavour to embed herself in these seams of all-male Protestant history, was almost inevitably going to be perceived as disruptive and transgressive. However, the sheer violence of the responses from the likes of Woodward and Goodwin, men who were, relatively speaking, her religious allies, requires further explanation. As other chapters show, some women could write controversial religious literature in this period that was met (at least initially) with praise rather than opprobrium. However, the prophetic modes of writing by women like Anna Trapnel, Elizabeth Poole, or Mary Cary afforded them a protection which is denied Chidley because of her generic choices. Where Poole, Trapnel and Cary write prophecy, Chidley writes animadversion.

Animadversion is an extremely common variety of pamphlet writing which proceeds through the absorption, reconfiguration and rebuttal of other printed texts and images. It has a rich Renaissance heritage having its roots in common humanist modes of argument. From its first appearance in the vernacular with Thomas More's confutation of William Tyndale, to its popularization in pamphlet form in the Marprelate controversy of the 1580s, right through to its proliferation and maturation in the pamphlet explosions of the 1640s, animadversion had always been attached to, but was not the exclusive property of, religious controversy.[43] Perhaps the most famous example of animadversion is Milton's *Animadversions Upon the Remonstrants Defence Against Smectymnuus* which was published in the same year as Chidley's *Justification* as a response to the royalist bishop Joseph Hall's *Defence of the Humble Remonstrance against the frivolous and false*

---

disobedience of English recusants; *A New Yeares Gifte Dedicated to the Popes Holinesse and all Catholikes Addicted to the Sea of Rome* (London, 1579).

[43] Given the welter of pamphlet controversies in the early modern period, surprisingly little work has been done on the rhetorical and historical contexts for animadversion. See Raymond, *Pamphlets and Pamphleteering*, pp. 206–14; Thomas Corns, *John Milton: The Prose Works* (New York, 1998), pp. 25–9; Maureen Thum, 'Milton's Diatribal Voice: The Integration and Transformation of a Generic Paradigm in *Animadversions*', *Milton Studies* 30 (1993), pp. 3–25; Thomas Kranidas, 'Style and Rectitude in Seventeenth-Century Prose: Hall, Smectymnuus, and Milton', *Huntington Library Quarterly* 46:3 (1983), pp. 237–69; Richard McCabe, 'The Form and Methods of Milton's *Animadversions Upon the Remonstrants Defence Against Smectymnuus*', *English Language Notes* 18:4 (1981), pp. 266–72; Michael Lieb, 'Milton's *Of Reformation* and the Dynamics of Controversy', in Michael Lieb and John T. Shawcross (eds.), *Achievements of the Left Hand: Essays on the Prose of John Milton* (Amherst, 1974). On the historical and rhetorical contexts for the Marprelate controversy see Raymond, *Pamphlets and Pamphleteering*, pp. 27–52; Smith, *Literature and Revolution*, pp. 297–304; R. A. Anselment, *'Betwixt Jest and Earnest': Marprelate, Milton, Marvell, Swift and the Decorum of Religious Ridicule* (Toronto, 1979); Peter Auski, 'Milton's "Sanctified Bitternesse": Polemical Technique in the Early Prose', *Texas Studies in Literature and Language* 19 (1977), pp. 363–81; James Egan, 'Milton and the Marprelate Tradition', *Milton Studies* 8 (1975), pp. 103–22.

exceptions of Smectymnuus.[44] The ingenuity of Milton's manipulation of the mode is emphasized in a famous moment from the pamphlet when the generically typical point-by-point refutation of Hall's *Remonstrance* suddenly takes a turn for the ludic and denunciatory:

> *Remon[strant].* No one Clergie in the whole Christian world yeelds so many eminent schollers, learned preachers, grave, holy and accomplish'd Divines as this Church of England doth at this day.
> *Answ.*   Ha, ha, ha.
> *Remon.*   And long, and ever may it flourish thus.
> *Answ.*   O pestilent imprecation! Flourish as it does at this day in the Prelates?
> *Remon.*   But oh forbid to have it told in Gath!
> *Answ.*   Forbid him rather, Sacred Parliament, to violate the sense of Scripture.[45]

As the prose moves from the traditional quotation of the opponent's discourse through a myriad of other registers (the carnivalesque, the imprecatory, the supplicatory) it reveals the multivocal, forceful potential of mid-seventeenth-century animadversion. Milton's appeal here, like that of Chidley's title page, resides in his self-conscious refusal of the clearly demarcated polite codes of religious controversy; by laughing scornfully and inveighing heartily he breaks the refined rules of engagement which ought to guide every honourable Christian animadvertist's reasoned response.

One of the reasons that Milton's counter-positioning of the popular and the elite in his *Animadversions* was so successful was because the genre itself had enjoyed immense popularity in the vernacular since the sixteenth century. Indeed the proliferation of printed animadversion in the period is such that the most recent account of early modern pamphlet culture offers a nine-part taxonomy of the mode as a way of making sense of its superabundance.[46] Despite this, it was not until the publication of Rachel Speght's *Mouzell for Melastomus* in 1617 that a woman set her name to an animadversion for the first time.[47] This was due in no small part to the fact that a number of early modern writers regarded animadversion as an antifeminist form of discourse. This became particularly evident after Chidley had

---

[44] The most concise summary of the dynamics of this controversy is in Corns, *John Milton: The Prose Works*, pp. 18–28.

[45] John Milton, *Animadversions Upon the Remonstrants Defence Against Smectymnuus* (1641), *CPW*, vol. 1, p. 726.

[46] Raymond, *Pamphlets and Pamphleteering*, pp. 210–14.

[47] However, Chidley's *Justification* deserves to be read as the first extended animadversion to be written by a woman since only one-fifth of Speght's work conforms to the typographic and generic conventions of this mode of critical cross-examination. Importantly, *Jane Anger her Protection for Women* (1589) appears to animadvert a pamphlet entitled *Boke his Surfeit in Love*. However, the author is pseudonymous and conceivably male. Furthermore, because the *Boke his Surfeit in Love* no longer survives, the extent and nature of Anger's animadversion are indeterminable.

written her *Justification* in 1641. When Josiah Ricraft penned his defence of *Gangraena* as an animadversion to John Goodwin's *Cretensis* in 1646 he criticized the latter's 'boisterous, inhumane, unchristian dialect' and, more particularly, the 'wilfull and importune spirits' that had propelled Goodwin beyond the strict generic confines of animadversion. 'Ignorant of Rhetoric and Logick', Goodwin had composed a 'heap of impudent lies' instead of a tightly focused, point-by-point critique of Edwards's heresiography.[48] Ricraft took offence at his opponent's expansive, unrestrainable style and, realizing that 'no conscientious Christian can approve of Mr Goodwin his unchristian language', threatened to put an end to their printed confrontation.[49] The only way forward was to enforce or break animadversion's strict reciprocal codes of proposition and rebuttal:

> I here make him a solemn promise, that I will never anti-pamphlet with him more: If he be wilful and resolved to have the last word, I shall not envy him the ignoble glory and privilege of a Scold.[50]

Numerous pamphlet writers reflected on the difficulty of maintaining the focus and strict order of animadversion; it is telling here, though, that Goodwin's inability to conform to the dictates of genre is figured as a characteristically female vice.[51] By continually wanting to have 'the last word', he betrays a degree of linguistic 'wilful[ness]' which rescinds his right to participate in formal theological dispute and transforms him into the equally unrestrainable 'Scold' who was so spectacularly and violently punished at practically every level of Renaissance culture.[52] However, as Ricraft tries to argue that the man who exceeds the bounds of animadversion is, rhetorically speaking, a shrewish woman his own

---

[48]   Josiah Ricraft, *A Nosegay of Rank-smelling Flowers* (London, 1646), pp. 6, 10.

[49]   Ibid., p. 23.

[50]   Ibid., p. 8.

[51]   For instance Francis Turner later recalled that 'it is one thing to strike at random, as commonly Polemical authors do, or to oppose those passages in their Adversaries book, which are ready to fall of themselves, and to pass by those which urge and press them harder; and quite another thing to keep one another to the point'; *Animadversions Upon a Late Pamphlet* (London, 1676), p. 26; cited in Raymond, *Pamphlets and Pamphleteering*, p. 214.

[52]   On the position and status of the scold in early modern England see Lynda E. Boose 'Scolding Bridles and Bridling Scolds: Taming the Woman's Unruly Member', in Ivo Kamps (ed.), *Materialist Shakespeare: A History* (London, 1993), pp. 239–79; David Underdown, 'The Taming of the Scold: The Enforcement of Patriarchal Authority in Early Modern England', in A. Fletcher and J. Stephenson (eds.), *Order and Disorder in Early Modern England* (Cambridge, 1985), pp. 116–36; M. Andressen-Thom, 'Shrew Taming and Other Rituals of Aggression: Baiting and Bonding on the Stage and in the Wild', *Women's Studies* 9 (1982), pp. 121–43.

(I')

THE
IVSTIFICATION
OF THE
Independant Churches of *CHRIST*,

Being an *Anſwer* to Mr.*Edwards* his *Booke*
Which he hath written againſt the *Government*
of Christs Chvrch, and Toleration of
CHRISTS Publike Worſhip.

Mr. *EDWARDS*,

 Underſtanding that you are a mighty Champion, and now muſtering up your mighty forces (as you ſay) and I apprehending they
muſt come againſt the Hoaſt of *Iſrael*, and
hearing the Armies of the Living God ſo defied by you, could nor be withheld, but that
I (in ſtead of a better) muſt needs give you
the meeting.

Firſt. Whereas you affirme, *That the Church of God (which is
his Houſe and Kingdome) could not ſubſiſt with ſuch proviſion as their
father gave them: which proviſion was* (by your owne confeſſion)
*the watering of them by Evangeliſts, and Prophets, when they were plan-
ted by the Apoſtles, and after planting and watering to have Paſtors and
Teachers, with all other Officers, ſet over them by the Apoſtles & their own
Election, yet notwithſtanding all this proviſion, the Father hath made for
them, it was evident* (ſay you) *they could not well ſtand of themſelves,
without ſome other helpe.*

This was the very ſuggeſtion of Sathan into the hearts of our
firſt Parents; for they having a deſire of ſome thing more then
was warranted by God, tooke unto them the forbidden fruit,
as you would have the Lords Churches to doe, when you ſay
they muſt take ſome others beſides theſe Churches and Officers,
and that to interpoſe authoritatively; and theſe ſomething elſe
you make to be Apoſtles, Evangeliſts, and Elders of other
A   Churches,

Figure 3: Katherine Chidley, *The Justification of the Independent Churches of Christ*
(1641) This is the typical page layout for Chidley's animadversions. She gives plentiful
typographical space to her opponent and mocks the militaristic tenor of religious
controversy.

writing begins to unpick itself. At such moments, which are reminiscent of those more familiar occasions when someone tells you that they are not speaking to you, the medium cannot bear the message and, according to the terms of his own logic, Ricraft effeminizes himself.

Whilst Ricraft was demeaning Goodwin and defending Edwards, Edwards himself was setting and policing animadversion's formal boundaries in a more precise, masculinist fashion:

> I suppose the excellencie of an Answer (as distinct from writing Tractates upon such a subject or such a point) consists in three things. 1. In not speaking whatever a man pleases, or bringing in whatever he hath a mind to, but in following the text before him, and in keeping all his discourse close to that. 2. In not omitting any materiall passages, skipping over the knots, passing by the hard arguments and falling upon the weake, snatching here and there, but going through all. 3. In labouring to take the Authors mind laid down in the words and scope, and in not wresting and fastning another sense upon the Author.[53]

Edwards's archetypal animadvertist knows when to respond and when to be silent, is focused, well-read and possesses that rigorous intellectual honesty which permits the unravelling of intricate arguments and, apparently, the recovery of authorial intention. As such 'he' is unambiguously male. Even John Goodwin found himself in agreement with his adversary on this matter when he opened his animadversion of *Antapologia* with a justification which could almost come from his opponent's text itself: 'As his Tractates or Books were his to write, so are they mine or any other man's to answer'.[54]

Justification Cannot Be Self-Justification

With such a densely complex network of masculinist interdiction and antifeminist prohibition in place, Chidley's two extant, extensive animadversions thus become anomalous and problematic. In what follows, I contend that Chidley writes forcefully in this hostile arena by deploying a rhetoric of self-effacement which pushes the structure of her chosen genre to its limits. What we might think of as her inclusive manipulation of animadversion's and humanism's first principles (that truth must be attained through dialogue) actually has its roots in a pro-toleration position which was daringly egalitarian and sought to uphold the fundamental democratic rights of virtually all citizens and believers irrespective of wealth and social status. We have already seen her defence of non-aristocratic mothers who were prey to both the physical demands of childbirth and the economic exigencies of prelacy. Perhaps unsurprisingly, given her concern for

---

[53] Edwards, *Antapologia*, sig. A2v.
[54] Goodwin, *Anapologesiates Antapologias*, sig. d2r.

those in subordinate subject positions, her views on religious toleration are similarly broad. Whilst Chidley was as virulently anti-Catholic as the next seventeenth-century puritan, she was, nonetheless, relatively unusual in her persistent assertion that:

> Jewes and Anabaptists may have a toleration also ... For my part I speake for myselfe, and I suppose that they may say as much for themselves ... as the Separates doe, for they maintaine their poore, and their Ministers, and the poore, and the Priests of the Church of England as well as we. And I think they are persecuted and hunted also; but I will leave them to plead for themselves.[55]

For Chidley, toleration and liberty of conscience are not about the simple promulgation of divinely sanctioned truths, but can be sensed instead in the unrestrained, dialogic interplay of a welter of different religious voices, in the gloriously cacophonous moment when Jew, Anabaptist and Separatist 'speake', 'say' and 'plead for themselves' beyond the confines of controlling texts and authors. The contrast with Edwards's anti-tolerationist, Presbyterian position could not be starker. Edwards seeks to curtail freedom of expression and goes so far as to envisage a restriction of the movement of dissenting saints:

> There ought to be no Toleration; everyone in their place; everyone in their place ought to be against it, the Magistrates, Ministers and the People. The permitting and suffering of evill, with the giving of any countenance to it, when men have power to hinder it, is to be partakers of sin ... Is it fitting that well meaning Christians should be suffered to goe and make Churches, and proceed to chuse who they will for ministers, as some Taylor, Felt Maker, Button maker, men ignorant, and low in parts, by whom they shall be led into sinne and error, and to forsake the publicke assemblies, where they may enioy worthy and pretious Pastors, after Gods own heart, who would feed them with knowledge and understanding.[56]

Here the strictures of anti-populism demand that Edwards replace Chidley's chaotic yet egalitarian scheme of diversely dissonant voices with the more orderly, uni-directional image of 'feed[ing]'. 'Well meaning Christians' have 'knowledge and understanding' given to them by 'Pastors' whose nourishing word is accorded a primacy and legitimacy denied the 'Taylor, Felt Maker' or 'Button maker'.

The implications that these positions have for Chidley's sense of agency in print controversy can be demonstrated by attending more closely to the dynamics of Edwards and Chidley's pamphlet dialogue. In an extended set-piece from his first Presbyterian text, Edwards lays bare the foundations for the anti-tolerationist position on the grounds that:

---

[55]   Ibid., p. 44.

[56]   Edwards, *Reasons Against the Independent Government*, p. 23.

toleration will not onely breede Divisions and Schismes, disturbing the peace and quiet of Churches and Townes, by setting them who are of different families ... against one another, but it will undoubtedly cause much disturbance, discontent, and divisions in the same families even between the nearest relations of husbands and wives, Fathers and children, brothers and sisters, Masters and servants: The husband being of one Church, & the wife of another ... and so all Oeconomicall relations and duties will be much disturbed, when as they of one house, and they in one bed shall be so divided, as that they shall not be of one Church, nor worship one God together ... but apart. O how will this overthrow all peace and quiet in families, filling husbands and wives with discontents, and setting at variance ... weakening that fervant love in those relations! O how will this occasion disobedience, contempt, neglects of Governours from the inferiors of the family! ... O how will this toleration take away ... that power, authority, which God hath given the husbands, fathers and masters, over wives, children, servants![57]

The eradication of the sects is the necessary purge upon which civil order, the nuclear family and the 'Oeconomic' well being of the entire nation depend. Edwards presents an argument which is thoroughly monologic; not only in that it sounds the Presbyterian voice whilst muting all others, but also in its repeated use of emotional exclamation through the repeated rhetorical figure of ecphonesis.[58] The ecphonetic force of 'O how' depends not upon reciprocal appeals to real, active participants in a dialogue, but rather draws its strength from the rapt attention of an imagined, pointedly silent, audience. Chidley responds to this section of Edwards's *Reasons* by engaging (instead of mastering and silencing) all voices in the controversy:

Againe you say, *(O how) this will occasion disobedience.*
    To this your Lamentation I answer. O that you would remember the rule that every servant ought to count his master worthy of all honour; and in the judgment of charitie beleeve that persons professing the Gospel will learne that lesson.

---

[57]   Edwards, *Reasons Against the Government of Particular Congregations*, p. 26.
[58]   The most extended consideration of the cultural importance monologism and dialogism is, of course, to be found in the work of Mikhail Bakhtin. See his *Problems of Dostoevsky's Poetics*, and *The Dialogic Imagination: Four Essays*, trans. Caryl Emerson and Michael Holquist (Austin, 1981). For further contributions to and criticism of dialogical theory see Sue Vice, *Introducing Bakhtin* (Manchester and New York, 1997); Michael Holquist, *Dialogism: Mikhail Bakhtin and His World* (London and New York, 1990); G. S. Morton and C. Emerson, *Mikhail Bakhtin: Creation of a Prosaics* (Stanford, 1990); Ken Hirschkop, 'Is Dialogism for Real', *Social Text* 30 (1987), pp. 102–13; idem., 'Bakhtin, Discourse and Democracy', *New Left Review* 160 (1986), pp. 92–113. At times Bakhtin's thoughts on monologism sound like an updated theorization of Edwards's Presbyterian position: 'Monologism at its extreme denies the existence outside itself of another consciousness with equal rights and equal responsibilities, another I with equal rights ... With a monological approach ... another person remains wholly and merely an object of consciousness, and not another consciousness.'; Bakhtin, *Problems of Dostoevsky's Poetics*, pp. 285, 292.

Next you say *O how will this take away that power and authority which God hath given to Husbands, Fathers, and Masters over wives, children and servants.*

To this I answer O! that you would consider the text in *1 Cor 7* which plainly declares that the wife may be a beleever & the husband an unbeleever ... if you have considered this text, I pray you tell me, what authority this unbeleeving husband hath over the conscience of his beleeving wife; It is true he hath authority over her in bodily and physical respects, but not to be a Lord over her conscience.[59]

In giving plentiful, typographically differentiated textual space to the directly quoted words of her antagonist, Chidley draws upon one of the stock humanistic tactics of print controversy in the period so that even cursory attention to the text leaves one with the sense that two distinct voices are clashing within the confines of her pamphlet. However her writing here is much more significantly dialogical than simple proposition and rebuttal. Through her parodic manipulation of Edwards's 'Oh!', she gives genuinely fresh dialogical impetus to traditionally uni-directional ecphonesis. She appeals now not to a silently captive audience but to an anonymous yet actively participating print readership who are free to weigh the profundity or levity of repeated words in multiple texts for themselves.

In thus inflecting the original Edwardsian lament back on itself, Chidley persuades by empowering a reading public who, through the application of reason, can ascertain the rational bases of congregational worship.[60] Her readers are encouraged to work for their insights by discerning the multivocal qualities of the written word. With the reference to I Corinthians 7, it soon becomes clear that the authoritative nature of Chidley's prose derives its poise and confidence from the fact that the controlling, enunciatory 'I' has problematically located itself on the threshold of both the Pauline epistle and the animadvertist's response.[61] The narratorial 'I' does not unambiguously register Chidley's inscribing presence, but simultaneously invokes another first person capable of sounding a biblical, epistolary mode of address. This tactic is all the more fascinating in that it is absolutely distinct from other forms of self-effacement upon which so much early modern women's prophetic writing depended. The Pauline text Chidley invokes lays claim to an authority which abjures any divine basis: 'speak I, not the Lord', Paul reminds his readers. Chidley's agency here, then, is not dependent on the more typical sublimation of the self or narratorial 'I' within Christ, a subordination of the medium beneath the message, but on the readiness to sound voices that are

---

[59]   Chidley, *Justification*, p. 26.

[60]   Chidley's writing thus gives further credibility to Raymond's argument that 'the idea of public opinion had been created, grounded in the most common form of print'; *Pamphlets and Pamphleteering*, p. 262.

[61]   The full text Chidley alludes to is: 'But to the rest speak I, not the Lord: If any brother have a wife that believeth not, and she be pleased to dwell with him, let him not put her away. And the woman which hath an husband that believeth not, and if he be pleased to dwell with her, let her not leave him. For the unbelieving husband is sanctified by the wife, and the unbelieving wife is sanctified by the husband', I Cor 7, vv. 12–14.

proximate to, yet historically distinct from, her own. Furthermore, in this particular example subtle narratorial self-effacement is performed at precisely the same moment as Chidley downplays the significance of female bodily presence (a husband may well be Lord over a woman in 'bodily and physical respects') in order to foreground the radically non-spectacular power of a woman's conscience. In fact, by enjoining her disputant and readers to engage in dialogue with and actively 'consider', remember, or locate for themselves (rather than merely read a reprinting of) the original Pauline text, Chidley may well have been aware that the original passage to which she alludes contained a much more daring reading than the one she explicitly offers here. Verse 4 makes a case for the rights of *both* sexes in marriage to exercise power over the partner's body: 'The wife hath not power of her own body, but the husband: and likewise also the husband hath not power of his own body but the wife'.

Agency for Chidley, as it was indeed for Trapnel, is thus fundamentally dependent on a willingness to stress the presence of others in the creative process. Her animadversions open up the confines of the genre by downplaying the importance of the individual, combative author-hero in favour of a complex exploration of the multiple agencies required to make pamphlet dialogue and (as importantly) religious toleration work. They do this by pledging a belief in the vital productiveness of the present moment. Whilst a number of early modern pamphlet writers sought imaginatively to reconstruct the scene of writing by creating an aura of bibliographic immediacy, or re-awaken an awareness of books, rooms and paper, Chidley's pamphlets go further than this by embracing what might be regarded as free invention in an open-ended present.[62] These are no stenographer's reports of finished altercations with Thomas Edwards, but are instead dynamic, dialogic texts written from the immediate present of the creative process, poised on the threshold between competing subjectivities and narratorial positions.[63] Thus, for example, Chidley begins a line of argument with Edwards about the sources of funding for the education of ministers which is pressed in direct opposition to the stock Presbyterian case for the necessity to levy tithes on parishes to fund the training of clerics. She focuses instead on 'the mighty Revenues', which the church already commands and advocates a ministerial educational system that is self-funded: 'you might rather have perswaded your Parish Priests to have bequeathed some of their large revenue [for] the maintenance of scholars' she informs her disputant.[64] Her argument proceeds through thorough-going materialist analyses of the impact that tithe payment and burial duties have on the lives of the poorest members of the parish, the way in which at times of mourning and grief the sum

---

[62] On early modern pamphlet writers' attempts to recreate the scene of writing see Raymond, *Pamphlets and Pamphleteers, passim.*

[63] The last two sentences have been similarly positioned in relation to a passage from Bakhtin's *Problems of Dostoevsky's Poetics*, p. 63.

[64] Chidley, *Justification*, p. 56.

total of 'Bearers wages, Grave diggers wages', 'the ground' and the dues of a 'twelve-penny priest' exact '7 or 8 shillings' from families who 'be not worth a shilling'.[65] However, when she recalls the specific material sufferings of 'wives and children, destitute of Calling and Maintenance' alongside the luxurious livings of a maintained national clergy, the logic of her finely plotted materialist argument begins to fragment. It is almost as if in the violent arena of printed religious dispute Chidley suddenly begins to try to unsettle her antagonist by extemporizing in diverse, unexpected ways. Thus she abruptly re-routes her argument to:

> confesse that I was overseene (in the entrance to this Discourse) when I moved you to perswade these men to bequeath something to their brethren (that are Schollers bred) for I did not consider that though they received much, yet they had but little to give, because it is not blessed for increase: but I should rather have comforted you, with giving you knowledge that God hath provided maintenance for his Ministers; as well as for his People, that they need not bow to you for a morsell of bread; for God taught his apostles to worke with their hands, as Paul saith.[66]

She thus refuses to interpose any reflective distance between herself, her text and her opponent but writes, as it were, from the immediate moment of the disputative-creative process. Arguments are penned as they are forged in the heat of the clash between Edwardsian, Pauline and narratorial voices. Thus the text is not a pristine moment of reflection, a sovereign point of meditation on things past, but rather expresses a belief in and commitment to the productiveness of present and future. Such optimism provides us with a new sense of the revolutionary polemical encounter as something genuinely open and full of potential.

Chidley's animadversions, like her public disputes, might therefore be thought of as wilfully unfinished or, indeed, unfinishable; they repudiate the generic closure, the rhetorical dead ends traditionally offered the polemicist in order to remain resolutely processal and defiantly open-ended. William Greenhill's repeated attempts to retreat from the 'wearying' dispute in Stepney with which this chapter began are just one graphic illustration of the fact that, for Chidley, dispute and dialogue are never over. The ending of her *Justification*, moreover, is similarly committed to the continuing proliferation of discourse:

> And now (Mr Edwards) for conclusion of the whole, I doe here affirme, that if upon sight of this Booke, you shall conceive that I have either misconstrued your words or accused you without ground ... or that I have mistaken any sense of any Scripture ... or that I have not answered you directly to the point (by any oversight) Then choose you sixe men, (or more if you please) and I will choose as many, and if you will we will agree upon a Moderator, and trie it out in a faire discourse.[67]

---

[65] Ibid., pp. 57–8.
[66] Ibid., p. 59.
[67] Ibid., pp. 80–1.

At one level, Chidley's invitation here demonstrates the long-standing interdependence of printed animadversions and formal set-piece disputations, those formal, elaborate, all-male confrontations that would have been commonplace to those who had completed a university or even grammar school education and that, presumably, did much to inhibit women's manipulation of the genre.[68] At another level she also offers a conclusion to her pamphlet that is really no conclusion at all. In an exquisitely open-ended and complex moment of self-effacement she downplays the finality and final importance of her agency in a speech act to leave the concluding words of her text full of potential on the threshold of 13 other addressees.[69]

Animadversion, thus rendered, lays bare the dialogic foundations of language and truth. Even if this insight had long been central to project of Renaissance humanism, the importance of such open-ended conclusions (the unfinished business) of Chidley's manipulation of the dominant mode of printed religious dispute ought not to be underestimated. By representing the encounter of the remonstrant and animadvertist as productively unfinished, we gain a new sense of the agency of the animadvertist as being based upon strategies of self-effacement. The unfinished quality of the text posits the absolute equality and centrality of the remonstrant's (and indeed all other potential respondants') discourses alongside her own and, indeed, the very title of her *Justification* itself reveals a reliance on and anticipation of other discourses. A pertinent passage from Mikhail Bakhtin's revision notes for his *Problems of Dostoevsky's Poetics* best unpacks the full implications of this:

> I cannot manage without another, I cannot become myself without another; I must find myself in another by finding another in myself ... Justification cannot be self-justification, recognition cannot be self-recognition. I receive my name from others, and it exists for others.[70]

---

[68]   On disputations see Ann Hughes, 'The Meanings of Religious Polemic', in F. J. Brenner (ed.), *Puritanism: Transatlantic Perspectives on a Seventeenth-Century Anglo-American Faith*, pp. 201–29; idem., 'The Pulpit Guarded: Confrontations Between Orthodox and Radicals in Revolutionary England', in Ann Laurence, W. R. Owens and Stuart Sims (eds.), *John Bunyan and His England, 1628–1668* (London and Roncevert, 1990), pp. 31–50. For a seventeenth-century perspective see John Ley, *A Discourse of Disputations Chiefly Concerning Matters of Religion with Animadversions on two printed Books* (London, 1653).

[69]   There is no evidence that Edwards ever responded to this particular challenge. Chidley persistently replicates the unfinalizable tactics of her *Justification*. For instance, the conclusion to an argument about the rights of lay preachers in her *Good Counsel to the Petitioners* concludes: 'therefore I ... wish it might please the Parliament to examine the gifts of such whom these call illiterate (so that it may appear how reasonable we are) ... by disputation between the Presbyters and them'; no sig. A similar invitation was made earlier in the century by Richard Hooker. See his *Of the Lawes of Ecclesiastical Politie* (London, 1617), sig. C6r.

[70]   Bakhtin, *Problems of Dostoevsky's Poetics*, pp. 287–8.

Likewise, Chidley's *Justification* can never be deemed simple *self-Justification*. According to the form and logic of all of her pamphlets, and in direct contradistinction to the dictates of Edwards's brand of Presbyterianism, authorship has nothing to do with the self-aggrandizing promulgation of apparently self-evident truths. Instead Chidley's work encourages us to see the pamphleteer as the selfless, pacifistic mediator of verbal exchange.

Chapter 2

Agency in Crisis:
Women Write the Regicide

Lord President. Sir, I must interrupt you, which I would not doe, but that what you doe is not agreeable to the proceedings of any court of Justice, you are about to enter into Argument, and dispute concerning the authority of this court, before whom you appear as a prisoner, and are charged as an High Delinquent; if you take upon you to dispute the Authority of the court, we may not do it, nor will any court give way unto it, you are to submit unto it, you are to give a punctuall and direct answer, whether you will answer your charge or no, and what your answer is.

The King. Sir, by your favour, I do not know the formes of Law, I do know Law and Reason, though I am no Lawyer profess'd, but I know as much Law as any Gentleman in *England*; and therefore (under favour) I do plead for the Liberties of the people of *England* more than you do, and therefore if...

Lord President. I must interrupt you, you may not be permitted ... you are not to dispute our Authority; you are told it again by the court. Sir, it will be taken notice of, that you stand in contempt of the court, and your contempt will be recorded accordingly.[1]

The epigraph to this chapter details an unusual exchange that took place on 22 January 1649 at the High Court of Justice at Westminster, in which the President of the Court, John Bradshaw, and Charles I brought the trial of the king to one of its many climaxes. Charles stood charged accountable for the depredations of the recent civil wars and the infringement of the rights and 'Liberties of the people of England'. He went to his death only eight days after making this utterance, continually disputing the 'Authority' of the court, and refusing accordingly to offer anything approaching a cogent line of defence against the court's charge of high treason.[2] It is questionable (after the collapse of the Treaty of Newport and once

---

[1] *A Perfect Diurnall* 287, 22–29 Jan. 1648/9, p. 2307. The *Diurnall* gave one of the fullest reports of the trial as its editor, Samuel Pecke, reprinted the official accounts of the court's proceedings. On the role of newsbooks during the trial and execution of Charles I see Joseph Frank, *The Beginnings of the English Newspaper 1620–1660*, (Cambridge, MA, 1961), pp. 169–75; Joad Raymond, *Making the News: An Anthology of the Newsbooks of Revolutionary England, 1641–1660* (Moreton-in-Marsh, 1993), pp. 124–7.
[2] Accounts of the events and debates surrounding the regicide can be found in Sean Kelsey, 'The Death of Charles I', *Historical Journal* 45:4 (2002), pp. 727–54; Jason Peacey (ed.), *The Regicides and the Execution of Charles I* (London, 2001); Sarah Barber, *Regicide and Republicanism: Politics and Ethics in the English Revolution, 1646–1659* (Edinburgh, 1998); Robert B. Partridge, *'O Horrable Murder': The Trial, Execution and Burial of*

the trial itself had been determined upon) whether the king could have offered any form of verbal defence that would have spared his life; but the manner in which he attempts to do so in the account from *The Perfect Diurnall* is significant.[3] Alongside the rights of the English 'people' and their elective body, also under contention is the ability of a man to govern through knowledge and his capacity to apply 'Reason' through its prime manifestation in the 'Law'. Charles's gesture of self-debasement at this critical moment is therefore telling: 'I do not know the formes of Law, I do know Law and Reason, though I am no Lawyer profess'd, but I know as much Law as any Gentleman in England'. He only accrues legalistic knowledge with a precipitate fall in social status, a process that enables him to eschew the traditional monarchical perspective wherein a king was seen to be beyond the scope or influence of the law due to the royal prerogative.[4] Yet whilst 'Law' and 'Reason' might be subtly bestowed via this rhetorical social levelling, such knowledge could only be fully grasped once the gender specificity of the

---

Charles I (London, 1998); Ian Gentles, *The New Model Army in England, Ireland and Scotland, 1645–1683* (Oxford and Cambridge, MA, 1992), pp. 266–314; Noel Henning Mayfield, *Puritans and Regicide: Presbyterian-Independent Differences Over the Trial and Execution of Charles (I) Stuart* (Lanham and London, 1988); David Underdown, *Pride's Purge: Politics in the Puritan Revolution* (Oxford, 1971); Wedgwood, *Trial;* S. R. Gardiner, *History of the Great Civil War 1642–1649*, 4 vols (London, 1987) vol. 4, pp. 233–330; J. G. Muddiman, *The Trial of Charles I* (Edinburgh and London, 1928); John Nalson, *The Trial of Charles the First, King of England, Before the High Court of Justice for High Treason* (Oxford, 1753); *King Charles His Tryall: Or a Perfect Narrative of the Whole Proceedings of the High Court of Justice* (London, 1649); *A Perfect Narrative of the Whole Proceedings of the High Court of Justice* (London, 1649).

[3]   There is much disagreement about the status of the king's death as an inevitable consequence of the trial. For recent accounts which dispute the unavoidability of regicide see Sean Kelsey, 'The Trial of Charles I', *English Historical Review* 118: 447 (2003), pp. 585–616; idem., 'The Death of Charles I'.

[4]   The position Charles advances here is atypical; elsewhere in the trial he continually asserted his kingly prerogative which he thought ought to exempt him from the proceedings of the High Court of Justice. However, asserting his gentlemanly status was perhaps the deftest rhetorical ploy of the entire trial. Whether or not a monarch was above the law was, of course, one of the major points of contention throughout the whole revolutionary period, and the argument that a king was actually within the scope of the law was one of the foundational arguments of the revolutionaries and regicides themselves. Charles's adoption of this strategy might therefore be seen as political suicide. However it exploited a tension in the regicides' logic. Alongside the argument that Charles was a mere man, or a 'gentleman of England' as Charles himself put it, was the charge that he was a tyrant, a difficult leap to make logically if one accepts Milton's definition of a tyrant as one who 'regarding neither Law nor the common good, reigns only for himself and his faction'. Thus allying himself with the gentlemen of England, ever the subject of law, Charles was, in effect, confuting the charge of tyranny on the regicides' own terms. See Barber, *Regicide and Republicanism*, pp. 40–65, 126–7. On the relationship between the king and the law throughout the revolutionary period, see Glenn Burgess, *The Politics of the Ancient Constitution* (Basingstoke, 1992); J. G. A. Pocock, *The Ancient Constitution and the Feudal Law* (Cambridge and New York, 1987), pp. 306–34. For Milton's definition of a tyrant see *The Tenure of Kings and Magistrates* in *CPW*, vol. 3, p. 212.

claim was made explicit. In the fraught proceedings of the High Court of Justice, Charles in effect appeals to his masculinity, his gentlemanliness, as much as his sovereignty, in an attempt to gain the right to speak in his own defence.

At one level, Lord President Bradshaw's continual reminder that he 'must interrupt' Charles to prevent him from speaking points to a prevalent fear of the popularity of the king amongst radicals.[5] However, it ought also to remind us of one of the more problematic silences in the proceedings of the High Court of Justice. In this dangerous, disputative arena, where even kings could be silenced as the 'Freedom and Liberty of the *People* of England' were defended, what happened to the freedom, liberties and voices of those women who played such crucial roles in the dramas of the civil wars? In the previous chapter we saw how debates surrounding religious toleration were predicated upon a cross-party conviction of the necessity of female silence. It is perhaps no surprise to discover that much the same atmosphere sustains the environment of regicide dispute. An incident from the High Court of Justice on 27 January is particularly revealing, therefore, in this regard. Almost certain of the dramatic course events were going to take in the next three days, the king entered the final session of the trial and instead of waiting until the Lord President had opened proceedings, attempted to offer a speech in defence of monarchy. The Lord President once again interrupted and countered: 'Gentlemen, it is well known to all, or most of you here present, that the prisoner at the bar hath been several times convened and brought before the Court to make answer to a charge of treason and other high crimes exhibited against him in the name of the people of England—'.[6] However, notwithstanding the legalistic homosociality of the address a masked woman, Lady Ann Fairfax, wife of the army's Lord General, called from the gallery 'Not a half, not a quarter of the people of England. Oliver Cromwell is a traitor'.[7] Lady Fairfax's interruption probably has less to do with her status as defender of the rights of seventeenth-century Englishwomen than her own Presbyterian fears concerning the danger and illegality of the High Court's proceedings; nonetheless it certainly suggests that around the time of the king's trial women's political consciousnesses were sensitively attuned to recent developments in matters of state, and that this enabled some to highlight the exclusive, unlawful and unprecedented nature of

---

[5]   The radical minority's fear of the king's popularity is something that has continually been underestimated by historians of the period. The army's *Remonstrance*, which was presented to parliament on 20 November 1648, continually stressed that public safety rested in the deposition of the king, acknowledged the king's 'reputation among the people' and was concerned that the majority 'will surely be more apt to join unanimously with him or let him have what he will, that there may be no war.'; cited in Gentles, *New Model*, p. 275.

[6]   Nalson, *Trial*, pp. 24–5; Wedgwood, *Trial*, p. 154.

[7]   Ibid; Clarendon, *History of the Rebellion*, vol. 4, p. 486. Wedgwood is more sceptical than either of the seventeenth-century chroniclers that the disputant was in fact Lady Fairfax.

legal procedure at the High Court.[8] In fact this was not the first time that Lady
Fairfax had interrupted the proceedings of the trial. On the opening day, as the
court's clerk John Phelps was reading the roll-call of the Commissioners, she rose
as he read out her husband's name and said 'He has more wit than to be here'.[9]
This determination to interrupt and intervene in the political process further
contributed to Lady Fairfax's unpopularity amongst the army, an unpopularity that
had intensified following the discovery in 1647 that she was relaying inside
information from the Army Council debates at Putney to Charles I. Indeed, shortly
after the trial one of Fairfax's female relatives was mistaken for the Lord General's
wife and received a death threat. In light of this, the response of the court is also
telling; Colonel Daniel Axtell, who was responsible for the security at the trial,
ordered his men to level their muskets at her, branded her a whore and promptly
bustled her out of the chamber.[10]

What is at stake at the High Court of Justice is more than the simple restraint of
a typological, gendered loquacity as a mark of respect for legal procedure, but can
be regarded instead as part of an attempt at the systematic exclusion of women
from the forum of regicide discussion. This may also be seen in a series of
sensational post-Restoration letters between Archbishop William Sancroft,
sometime Dean of St Paul's and Archbishop of Canterbury, and his doctor Dr John
Levett. These unofficial documents reconstruct a brief narrative of some of the
events at the High Court of Justice and according to Levett are ratified by a
number of eminent Restoration courtiers: 'Colonel Grey, ... Mr Andrew Cole (one
of his Majesty's Querries) [one of the keepers of the king's horses], Mr Robinson,
the Duke of York's chirurgion ... confirm the same for truth'.[11] They report that on
the same day that Lady Fairfax made her acerbic comment about her husband's
absence from the High Court, one Anna De Lille, daughter of William Fowler
(poet, secretary and master of requests to Anne of Denmark) ventured a public
intervention in the king's defence. As the court's solicitor read the charges of 'high
treason and other high crimes' against the king 'on behalf of the people of
England', De Lille is rumoured to have stood up and declaimed that these
accusations were levelled only by 'traytors and rebells'.[12] Whereas the High
Court's response to Lady Fairfax's interruption was swift and censorious, De
Lille's treatment was altogether more severe. Levett claims that she was seized by
Colonel John Hewson, one of the signatories on Charles's death warrant, and was

---

[8]   On Lady Fairfax and her relationship with her husband see John Wilson, *Fairfax: A Life
of Thomas, Lord Fairfax, Captain-General of all the Parliament's forces in the English
Civil War, Creator and Commander of the New Model Army* (London, 1985), pp. 11–12,
96–97, 159–162; Wedgwood, *Trial*, pp. 126–8, 154–5; Underdown, *Pride's Purge*, pp.
187–93.

[9]   Clarendon, *History*, IV, p. 486.

[10] Wedgwood, *Trial*, p. 155.

[11] BL Harl. MS 3784 f. 287.

[12] BL Harl. MS 3784 f. 271.

burned with hot irons, perhaps implausibly, 'in open court'.[13] The branding is reported to have left a hand-sized scar on her shoulder and the incident was apparently witnessed by many present. Basil Feilding, the Earl of Denbigh, who had long been opposed to the trial, was apparently so appalled at De Lille's punishment that some time later he is supposed to have 'kissed her wounds and condemned the then baseness of the Lords that she should be the only assertor of loyalty'.[14] Even more striking, the king himself is alleged to have looked up at De Lille from the floor of the court and 'seeing her flesh smoake and her haire all of a fire for him by their hot irons, much commiserated her, and wished he could have been able to have requited her.'[15]

We will return to the significance of sympathetic relationships between women and the king in due course. There is, however, a striking parallel in the fact that as women were silenced at the High Court of Justice, so too their voices can scarcely be heard in the proliferation of pamphlet discussions of the trial and execution of the king that helped give definition to the mid-seventeenth-century public sphere. Even Henrietta Maria, who made two written appeals to both Fairfax and parliament imploring permission for her presence at her husband's trial, was excluded.[16] However, the king's own approach to his trial and the treatment he received as a result of it ought to instruct us that silences are especially difficult to interpret in this context. As has already been mentioned, Charles did not acknowledge the authority of the High Court of Justice and came to the first day of the trial desperate to 'know by what Power I am called hither ... let me know by what lawful Authority I am seated here, and I shall not be unwilling to answer. In the meantime ... I will not ... answer to a new unlawful Authority.'[17] Ultimately, he did not answer at all. The regicides had long predicted that the king would refuse to plead in response to the charges levelled against him and, after some dubious legal chicanery, they executed him nonetheless some eight days later. Faced with the king's obdurate silence in the face of treasonous charges, they had already agreed to convict him *pro confesso*, that is, as if he had freely confessed to them. In other words, the regicides were determined to read Charles's silence as profound. For them it did not merely speak of a refusal of the authority of the High Court of Justice, it also, by extension, resonated with a wilful rejection of the will

---

[13] R. B. Partridge is less sceptical about this incident and has speculated that 'exactly why hot brands should be so readily available in the court must be a matter of conjecture. It was a cold January and there may have been some form of heating installed in the hall, or it is possible that they were used for the melting of sealing wax', *O Horrible Murder*, p. 63. J. G. Muddiman is also convinced that this took place; see *The Trial of Charles the First*, pp. 80–81.

[14] BL Harl. MS 3784 f. 287.

[15] Ibid., f. 271.

[16] Clarendon, *History*, vol. 4, p. 472; Wedgwood, *Trial*, pp. 90–91. See also Lois Potter, *Secret Rites and Secret Writing: Royalist Literature, 1641–1660* (Cambridge, 1989), p. 132.

[17] Nalson, *The Trial of Charles I, King of England*, pp. 6–7.

of the people and (providentially speaking) God.[18] Given the widespread disquiet about the illegality of the High Court, such arguments were rather tenuous, but they vividly illustrate the problematic nature of silence in the forum of regicide dispute. This chapter attempts, therefore, to sound out regicidal silences in order to investigate the manner in which they might have been conducive to verbal strategies and rhetorical formulations that women could then adapt.

'Womanish Pity' and the Symbolic Economy of Regicide

What, therefore, might be considered the general determining factors for the interdiction of female opinion in the regicide debate? Lady Fairfax implicitly draws attention to part of the problem in her interruption of the High Court of Justice, querying the manner in which the 'people of England' constitute an adequate label for those pursuing the trial of Charles. Yet whereas it is likely that she voices her discontent at the exclusion of the Presbyterian and middle group Independents from the political process which led to the execution of the king, many modern historians of gender would hear in her disclaimer the voice of a woman speaking out against an early modern English political culture which defined the politically participating subject in exclusively masculine terms.[19] It is beyond the scope of this chapter to review the classical and medieval provenance of the masculinization of the political subject, but by the mid-seventeenth century the notion that the political animal was a universal 'man' had become an orthodoxy propounded by royalists, parliamentarians and republicans alike.[20] This found particularly forceful expression in theories of social contract between governments and their subjects. Contract theory, with its central argument that the safety of the people should be the supreme concern of all law givers (or *salus*

---

[18]   The *pro confesso* charge was one of the earliest aspects of the trial to be decided; indeed it was probably resolved upon as early as 30 Dec. 1648. See *Mercurius Pragmaticus* 26 Dec. 1648–49 Jan. 1649, no sig.; Barber, *Regicide and Republicanism*, pp. 124, 129, 141.

[19]   See Carol Pateman, *The Sexual Contract* (Cambridge, 1989); Susan Moller Okin, *Women in Western Political Thought* (Princeton, 1979); Hilda L. Smith 'Women, intellect and politics: their intersection in seventeenth-century England', in idem., (ed.), *Women Writers and the Early Modern British Political Tradition* (Cambridge, 1998), pp. 1–14. For a less restrictive account of women's involvement in politics, specifically those of the English Civil War, see Katharine Gillespie, 'Table Talk: Seventeenth-Century English and American Women Writers and the Rhetoric of Radical Domesticity', an unpublished Ph.D. dissertation (SUNY Buffalo, 1996) that amply demonstrates that Pateman focuses too exclusively on the tradition of male-authored social contract theory, and pays little attention to women's experiments with voluntary religion. See also Sharon Achinstein, 'Women on Top'.

[20]   For a fascinating discussion of the deleterious effects such false universals have for women's agency see Hilda L. Smith, *All Men and Both Sexes: Gender, Politics and the False Universal in England, 1640–1832* (Philadelphia, 2002).

populi, suprema lex as it was more commonly known following Cicero in *De Legibus*), was essential to supporting the cases both for and against regicide.[21] Thus Charles refused the authority of the High Court in order to 'defend as much as in me lies the ancient Lawes of the Kingdom' and safeguard 'the Liberties of my *People*'.[22] Milton set out the regicides' position using terms remarkably similar to the king, but was forthright in maintaining that such liberties had only ever been a male privilege. Tracing the history of the social contract in *The Tenure of Kings and Magistrates*, he reminds his readers that:

> No man who knows ought, can be so stupid to deny that all men naturally were born free, being the image and resemblance of God himself, and were by privilege above all the creatures, born to command and not to obey: and that they lived so. Till from the roots of Adam's transgression, falling among themselves to doe wrong and violence, and foreseeing that such courses must needs tend to the destruction of them all, they agreed by common league to bind each other from mutual injury ... Hence came Citties, Townes and Common-wealths. And because no faith in all was found sufficiently binding, they saw it needful to ordaine som authoritie, that might restrain by force and punishment what was violated against peace and common right.[23]

As he outlines the importance of the social contract for preserving the 'common right', Milton gives voice to the exclusion, even the coercion, that is inherent in the supposed liberalism of contract theory. Men (and only men, it would seem) have always been political animals; it is they who come together in the 'common league' of towns, cities and commonwealths in order to preserve the peace of the human species. If civil government is a post-lapsarian phenomenon, it is nonetheless an institution that is born through an exclusively male 'transgression'. In an interesting rendition of biblical history, which differs markedly from the representation of the first parents in *Paradise Lost*, Eve and her daughters are entirely absent from Milton's republican narrative of human socialization and the rise of the political society. If men were 'naturally born free' we are left wondering, on these terms at least, if women were ever born at all. At very best they are silent presences, born to obey and not to command.

Whenever such masculinist theories are used, and they were continually appropriated in regicide discussion in the late 1640s, the opportunity for any form

---

[21]   W. D. Pearman (ed.), *Cicero: De Legibus Libri Tres* (Cambridge, 1881), pp. 112–3. On contract theory see Jane S. Jaquette, 'Contract and Coercion: Power and Gender in Leviathan', in Smith (ed.), *Women Writers and the Early Modern British Political Tradition*, pp. 200–19; Gordon Shochet, *Rights in Context: The Historical and Political Construction of Moral and Legal Entitlements* (Lawrence, KS.: 1998); Pateman, *The Sexual Contract, passim*. For an important discussion of *salus populi* arguments in this context see Barber, *Regicide and Republicanism*, pp. 14, 71, 82, 86, 98.

[22]   Quoted in the account of the trial reprinted in *A Perfect Diurnall* 287, 22–29 Jan. 1649, p. 2309.

[23]   Milton, *The Tenure of Kings and Magistrates*, in *CPW*, vol. 3, pp. 198–9.

of female subjectivity is all but obliterated. Instead of acting as political agents in the momentous events surrounding the trial and execution of the king, women feature instead as symbols in the male-authored texts of revolutionary politics; they figure as symptoms of the nationwide malaise that afflicts and imperils the body politic. One of the most noticeable features of the pamphlet culture after the regicide was a royalist martyrology epidemic which foregrounded the impenetrable, deific aspects of kingship.[24] In these cheaply printed accounts 30 January 1649 becomes Good Friday, Charles's treatment and demeanour on the scaffold become Christ's agonies on Golgotha and (just as in the gospel accounts of the crucifixion) strange signs and evil omens are seen throughout the country. The portentous symbolism of the execution included tales of ducks forsaking their long-time home on the pond at St James's to flutter mournfully around the scaffold and stories of Fairfax and Cromwell being haunted by evil spirits. [25] Like these ducks and ghosts, women assume a central place in the image-stocks of regicide as evidenced by several pamphlets which tell of Charles's Christ-like apotheosis in striking terms:

> As women, beholding Christ's passion wept: so many women, beholding their Sovereign on a Scaffold, wept bitterly; unto whom he might have said (as our Saviour said unto the other) *Weep not for me, ye Daughters of Jerusalem, but weep for yourselves.*[26]

Charles does not appear to have actually uttered these words from Luke's gospel account before his death. Importantly, however, as the 'daughters of Jerusalem' are

---

[24]   The king himself laid the foundations for the royalist conception of the martyr king. Shortly before his death on the scaffold he is said to have claimed 'I needed not to have come here, and therefore I tell you ... that I am the Martyr of the People', *King Charls His Speech Made Upon the Scaffold at Whitehall-Gate* (London, 1649), p. 6. For a flavour of the royalist martyrology epidemic see *The Life and Death of King Charles the Martyr, Paralleled With our Saviour in All His Sufferings* (London, 1649); Henry Leslie, *The Martyrdom of King Charles, Or His Conformity With Christ in His Sufferings* (London, 1649). The best recent treatments of Charles-as-martyr are Andrew Lacey, *The Cult of King Charles the Martyr* (London, 2003); Lois Potter, 'The royal martyr in the Restoration', in T. N. Corns (ed.), *The Royal Image: Representations of Charles I* (Cambridge, 1999), pp. 264–87; Nancy Klein Maguire, 'The Theatrical Mask/Masque of Politics: The Case of Charles I', *Journal of British Studies* 28 (1989), pp. 1–22.

[25]   'It was thought very prodigious that when he sufered, the Ducks forsook their pond At St James's, and came as far as Whitehall, fluttering about the scaffold; so that our Soveraigne might have said unto his murderers, as it is in Job 12.7 *Ask the beasts and they will tell thee, ask the Fowles of the Heaven and they will instruct thee* what an unnatural murder ye are now committing'; Leslie, *The Martyrdom of King Charles* (London, 1649), p. 18. Such narratives were not solely confined to martyrological texts, but also featured in royalist newsbook accounts. See, for instance, *The Man in the Moon* 2, 16–23 April, 1649 pp. 13–14.

[26]   *The Life and Death of King Charles the Martyr*, p. 6. These words are reproduced verbatim in Leslie, *The Martyrdom of King Charles*, p. 18.

transformed into an obscure, indistinct 'other', women more generally are subsumed within the purely symbolic economy of the regicide; it is as if the evils of the execution find their most appropriate imaginative correlate in the extreme emotional responses of women. This is also seen in the most famous contemporary artistic representation of the execution, Weesop's 'The Execution of Charles I' (see figure 4). Given the title, we might anticipate the focus of the painting to be the effects of the events of 30 January on the king himself. However, viewers' expectations are immediately disrupted by the disproportionate predominance given to a swooning woman's emotional reaction in the centre foreground and the relegation of the execution itself to a tableau played out by curiously indistinguishable men in the background. The physical response of a woman to the regicide thus becomes the primary symbolic focus of the principal scene, something that is carefully accentuated by the knowing composure of the male spectator who engages our gaze in the right foreground. The only other appropriate reaction for a woman is, it would seem, to fan herself or look away and pray. Even the narrative offered by the series of inset paintings (which we might expect to correct the skewed perspective of the central action) places unthinking women centrally at the culmination of the trial and execution with two women scavenging for relics in the dirt before the scaffold.[27]

Women's extreme emotional and immediate physical responses are recorded elsewhere. Sir William Sanderson, the royalist historian, recalls that 'women miscarried' on hearing the news from Whitehall.[28] In her autobiography, Mary Rich, Countess of Warwick, recounts her own peculiarly virulent reaction to the regicide:

> God was pleased in the year 1648 to make me fall dangerously ill of the small-pox. My distemper at the first made Dr Wright, my physician, believe I would die, but it pleased God, by his means, to save my life, yet when I was, as he thought, almost past danger, that barbarous and unheard of wicked action of beheading King Charles I was of a sudden told me, which did again endanger me, for I had a great abhorrence of that bloody act, and was much disordered at it.[29]

However, perhaps the most striking rendition of a woman's physical and emotional response to Charles I's death comes in a volume of manuscript verse

---

[27] Narrative coherence demands that we read the inset paintings from top left to bottom right. The first represents Charles at his trial; the second his progression to the scaffold, the third, focuses on the executioner with his spoils and the final scene details the aftermath at Whitehall. I am grateful to Robert Jones for a valuable discussion of this painting.

[28] W. Sanderson, *A Compleat History of the Life and Reign of King Charles: From His Cradle to His Grave* (1658), p. 1139.

[29] T. Crofton Croker (ed.), *Autobiography of Lady Warwick* (London, 1848), pp. 24–5.

Figure 4: Weesop, 'The Execution of Charles I'
The swooning woman is at the symbolic centre of the regicide.

written by Lady Hester Pulter, an ardent royalist from Hertfordshire. In *Poems Breathed Forth by the Noble Hadassas*, Pulter places her response to the regicide at the symbolic heart of a series of poems about loss – of her own children in childbirth, the royalist cause in the civil wars and, more comically, Sir William Davenant's nose to syphilis.[30] Stridently anti-populist in tone, her poems condemn the 'Ffierce hydras' of parliamentary rule and consistently trope tears and prayer as the most appropriate female responses to violence against the king: 'Then ask noe more why I'm in tears dissolv'd / Whilst our good king with sorrow is involvd' the speaker opines in one elegy.[31] In another poem, however, she reflects upon the problematic nature of women's tears in the wake of the regicide; tears also, it would seem, threaten to violate models of aristocratic decorum and detachment with the result that the speaker fantasizes about a very different kind of intense physical reaction to recent events:

> Let none presume to weep, tears are to weak
> Such an unparreld loss as this to speak
> Poor village Girles doe soe express their grief
> And in that sad expression find relief
> When such a Prince in such a manner Dies
> Let us (ay mee) noe more drop teares but eyes
> Nor let none dare to sigh or strike their breast
> To shew a grief that soe transcends the rest

---

[30]   *Poems Breathed Forth by the Noble Hadassas*; Brotherton Library, University of Leeds, MS Lt q. 32.
[31]   Ibid., f. 44v ; f. 33r.

Pleabeans soe each vulgar loss deplore
Wee doo too little if we doo noe more
When such a king in such a manner dies
Let us suspire our Soules, weep out our eyes.[32]

Women's weeping has become a symptom of, as well as an appropriate reaction to, the current crisis. Tears dissolve class boundaries, making the noblewoman look every inch the distressed village girl and perhaps reminding royalist readers that Charles's own troubles took place against a backdrop of similarly unstable hierarchies. Pulter thus endeavours to reinstate social distinction and reaffirm aristocratic women's affinities with the king's cause through images of scarcely conceivable suffering. The pain of a monarch's execution can only be equated with the impossible situation of a trauma victim weeping so intensely that her eyes are squeezed from their sockets.

Seventeenth-century parliamentarians and republicans were not slow to notice that women formed an integral part of the royalist symbolic economy at the time of the regicide, and they were quick to accord them a passive status in their own political world. Alongside republican masculinism, many male-authored, non-royalist pamphlets discuss the nature of the trial and execution of Charles in terms whereby anti-monarchism and antifeminism appear to be almost synonymous.[33] Thus, according to Milton, those who mourned the death of the king were not only the 'blockish vulgar' of 'the Common sort', but were also predominately female. Hence he draws parallels with the *Iliad*'s 'captive women' who 'bewaild the death of *Patroclus* in outward show', but were actually grieving for their own enslaved condition.[34] If these women were supposedly disingenuous and deceitful in their grief, others who 'cri'd out for justice' for the king at the trial were indicative of the national moral bankruptcy of the dying monarchical regime. They were:

---

[32] Ibid., f. 34r.

[33] This is not to assert that masculinism and republicanism are synonymous, merely that in its early English manifestation republican culture was a far from ideal environment for women. David Norbrook's brilliant account of seventeenth-century republicanism has contrasted it with the public sphere of royal court culture which offered women 'significant avenues for political influence and cultural practice'. See David Norbrook, *Writing the English Republic: Poetry, Rhetoric and Politics, 1627–1660* (Cambridge, 1999). For the gradual feminization of republicanism in the eighteenth century see Kate Davies, 'Gender and Republicanism in America, 1760–1785', unpublished D.Phil. thesis (University of York, 1999).

[34] John Milton, *Eikonklastes in Answer to a Book Intitl'd Eikon Basilike*, in *CPW*, vol. 3, p. 345. Briseis and the other women have just been surrendered to Achilles at this point by Agamemnon. Her impassioned speech is genuinely motivated by her remembrance of Patroclus's kindness to her when she was initially captured by Achilles and therefore constitutes, despite all of Milton's protestations to the contrary, a very good parallel example of ritualized grief; Homer, *The Iliad*, xix ll. 333–58, trans. Robert Fagles, (Bath, 1997), pp. 497–8.

Court Ladies, not the best of Women; who when they grow to that insolence as to appear active in State affaires, are the certaine sign of a dissolute, degenerat, and pusillanimous Common-wealth.[35]

National degeneracy and dissolution are not merely the effects of the corruption of the Caroline court, then; they are also born when women are 'active in State affaires'. In the republic, the militaristic or masculine ideal of Machiavellian *virtù* would presumably silence all such unlicensed public female assertions. The reference to 'Court Ladies' has led at least one critic to suggest that Milton here echoes Thomas May's version of female participation at Strafford's trial where women, 'filling the Galleries at the Tryall' were 'moved by pitty, proper to their sex' which led them to be 'all of his [Strafford's] side'.[36]

This motif of women's instinctive sympathy for inappropriate royalist causes is the satiric, parliamentarian counterpart to the figure of the woman prey to violent bodily and emotional reactions to the regicide. It was a trope manipulated by John Cook, the High Court's solicitor general, who must have been especially sensitive to women's interruptions of the High Court's proceedings as he himself had been denied the right to speak for the prosecution because of the king's refusal to plead. From the very title page of his *King Charls, His Case* he equates women with an irrational longing for monarchy and in a collection of legal maxims taken from Sir Edward Coke's *Institutes* and other seventeenth-century aphorisms he contends that:

Justice is an excellent vertue:
Reason is the life of the Law.
Womanish pity to mourn for a Tyrant,
Is a deceitful cruelty to a City.[37]

Later in the seventeenth century, Spinoza would add philosophical respectability to the aphoristic quality of 'womanish pity' when he discussed it in his *Ethics*; Cook is merely anxious here, however, to use the epithet in a gendered deprecation of the many outpourings of anguish and nostalgia for the recently executed king.[38] He does so by associating grief for monarchy's cause with cruelty and deceit, values

---

[35]   Ibid., p. 370.

[36]   Thomas May, *The History of the Parliament of England: Which began November the third, M. DC. XL. With a short and necessary view of some precedent years* (London, 1647), p. 92. The parallel between the trials is first suggested by Merrit Hughes in *CPW* 3, p. 370.

[37]   Cook, *King Charls, His Case*, title page.

[38]   Spinoza genders irrationality in a discussion of the relationship between intellect and will: 'everyone [should] be content with his own, and be helpful to his neighbour, not from any womanish pity, from partiality or superstition, but by the guidance of reason alone'. Similarly, he inveighs against the illogic, 'empty superstition and womanish tenderness' of those who object to the slaughtering of animals. Benedict de Spinoza, *Ethics*, ed. James Gutman (New York, 1949), pp. 125, 215.

axiomatically associated with women in the amorous verse of the period. The intent and effect of Cook's arguments become clearer as he inveighs against Charles's supporters:

> Blessed God, what ugly sins lodge in their bosoms, that would have this man to live! But Words are Women, Proofs are Men; it is Reason that must be the Chariot to carry men to give their concurrence in this judgement.[39]

Cook thus presents monarchistic sympathy after the regicide as a crisis of signification. The attractiveness of the female form belies the 'ugly sins' it contains, in just the same way that language has become deceptive in that it is no longer the cipher for truth. Pointedly, these 'Words are Women' and truth can only now be achieved via the male 'Proofs' of 'Reason'. The exclusive and masculinist rationality of Cook's argument is emphasized by the fact that he is actually reworking the proverbial expression 'words are women, *deeds* are men', or *fatti maschii, parole femine*, at this point. Yet whereas the proverb advances the troubling possibility of women's verbal mastery and expresses male fears about the influence of women's words, Cook intensifies the antifeminism of the aphorism by translating it into a version of the 'irrationality of all women' *topos*. His innovation significantly locates male supremacy in the realm of logic rather than in more traditionally masculinized spheres of physical and public 'deeds'.[40] This stress on 'Reason' is an explicit attempt to exclude all women from regicide debate and is a strategy supported by Cook's rhetorical technique. By persistently employing forensic rhetoric, which stresses the rule of logic and therefore can only be addressed to readers and listeners who are willing to reason from shared assumptions and premises, he excludes both royalists and, by extension, women from discussion of the king's trial and execution.[41] However, if words are indeed women, the rhetorically strained structures of Cook's argument significantly belie its claim to rational objectivity.

The misogynistic tenor of these images and arguments aside, is there any justification in the persistent assertion that women uniformly appropriated the king's cause as their own in 1649? The answer to this is far from simple. After the Restoration, Lucy Hutchinson briefly (and disapprovingly) recalled Charles's wilful behaviour at this trial and presented her husband's signature on the death warrant as divinely sanctioned: he signed 'according to the dictates of conscience

---

[39] Cook, *King Charls, His Case*, sig. A2v.
[40] For a brief discussion of this proverb see Mendelson and Crawford, *Women in Early Modern England*, p. 215.
[41] Elizabeth Skerpan makes a case for the rhetorical failure of the revolutionary party as being based on the failure of their exclusive forensic techniques to oust the more inclusive royalist epedeitic genre, 'Writers-Languages-Communities: Radical Pamphleteers and Legal Discourse in the English Revolution', *Explorations in Renaissance Culture* 16 (1990), pp. 37–56.

... and accordingly the Lord did signalise his favour afterwards to him'.[42] More than two years after the momentous events at Whitehall, the Fifth Monarchist Mary Cary dedicated an extensive exegetical pamphlet to the wives of some of the leading opponents of the king, Elizabeth Cromwell, Bridget Ireton and Margaret Rolle (wife of Sir Henry Rolle). In it she presents the late king's demise as the glorious fulfilment of the scriptural prophecies of Daniel 7 and embraces the fact that wholehearted support for the regicide was a minority position:

> How could they which are so few in number, and in the eies of the world despised and despicable creatures, have carried on that work so effectually, as to have cut off the late King; though it was verily believed, and it is very probable, there was at that very time, twenty to one in this Nation of England, that were against it; had not the Lord assisted them with thousands of Angels and evidently manifested himselfe to bee with them?[43]

For Cary, 1649 was undeniable proof that God had 'lifted up the heads of his saints' and 'owned ... Roundheads, Puritans, Independents, Presbyterians, Anabaptists, Sectaries, Prescisians, and what not.'[44] However, she anxiously acknowledges that she failed to publish her pro-regicide pamphlet in the immediate context of the trial and execution, repeatedly justifying this with the explanation that 'these things are come to pass and all prophecies are best understood when they are fulfilled'.[45] This perhaps suggests Cary's awareness that very few women had actually spoken up in defence of the regicide in 1648–49.[46] Indeed, women who we might expect to have supported Charles's execution failed to do so in the weeks preceding and months following the momentous event. Even

---

[42]   Lucy Hutchinson, *Memoirs of the Life of Colonel Hutchinson*, ed. N. H. Keeble (London, 1995), p. 235. For Hutchinson's comments on the 'disdainful' behaviour of the king at his trial see ibid., p. 234.

[43]   Mary Cary, *The Little Horns Doom & Downfall: Or A Scripture Prophesie of King James, and King Charles, and of this present Parliament Unfolded* (London, 1651), pp. 31–2. See also idem., *A New and More Exact Description of New Jerusalem's Glory* (London, 1651).

[44]   Ibid., p. 22.

[45]   Ibid., p. 44. She makes exactly the same argument a handful of pages later: 'seeing as I have said, that all Prophesies are best understood in the fulfilling of them; the truth of these things will doubtlesse now be the more prevailing with Saints'; ibid., pp. 46–7.

[46]   A notable exception here is Lady Eleanor Davies whose apocalyptic reading of Belshazzar's feast (from Daniel 5) was republished in 1649 with new, extensive marginal glosses. Whereas earlier versions of the tract had merely been highly critical of the Laudian regime, the marginalia of the later edition maintained that the doom-laden writing on the wall at Belshazzar's banquet actually foretold the trial and execution of Charles I. According to Davies's most recent biographer, however, Lady Eleanor did not write the marginalia. See Lady Eleanor Davies, *Given to the Elector Prince Charles of the Rhyne* (Amsterdam, 1633); idem., *Strange and Wonderfull Prophesies By the Lady Eleanor Audley; who is yet alive, and lodgeth in Whitehall* (London, 1649); Esther S. Cope, *Handmaid of the Holy Spirit: Dame Eleanor Davies, Never So Mad A Ladie* (Ann Arbor, 1992), p. 147.

Cromwell's sister, Katherine Whitstone, was condemned as a royalist because of her sympathy for the king. In a letter to a friend written in February 1649 she confesses 'I was much troubled at the stroke which took the head of this poor kingdom from us, and truly had I been able to have purchased his life, I am confident I could with all willingness have laid down mine'.[47] This absence of women's voices from the earliest defences of regicide is striking and goes some way towards explaining the prominent position accorded to women in the symbolic economy of regicide.

Yet there is surely more at stake in this process than the anti-feminist conferral of supposedly stereotypical female attributes; might not 'womanish pity' be reconceived as a motive of empathetic self-recognition? Several factors present us with the possibility of a positive answer to this question. Firstly, the various moments of enforced silencing at the trial suggest a strong affinity between the king's treatment and female agency. Whilst issuing the essential proviso that the king's silence was predicated by the 'wilful' decision not to plead at the trial – that is, the broader male prerogative of not speaking when the opportunity affords itself – and is therefore fundamentally different to the suppression of a female voice, a number of seventeenth-century women were willing to make comparisons of this kind. On 23 April 1649, following the imprisonment of the Leveller leaders, hundreds of women, possibly lead by Katherine Chidley, besieged the House of Commons presenting a petition demanding the release of John Lilburne, William Walwyn, Thomas Prince and Richard Overton.[48] After being pushed down the stairs at gunpoint and having squibs thrown among them by the attendant soldiers, twenty women were eventually permitted to enter the lobby to present the petition to the members.[49] Their reception at the hands of some of the members is detailed by a contemporary newsbook:

> a member of the House coming out and demanding what was the matter with the women, the Gentlewoman that was to present their Petition, answered, they were come with a Petition; he told her that it was not for women to Petition, they might stay at home to wash their dishes; she answered, Sir we have scarce any dishes left us to wash, and those we have we are not sure to keep them. Another member told her it was strange that women should petition: she answered, Sir that which is

---

[47] Reprinted in Patricia Crawford and Laura Gowing (eds.), *Women's Worlds in Seventeenth-Century England: A Sourcebook* (London and New York, 2000), pp. 252–3.

[48] *To the Supreme Authority of this Nation, the Commons Assembled in Parliament: The Humble Petition of Divers Wel-Affected Women* (London, 1649); *Mercurius Militaris* 1, 17–24 April, pp. 13–14; Ellen A. McArthur, 'Women Petitioners and the Long Parliament', p. 706. Chidley's involvement in the composition and presentation of this petition is charted in Katherine Gillespie, 'A Hammer in her Hand', pp. 225–9; Ian Gentles, 'London Levellers in the English Revolution', p. 292.

[49] *Mercurius Militaris* 1, p. 13; McArthur, 'Women Petitioners', p. 706. For a different version of events see *Perfect Occurences of Every Daie* 121, 20–27 April 1649, p. 997.

strange is not therefore unlawfull, it was strange you cut off the Kings Head, yet I suppose you will justifie it.[50]

Public and private, domestic and political economies all collide here and there is a sense in which the king's cause becomes very much the Leveller women's (and there is surely more in play here than simple Leveller nostalgia for a monarch whose ambition they perceived now to be less than that of their future Protector). Radically, the exclusion of women from the public sphere is viewed as just as 'unlawfull' as the regicide itself. Moreover, it is possible to see such affinities running back to the proceedings of the trial itself, affinities that stem from Charles's occasional argument that he was subject to (rather than above) the law. From such a perspective it becomes apparent that whether above or simply beyond the consideration of the law, those who stood outside it, whether kings or women, appear to have to suffer the same consequences of enforced silence when entering into it. In an effort to scrutinize the precise terms of this sympathetic alliance, we must now turn to the pamphlets of those royalist women who discussed the regicide in the immediate context of the king's death.

Mary Pope: Negotiating the Restraints on a Woman's Tongue

When Lady Fairfax made her masked intervention at the High Court of Justice, intrigue abounded for some time as to the identity of the woman who had so daringly interrupted the trial. She was apparently unknown to the man who had sold her the seat, and the newsbooks were keen to speculate as to who was the most likely disturber of the High Court of Justice's peace. One of the commonest theories advanced was that it was Mary Pope, a largely unknown salter's widow who, according to rumour, had not only announced her desire to intervene in person at the trial but was so convinced about the impossibility of the king's condemnation that she was willing to wager an amazing £15 on Charles's restoration to his throne within six weeks of the trial's commencement.[51] However, doubtless impeded by the prohibitions on public female regicide discussion we have already traced, Pope did not feature at the trial, but opted instead to try to write herself into the debate. A staunch royalist, she published two pamphlets in

---

[50]   *Mercurius Militaris* 1, p. 13.
[51]   Biographical details for Pope are few. See *Perfect Occurences* 26 Jan.–2 Feb., 1649, p. 814; Wedgwood, *Trial*, pp. 150–51, 154. Interestingly, *Perfect Occurences* couples Pope's supposed visit 'to plead in behalfe of the King' with that of one 'Mrs Levingston (not she that was the Lady Odondy)'. Like Lady Fairfax both were 'put out'. Another potential disturber of the High Court's peace was thought to be Lady Newburgh, formerly Lady Catherine Howard. Notoriously royalist, she was well accustomed to making interventions in the world of politics having been instrumental in hatching plots to seize London for the royalists in 1643, and later free the king from his imprisonment. She had also carried concealed messages to him through enemy lines. See Wedgwood, *Trial*, p. 65.

January 1649 which condemn the proceedings of the army and purged parliament as utterly illegal.[52] She condemned all pro-regicide discussion as the 'blasphemous arrogancy of servill parasites' whose sole intention was to 'pull down the Lawes of God and Men' advancing instead 'the absolute impunity of Kings that they are not accountable to any on earth'.[53] Whilst Pope continually dwells on the manner in which 'law' and 'lawgivers' ought to intervene in the crisis, it soon becomes apparent that because, as she puts it, 'the laws of the land I doe not well know them', her legalistic theories all involve a substitution of the secular for the sacred.[54] Thus magisterial impunity is not deduced from legal and historical precedent but from biblical injunctions (such as Hebrews 13.17, wherein all are enjoined to 'obey all that have oversight of them') and biblical history so that just as Moses honoured the supremacy of the Pharaoh so too:

> when our Saviour Christ was born and *Herod* made king over the Jews by *Caesar Augustus*, we read in holy writ that many male children Herod slew thinking thereby to destroy Christ; yet for all that blood he shed, God did not take him away till the full time of his dayes were expired: Nay God used *Joseph* to carry his own sonne Christ into *Ægypt* till *Herod* was dead.[55]

In the strictest sense, Christianity entails loyalism and an absolute submission to the awful truths of providentialist historiography. Furthermore, Pope's particular exemplification of that submission limits the impact of the blood guilt argument which raged around Charles throughout the revolutionary period; if Herod's massacre of the innocents was unpunishable by immediate death, why should the king's more contestable evils be subject to that ultimate sentence?[56]

In fact, as Pope's providentialist vision shifts from biblical history to that of the seventeenth century, she explicitly transfers the guilt for the blood shed throughout the civil wars onto the parliamentarian cause:

---

[52]   Mary Pope, *Behold, Here is a Word or an Answer to the Late Remonstrance of the Army* (London, 1649); idem., *Heare, Heare, Heare, A Word or Message from Heaven to all Covenant Breakers* (London, 1649).

[53]   Pope, *Behold, Heare is a Word*, p. 2.; *Heare, Heare, Heare*, p. 21.

[54]   Ibid., p. 15. Pope's continual substitution of the sacred for the secular ought, of course, to be distinguished from the prevalent technique of other regicide writers who sought instead to buttress secular arguments with scriptural exemplification and vice versa. Thus, for example, Milton's discussion of tyrannicide begins with quotations from Seneca and other 'prime Authors' of 'the Greeks and Romans' who 'held it not onely lawfull, but a glorious and Heroic deed'. Then, however, 'lest it bee objected they were Heathen' Milton works through a different series of texts which justify tyrannicide but also 'show knowledge of the true Religion'. Thus he follows his analysis of Seneca with an exegetical reading of Ehud's murder of Eglon in the Book of Judges; Milton, *Tenure*, pp. 212–13.

[55]   Pope, *Heare, Heare, Heare*, p. 9.

[56]   For a discussion of the status of the blood guilt argument see Patricia Crawford, '"Charles Stuart that Man of Blood"', *Journal of British Studies*, 16 (1974), pp. 41–61.

if the Kingdome and the people had obeyed their supreame King in doing what he commanded, and had payed the Knight-hood money, and Conduct money, and Ship money, and according to God's commandment you had feared God and honoured the King, and ... yeelded up those Members of Parliament when they were required by the King, (though it may be it was illegal) yet if you had done so, you had been obedient servants to God and man; but your height of disobedience in resisting Gods command hath brought all this blood upon the Land.[57]

Not even Edward Hyde, Earl of Clarendon, one of Charles's most devoted advisors, would have gone this far in pressing his loyalty to the king. The incident involving 'those Members of Parliament' was viewed as more than simply 'illegal'; all commentators were unanimous in their assessment that Charles's attempt to arrest the Five Members on 4 January 1642 displayed monarchical statecraft at its unsanctionable worst.[58] In this context of ultra-loyalism it is therefore surprising that Pope should never once refer to the position of women, or give a new positive evaluation to feminized loyalty, or 'womanish pity', for the king's cause. This would not only ally women with monarchy but could, in her own terms, have given them a radically ascendant role in a heavenly hierarchy. Instead, women remain in curiously silent subordination on the margins.

This implied feminine silence is obviously at odds with Pope's own volubility on the subject of regicide. She accounts for the genesis of her pamphlet in the following terms:

And this I should at this time have made fully cleare unto you; but that I have laine among the pots, under disgrace because of my book of *Magistracy*, which God enabled mee to set forth for the good of his people. And this matter that I have last spoken of should have followed it, which hath been finished almost three quarters of a yeare agoe ... why it came not out at the appointed time was because the wings of my desires were clipt by reason of the frownes and strange speeches of those who were my familiar friends. And now God hath gilded my wings with confidence in his promise, and raised up my spirits.[59]

Once again, even 'familiar friends' disapprove not just of women's participation in regicide debate but of their verbal activity in the public sphere *per se*. Despite a willingness and ability to write, her current work has been confined within the accepted bounds of female privacy for near nine months. The 'pots' Pope has been confined with seem most plausible as an index of enforced female privacy and

---

[57] Pope, *Heare, Heare, Heare*, p. 22.

[58] Clarendon refers to himself as being amongst a group of the king's closest supporters who 'were so much displeased and dejected' by the incident 'that they were inclined never more to take upon them the care of anything to be transacted in the House', *History of the Rebellion*, vol. 1, p. 487.

[59] Pope, *Heare, Heare, Heare*, p. 32; idem., *A Treatise of Magistracy, Shewing the Magistrate hath been, and for ever is to be the Chiefe Officer in the Church* (London, 1647). Ostensibly on the subject of church government, the pamphlet is ultra-royalist in tone, stressing the absolute necessity of monarchical order

domesticity following the 'disgrace[ful]' publication in 1647 of her 130-page pamphlet entitled *A Treatise of Magistracy*.[60] publication in 1647 However, lurking behind this account is a biblical passage which permits a radically different reading of the extract. If we consider verse 13 from Psalm 68 ('Though ye have lien among the pots yet shall ye be as the wings of a dove, covered with silver and her feathers with yellow gold'), those 'pots' which once connoted privation and punishment for illicit verbal acts now insinuate imminent glory and salvation. That God is behind Pope's words is the ultimate force of her account, yet in this variation of the instrumentality of the prophetess *topos* – which would attribute the agency of female prophetic activity unproblematically to God – divine ordinance would seem to prescribe feminine domesticity as an absolute prerequisite of female instrumentality. Accordingly female political agency becomes self-cancelling; the woman who would write of regicide can only ever pen a word which tells of imminent salvation through a woman's domestic attention to her 'pots'. Pope deploys this strategy in a monarchistic account of recent history:

> And those that have adhered to the King, according to God's commandment are and have been punished by man, and threatened to be. And seeing the business is carried so, and the work set up, I shall not now restrain my tongue by the power of God any longer, seeing pride, loftines, and arrogancy hath possessed you.[61]

The violence offered to the monarchistic cause is ostensibly what impels Pope into print. However, if her extreme loyalism is re-routed to its proximate (and logical) conclusion, there could, of course, be no justification for women writing or acting publicly in the first instance. A divinely sanctioned, absolute subordination to God, to king, and to husband would place that woman in a position of servitude at the bottom of the heavenly hierarchy.[62] Pope's narrative takes this into account as she manages to encompass the double-bind placed on the woman who would write her loyalism. Her text is the result of the release of a 'restrain[t]' placed on her 'tongue', yet it is far from certain as to who or what is placing that restraint. We have already seen that Pope's own 'familiar friends', in accordance with a prevalent attitude concerning female intervention in the crisis surrounding the king, were especially keen to restrict her public words on regicide, yet it would

---

[60] Mary Pope, *A Treatise of Magistracy, Shewing the Magistrate hath been, and for ever is to be the Chiefe Officer in the Church* (London, 1647).

[61] Ibid., p. 21.

[62] Sir Robert Filmer's *Patriarcha* is the most famous early modern instantiation of a loyalist logic which co-opts and combines theories of monarchism and patriarchalism, antipopulism and antifeminism. Just as, according to Filmer's virulent antifeminism, a woman is deemed naturally inferior and necessarily subordinate to a man, so too 'the people' are naturally inferior to their king: 'to serve the king ... is not only agreeable to the nature of subjects but much desired by them, according to their several births and conditions. The like may be said for the offices of women servants', *Patriarcha*, p. 36. On political patriarchalism see Susan D. Amussen, *An Ordered Society: Gender and Class in Early Modern England* (Oxford and New York, 1988); Gordon J. Schochet, *Patriarchalism in Political Thought* (Oxford, 1975).

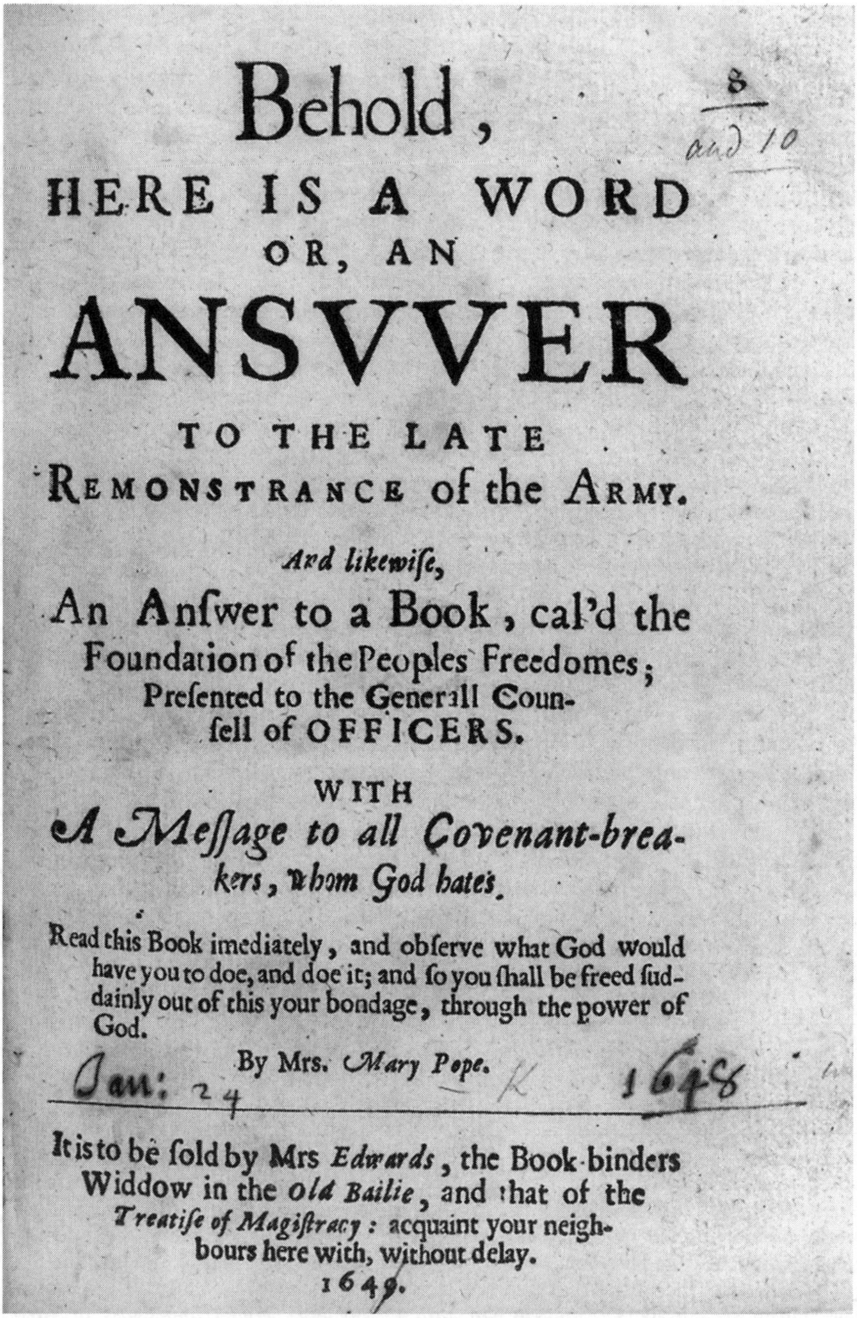

Behold,

HERE IS A WORD
OR, AN

ANSVVER

TO THE LATE
REMONSTRANCE of the ARMY.

And likewise,

An Anſwer to a Book, cal'd the
Foundation of the Peoples Freedomes;
Preſented to the Generall Coun-
fell of OFFICERS.

WITH
A Meſſage to all Covenant-brea-
kers, whom God hates.

Read this Book imediately, and obſerve what God would
have you to doe, and doe it; and ſo you ſhall be freed ſud-
dainly out of this your bondage, through the power of
God.

By Mrs. Mary Pope.

It is to be ſold by Mrs *Edwards*, the Book-binders
Widdow in the *old Bailie*, and that of the
Treatiſe of Magiſtracy : acquaint your neighbours here with, without delay.
1649.

Figure 5: Mary Pope's *Behold Here Is a Word* (1649), title page

seem that the specific circumstances involving the appearance of Pope's text also involves 'the power of God'. Whilst an instrumentality *topos* traditionally dictated that God features in the *production* of the prophetic text ('God' gilds the wings of all prophetesses 'with confidence') it is by no means certain that Pope presents this as the case here. In fact, the syntactical structure of the previous passage would appear to conspire against a divinely inspired reading of her words. It is 'godly power' as much as earthly patriarchal prohibition and required feminine modesty that would 'restrain' the publication of her text: the power of God helps her, she also implies, to restrain her tongue. Pope's extreme loyalism therefore effectively prohibits its own promulgation, and at the moment she pens anti-regicidal work, the female activist endeavours to write herself out of her own text.

'A woman of great wisdom and gravity' or 'a monstrous Witch full of deceiptfull craft'? Elizabeth Poole and the General Council of the Army

Alongside Lady Fairfax and Mary Pope, the most famous female regicide disputant is Elizabeth Poole.[63] As with most non-aristocratic women in this period, the biographical details surrounding Poole's life are scarce and the information we do have comes not from official records but Poole's own writings.[64] From

---

[63]   The more detailed and recent treatments of Poole are Gillespie, *Domesticity and Dissent in the Seventeenth Century*, pp. 115–65; Manfred Brod, 'Politics and Prophecy in Seventeenth-Century England: The Case of Elizabeth Poole', *Albion* 31:3 (1999), pp. 395–412; Ann Hughes, *Women, Men and Politics in the English Civil War* (Keele, 1999); Stevie Davies, *Unbridled Spirits: Women of the English Revolution: 1640-1660*, (London, 1998), pp. 136–49; Suzanne Trill, 'Religion and the Construction of Femininity', in Helen Wilcox (ed.), *Women and Literature in Britain 1500–1700* (Cambridge, 1996), pp. 43–4, 53, 54; Crawford, *Women and Religion*, pp. 107–112.

[64]   Poole has four printed works to her name: *A Prophesie Touching the Death of King Charles* (London, 1649); *An Alarum of War, Given to the Army and their High Court of Justice* (London, 1649); *An Alarum of War* (2nd edn London, 1649); *A Vision: Wherein is manifested the disease and cure of the Kingdome* (London, 1648). The copy of *A Prophesie* held in the University of Minnesota's Library is actually a collation of the two earlier editions of *An Alarum* printed under a different title and bearing the text from Isaiah 14 on its title page, the same text which Hugh Peter preached upon before the soldiers quartered a St James's Palace on 28 January. No record survives for Elizabeth Poole in the Baptist archive of The Angus Library at Regent's Park College, Oxford. Maureen Bell et al. contend that Poole was an active preacher in the early 1650s and was narrowly saved from being stoned for her message in 1653; Bell et al., *Biographical Dictionary of Women Writers*, p. 159. This is conjectural and rests on a misreading of the newsbook accounts of the woman preacher. Whereas *The True and Perfect Dutch Diurnall* only records that 'one Mrs Poole preached at Summerset-house Chappel, and uttered many strange expressions, to the great grief of the people', *The Weekly Intelligencer of the Commonwealth* carried the same story that week, specifying the woman was 'a Gentlewoman, one Mrs Anne Poole'. *The True and Perfect Dutch-Diurnall* 19–26 July 1653, p. 11; *The Weekly Intelligencer* 129, 19–29 July 1653, p. 930.

Abingdon, it would appear that she was a member of William Kiffin's Baptist congregation who had been 'cast out' due to what the congregation perceived as 'scandalous evils'; as a result of this imputation she was cast upon poorer times and had 'no livelihood amongst men, but what she earns by her hands'.[65] It would seem that Poole's poverty was such that despite the fact that she clearly felt that she had cause to prosecute a defamation case against Kiffin she could not afford to and instead enjoined Kiffin to bring the case to 'Civill Law'.[66] Notwithstanding all of this, Poole had, by the end of 1648, attained a sufficient degree of respectability that she was permitted to appear before the General Council of the Army to offer a view on which line the army should take in its proceedings with the king. She first appeared on 29 December 1648, when she presented herself as an army 'sympathiser', criticized the ousted monarch for his betrayal of the people's trust and delivered a vision to those assembled as to how 'the weake and imperfect distressed state of the land' would be relieved following the *de facto* transfer of power from king to parliament and thence to the army.[67] A pro-army pamphlet sketched her relationship with the General Council in positive terms:

> Out of Hartfordshire unto the General Council of the Army is come a woman of great wisedome and gravity, who told them she had a message to them from God, and desire they should heare her which they accordingly did with much acceptation; She saith they shall surely be prosperous and attain their desires for a speedy settlement of the Kingdome, and that all powers shall be subdewed under their feet.[68]

However, in concluding the matter here the pamphleteer here falls prey to the processes of selective memory, since after her first prophecy Poole was invited back to address the Council again on 5 January 1649. This time her message was less to the army's satisfaction. After pandering to the army's belief that they had

---

[65] *An Alarum*, p. 8. Earlier in the work she inveighs against 'diverse false witnesses, viz. W.K. Mr P. And Mr John Fountaine, but none of these stood to the publicke test but Mr Fountaine ... charging her with some follies committed many yeares agoe, and long since repented of, and with other things she knew not', p. 7.

[66] Ibid. On women, public insult and defamation cases in early modern England see Laura Gowing, *Domestic Dangers: Women, Words, and Sex in Early Modern London* (Oxford, 1996); idem., 'Language, power and the law: women's slander litigation in early modern London', in Jenny Kermode and Garthine Walker (eds.), *Women, Crime and the Courts in Early Modern England* (London, 1994), pp. 26–47. For the changing patterns of sexual slander after the Restoration see Robert B. Shoemaker, 'Reforming Male Manners: Public Insult and the Decline of Violence in London, 1660–1740' in T. Hitchcock and M. Cohen (eds.), *English Masculinities, 1660–1800* (London, 1999).

[67] The text of the vision presented on Poole's first appearance is reprinted in her *A Vision* pp. 1–3. A transcript of what she actually delivered followed by the army's discussion thereof can be found in C. H. Firth (ed.), *The Clarke Papers*, 2 vols (London, 1992), vol. 2, pp. 151–4.

[68] *The Manner of the deposition of Charles Stuart, King of England, by the Parliament, and the Generall Councell of the Army* (London, 1649), pp. 5–6.

been abused by all parties during the civil wars, she actually went on to assert that the best way of resolving the current crisis was to spare the king's life.[69] She was subsequently ridiculed by some of the officers and received no further offers to address the General Council.

How and why she appeared before the Council has been the subject of debate. In his study of the New Model Army, Ian Gentles attributes her appearance to Colonel Nathaniel Rich, whom he claims 'is the logical candidate' because of comparable religious beliefs, whilst David Underdown has advanced the theory that her presence was stage-managed by Cromwell, who 'may have detected in her some possible political value'.[70] Furthermore, Gentles also advances the interesting thesis that her appearance may have been due to Fairfax, whose 'views and piety ... corresponded exactly' only to discount it because 'he does not seem to have attended either session where she spoke'.[71] Although the logic in arriving at Rich as the most likely candidate is sound, discounting Fairfax on these grounds does seem suspect. As we have already seen, Lady Fairfax's intervention at the High Court of Justice was made in her husband's absence. Their views undoubtedly concurred and he does not appear to have attempted to distance himself from her comments. Lack of evidence makes the issue indeterminable, although this lack of certainty has been largely used against Poole to suggest that she had no agency whatsoever in what proceeded at Whitehall. Thus Underdown refers to her as 'the demented widow', an epithet which leaves her subject if not to Cromwell's machinations then to the vagaries of lunacy.[72] An earlier misogynistic assessment came in 1651 when a royalist pamphlet asserted that in order to further his supposedly crypto-Spanish designs, Cromwell had attempted to unite the General Council behind him by:

> provid[ing] a monstrous Witch full of deceiptfull craft, who being put into brave cloaths, pretended she was a Lady that was come from a far Countrey, being sent by God to the Army with a Revelation, which she must make known to the Army, for necessity was laid upon her: this Witch had a fair lodging prepared for her in White-Hall where she was very retired.
> This Witch had her lesson taught her beforehand by Cromwell and Ireton, by whose order she was entertained at Whitehall.[73]

Poole's motivation is, apparently, simultaneously infernal and material. In exchange for learning Cromwell and Ireton's prophetic script she receives new

---

[69]   *Clarke Papers*, vol. 2, pp. 163–9; *A Vision*, pp. 4–5.
[70]   Gentles, *New Model Army*, p. 301; Underdown, *Pride's Purge*, p. 183.
[71]   Gentles, *New Model Army*, p. 301.
[72]   Ibid. Even supposedly sympathetic critics have seen Poole's speech at Whitehall as beyond the scope of reason. For instance, Stevie Davies in part attributes it to Poole's 'undeniable tendency to witter'; Davies, *Unbridled Spirits*, p. 138.
[73]   *A Brief Narration of the Mysteries of State Carried on by the Spanish factions in England* (London, 1651), pp. 68–9.

clothes and temporary accommodation in Whitehall. Whilst, as we will see with the case of Elizabeth Alkin, some women did actually receive Whitehall lodgings as recompense for services to the Commonwealth, there is little reason to trust this report. Firstly, the records of the General Council demonstrate that Poole's true identity was known as she addressed the assembled army members. It is immediately stated that she is 'of Abingdon' which if a 'far Countrey' was in reality only a few miles further a 'Countrey' from London than Oxford, the seat of royalist power during the civil war.[74] Secondly, if her 'lesson' was taught her by Cromwell and Ireton, it was a lesson to which she was not fully attentive since in advancing a theory of clemency towards the king she would have in fact been alienating her regicidal teachers. However impossible it would have been for Poole to address the General Council without some kind of invitation, the 'lesson' she preached on her two visits was very much her own and attempts to wrest it from her constitute a misreading of her rhetorical strategies.

In order to evaluate such strategies fully it is paramount that the distinction between Poole's two visits to the General Council be preserved. Her visit on 29 December is the one generally recalled by royalist writers in that it is unproblematically pro-army. In it she offers the view of the army as the only possible remaining agents of reform of the 'distresses of this Land', and encapsulates this in the following image:

> after many daies mourning, a vision was set before me, to shew her [i.e. 'this Land's'] cure, and the manner of it, by this similitude: A man who is a member of the Army, having sometimes much bewailed her state, saying *He could gladly be a sacrifice for her*, and was set before me, presenting the body of the Army, and on the other hand, a *woman crooked, sick, weak and imperfect in body* to present unto me, the weak and imperfect state of the Kingdom: I having the gift of faith upon me for her cure, was thus to appeal to the person on the other hand, That he should improve his faithfulnesse to the Kingdom, by using diligence for the cure of this woman, as I by the gift of faith should direct him. Nevertheless it is not the gift of faith in me, say I, nor the act of diligence in you, but in dependence on the divine will which cals me to believe and you to act ... look how farre you shall act, as before the Lord, with diligence for her cure, you shall be made partakers of her consolation.[75]

Poole's represented position is a passive one, and in much the same way as Pope styled herself as mere 'Instrument' or channel for the Word, the message she delivers here is one 'set before' her. In it the activism of the male army in the current political situation is presented as the natural correlate of a physical, masculine superiority. As the entire country is reduced to the form of a decrepit, 'imperfect' female body, only male military intervention can cure it. With the nation pervasively anatomized and figured female, Poole presents her logical

---

[74]   *The Clarke Papers*, vol. 2, p. 150.
[75]   *A Vision*, p. 1; *Clarke Papers*, vol. 2, p. 151.

extension that the public realm of action be exclusively masculinized whilst the more private worlds of faith and belief remain the province of herself and presumably the rest of womankind. Accordingly, it is this gendered segregation of public and private duties, as much as the imperative of the divinely sanctioned image itself, which 'calls me to beleeve, and you to act'. The succession of passive constructions effectively strips Poole of any agency in the vision and one has the sense that the only reason she delivers it is because she is bound by the reciprocal obligation inherent in the economy of patriarchal 'gift' exchange. As 'the Lord' bestows the 'gift of faith' upon her she is obliged to repeat the act of generosity by giving her vision to the army officers.[76] Yet lurking beneath this reading is one that offers fundamentally different evaluations of passivity; accordingly, the army responds with action but it is presented as a crudely mechanistic form of agency alongside the promptings of imagination and reason from Poole/God, so that faith and intellect become the true curative agents of the nationwide malaise and the army merely the instrument through which that relief is effected.[77] Indeed the image of the passive female might actually attain a radical forcefulness if one considers the image of the whole of England as a 'crooked, sick weak' woman to be an image of deformity or 'imperfect[ion]' only in relation to the masculine 'body of the Army' so that the image of femininity becomes less weak and restrained than insistent and vivid.

As has already been mentioned, Poole's vision on this occasion was gratefully received. Colonel Rich was delighted with the message of military supremacy: 'I doe rejoice to heare what hath been said, and itt meetes much with what hath been upon my heart heretofore ... and shall rejoice to see itt made out more and more in others'.[78] Thomas Harrison similarly approved of the message but enquired as to the particular means wherewith the army should effect this 'cure'. Poole denied that there was any specific plan informing her vision claiming instead 'but by the guift and faith of the Church shall you bee guided, which spirit is in you, which shall direct you'.[79] Ireton's response was the most telling:

> I see nothing in her but those [things] that are the fruites of the spiritt of God, and am therefore apt to thinke soe at the present, being not able to judge the contrary, because mee thinkes it comes with such *a spiritt that does take and hold forth humility and self deniall*, and that rules very much about the whole that shee hath deliver'd, which makes mee have the better apprehension of itt for the present. Itt is only God that can judge the spiritts of men and women.[80]

---

[76]   Albeit in an earlier humanistic context, on the status of women within a patriarchal culture of reciprocal generosity see Hutson, *The Usurer's Daughter*.

[77]   Such an assessment of Poole's role in this visionary economy is evocative of Bacon's assertion of the value of the imagination's mediatory role between truth and the senses; see Francis Bacon, *The Advancement of Learning* (New York, 1955), p. 284.

[78]   *Clarke Papers*, vol. 2, p. 153.

[79]   Ibid., vol. 2, p. 154.

[80]   Ibid; emphasis added.

Faced with the equality of all men and women in God's judgement, and his own ignorance as to the validity of the prophecy, Ireton evaluates the vision in terms he can 'judge', that is, in those concerning the relationship between the sexes in the public sphere. Therefore, he gives credence to Poole's words because amid all her talk of a national female body and its relationship with 'body of the Army', they appear to erase her physical presence before the army Council. Thus, for Ireton, those words are spoken, not only with great 'humility' but are also 'self-denying'.

However, Poole's words here do not necessarily betoken the abject self-denial that Ireton found so comforting. For in spite of all her protestations about the supremacy of the army and the unspecific nature of her vision as to how they should effect the 'cure' of the 'distressed' nation, when she was invited to return to the Council one week later her message had fundamentally altered. No longer simply the enigmatic vessel of God's word, she claims that her speech is this time motivated by her *reading* of the Council of Officer's *Agreement of the People* which she believes represents a dereliction of the army's duty as 'stewards of the guift[s] of God in and upon this Nation'.[81] Thereupon she declaims that she has 'yett a[nother] message to declare, which itt's very possible may be strangely look't upon; butt in the law of the Lord I present myself to tender itt, and let itt finde acceptance as itt is'.[82] Instead of uttering a prophecy from the spirit of God, though, she presents the Council with 'a paper' against the king's execution which the officers promptly read and question her upon. The contrast with her first visit to Whitehall could not be starker. Poole offers a specific political message on the resolution of the present crisis surrounding the king, 'tender[s] itt' herself, that is, directly and personally, in a way that refuses to be enshrouded in and reduced to the mystery of the revealed Word. In effect, she moves from prophecy to polemic. The officers were quick to spot and ridicule Poole's manipulation of genre:

> *Col. Deane*: I must desire to aske one question: whether you were commanded by the spiritt of God to deliver itt unto us in this manner.
> *Woman*: I believe I had a command from God for itt.
> *Col. Deane*: To deliver this paper in this forme?
> *Woman*: To deliver in this paper or otherwise a message.
>
> *Col. Deane*: And so you bringe itt, and present itt to us, as directed by his spiritt in you, and commanded to deliver itt to us?
> *Woman*. Yea Sir, I doe.
> ...
> *Mr Sadler*: doe [you] offer this paper or from the Revelation of God?

---

[81]   Ibid., p. 163; *Vision*, p. 2. As the text of *An Agreement of the People* was only published and presented to what remained of the Long Parliament on 20 January, it seems more likely that the pamphlet Poole refers to is in fact the *Foundations of Freedom: or an Agreement of the People*. For a discussion of the *Agreement* in its various stages see Barbara Taft, "Communications: The Council of Officers" *Agreement of the People*, 1648/9', *The Historical Journal*, 28:1 (1985), pp. 169–85.

[82]   *Clarke Papers*, vol. 2, p. 164.

Woman: I saw noe vision, nor noe Angell, nor heard no voice, butt my spiritt being drawne out about those thinges, *I was in itt.* Soe far as it is from God I thinke itt is a revelation.[83]

Colonel Deane's incredulity registers his inability to come to terms with a woman acting politically, publicly and in print, whilst Poole's answer to the questions reveal the verbal traces of self-effacing agency. She maintains the effect of heavenly intervention in her utterances, but is far less forthright in its assertion. She 'believe[s]' God commanded it, but sounds less convincing on the specific nature of the command; the extensive use of the first person pronoun in her short answers effectively forces a space for herself in the ecstatic visionary economy. In tandem with this her response to Sadler's question dismisses all of the typological sensory experience of the prophetess, there was 'noe vision ... noe Angell ... no Voice', and she can instead assert that it was her 'spiritt', and not the divine one, that figured most prominently in the moment; 'I was in itt', as she puts it when triumphantly moving to conclude.

If we move from Poole's oral testimony at Whitehall to her own written record in her pamphlets, a more intricate picture of political agency emerges. The fact that her four texts are simply differently compiled accounts of the two visits at Whitehall demonstrates that both Poole and her publisher carefully evaluated the material as well as the symbolic force of her appearance before the General Council. Whilst there is almost a verbatim correspondence between Poole's writings and William Clarke's record for Poole's first, meeker visit to the General Council, Poole's account and the 'official' one diverge when it comes to her more forceful second appearance, the prophetess's own relation being much fuller than that of the Council's secretary. As we have already seen, Clarke's record presents Poole's second visit in far from subtle terms. It is, apparently, as if Poole had simply and wilfully changed her mind by the time of her second visit. Much more effort is taken to report the officer's discussion and ridicule of Poole's significantly unrecorded anti-regicide message. The patriarchal impetus behind such selective reportage is self-evident and is bound up once again with the attempt to silence the subversive female voice in the public sphere. However, one senses that if Poole's text had been reproduced in the record, a much more finely nuanced picture of her attempts to gain publicity and convince the army to spare the king would have emerged. Hence Clarke's account of Poole's second vision opens with the disarmingly colloquial report that she 'called in', a phrase which intimates at unfit intimacy, neighbourliness, or privacy and sets up a parallelism wherein the inappropriateness of private diction and public action is implied. By contrast, Poole's pamphlet records the opening of her second address as follows:

---

[83]   Ibid., pp. 164–5, 167–8.

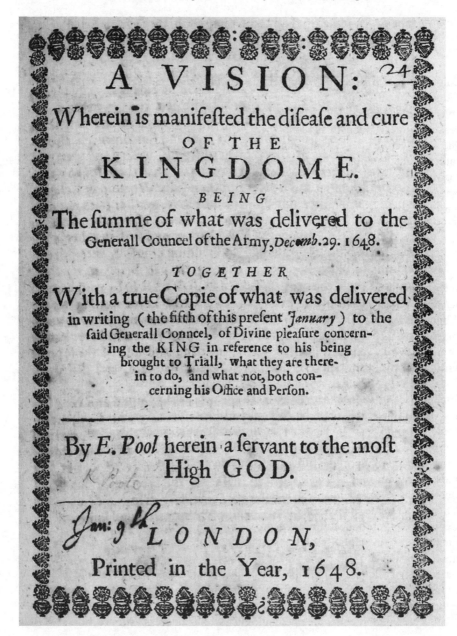

A VISION: 24

Wherein is manifested the difeafe and cure

OF THE

KINGDOME.

BEING

The fumme of what was delivered to the

Generall Councel of the Army, *Decemb*.29. 1648.

TOGETHER

With a true Copie of what was delivered

in writing (the fifth of this prefent *January*) to the
faid Generall Conncel, of Divine pleafure concerning the KING in reference to his being
brought to Triall, what they are therein to do, and what not, both concerning his Office and Perfon.

By *E. Pool* herein a fervant to the moft

High GOD.

LONDON,

Printed in the Year, 1648.

Figure 6: Elizabeth Poole, *A Vision* (1649), title page

Dear Sirs,

Having already found so free admission into your presences, it hath given me greater incouragement (though more peculiarly, the truth perswading me thereunto) to present you with my thoughts in the following lines. I am in divine pleasure madesensible of the might of the affaires which lye upon you; and the spirit of sympathie abiding in me, constraineth me to groan with you in your pains ... Now therefore my humble advice to you is, that you stand in the awfull presence of the most high Father, acting your parts before God and man, you stand in the place of interpreters, for many hard sayings present themselves to you, and will do, look for it.[84]

It would seem that the dictates of 'truth', 'divine pleasure' and the officers themselves provide Poole with the justification to write and publish. However, if one looks more closely at her introduction, the power relationship she envisages as the engine of the creative process is much more egalitarian than it initially appears. There is no godly, veracious, or military imperative to write, merely 'incouragement', a noun which implies that all parties are complicit in the recognition of Poole's political agency. From such sure footing it becomes a relatively easy leap to ascribe a degree of equality amongst the politically literate, so that whether a woman from Abingdon or a member of the General Council of the army, all become 'interpreters' of the divine will and the political process. Furthermore, Poole appears to be momentarily rewriting what we have seen to be the stock pro-regicide trope of 'womanish pity' or, as here, 'sympathy' for the king in his suffering. Instead she not only re-routes this affinity along parliamentarian lines, but actually makes the entire political crisis a peculiarly feminine condition; she is 'constrain[ed] to groan' with the army in their labour to effect a settlement, and share the 'pains' which afflict the whole nation, a nation she imagined female on her first visit.

Agency, Regicide and Domestic Violence

Arguing from such a heightened rhetorical position merely serves to demonstrate the intricately ordered, fantastically dextrous progression of what Poole reveals to be her anti-regicide argument. As I have already argued, the motives behind such an argument may have been particularly feminine, but it is also likely that they stem from beliefs which had formerly allied her to William Kiffin's Particular Baptist Congregation. About two years before her appearance at Whitehall, Particular Baptist groups had been instrumental in supporting the *Heads of the Proposals*, the peace proposals of the army grandees, which advocated dialogue with the king (and sought assurance that he would guarantee a form of religious

---

[84] Poole, *A Vision*, p. 3.

toleration) in order to resolve the crisis.[85] Kiffin himself was especially active in negotiations and actually met Charles at Hampton Court in September of 1647 in order to draft a petition for a personal treaty with the king.[86] It seems unlikely that Poole's anti-regicide message actually constitutes a public attempt on her part to make her peace with Kiffin (especially given her requests that he bring the whole matter to law), but the terms in which she argues for the sparing of the king's blood are fascinating. She now reconfigures her vision of the General Council; she deploys an image of them as a gravid woman, wishing them 'rest' from their 'labours' and then offers a view of the political landscape in highly domestic terms:

> That you give unto men the things that are theirs, and upon God the things that are his, it is true indeed, as unto men (I know I appeale by the gift of God upon me) the king is your Father and your husband, which you were and are to obey in the Lord, & no other way, for when he forgot his Subordination to divine faithood and headship, thinking he had begotten you a generation to his own pleasure, and taking you a wife for his own lusts, thereby is the yoake taken from your necks (I mean the neck of the spirit and Law, which is the bond of your union, that the holy life in it might not be prophaned).[87]

The abuses of king on country are reworked so as to figure as the libertinism of a husband who marries for mere 'pleasure' and 'lust', who refuses to permit his desire to be trammelled by the constraints of religious belief. Whilst this obviously panders to the typological depiction of royalist decadence and conspicuous consumption, it also sets the image of the people and parliament of England as the monarch's gravid wife into sharp relief. However, the text conspires against the blithe attribution of any kind of feministic pro-regicide sentiment to this depiction of nationwide feminine oppression within Poole's visionary economy. In the scene Poole sketches, patriarchal force would appear to be wielded not only by the lascivious Charles, but also by that 'divine ... headship' which ought to hold the king in 'Subordination'. Robert Filmer would, of course, give the most systematic expression of this view when *Patriarcha* was published some thirty years later, but it is telling that Poole should reveal that she too is favoured by a 'gift' within this masculine environment. Poole's own femininity is problematized once one realizes that in introducing her vision she echoes Christ at one of his most explicit moments of political commentary in the gospels. When she commences with the remark that 'you give unto men the things that are theirs, and upon God the things that are his', an early modern audience would have instantly conjured up the

---

[85]   Barber, *Regicide and Republicanism,* pp. 99, 113.
[86]   On Kiffin's negotiations with the king see Tolmie, *The Triumph of the Saints*, pp.164–5. Barber contends that two years later, guilt at their complicity in promoting negotiations with the king in 1647 impelled some Particular Baptists to be especially vociferous in their calls to bring Charles to justice; *Regicide and Republicanism*, pp. 100, 114.
[87]   Poole, *A Vision,* p. 6.

biblical passage where Christ is questioned by the chief priests about the legality of the Jewish 'tribute' to the Roman empire. There, instead of falling into the trap of advocating non-payment, which would have been conceived by his audience as a deliberate act of zealotry, Christ issued the quietistic injunction that all ought to 'Render therefore unto Caesar things which be Caesar's, and unto God the things which be God's'.[88] I am not suggesting here that Poole is deliberately eschewing her femininity (Christ's gender identity has often been portrayed as far from simply masculine). Rather, through subtle deployment of the *topos* of the instrumentality of the prophetess, she was able to gain some feminine political leverage by pitting patriarchal arguments concerning the public position of women against their main proponents.

In any case, the deliberate echo of Christ's abjuration of political radicalism prepares us for Poole's own solution to the crisis surrounding the king. Thus detailing the army's relationship with Charles she contests that 'in Subordination you owe him all that you have and are, and although he would not be your Father and husband, Subordinate but absolute, yet know that you are for the Lord's sake to honour his person. For he is the father and husband of your bodyes.'[89] This further feminization and domestication of the army makes the manner in which she offers her moderate argument of consensual pacific appeal for a non-violent resolution to the revolution particularly noteworthy. The daughterly and wifely obedience of this represented position precludes any physical violence against the spouse and, furthermore, by playing with prevalent misogynistic notions of the anarchy inherent in female disruption of the domestic sphere, Poole offers an argument against regicide on variants of what we have seen to be the regicides' own terms. As Frances Dolan has shown, the commonplace analogy between the household and the commonwealth was based on an imposed fluidity in the boundaries between the private and public spheres.[90] Thus from as early as 1352 statutes were in place that constructed a wife's murder of her husband as a kind of treason, whilst a husband's murder of his wife remained simple murder. Although structures were present that enabled the law to distinguish between various kinds of treasonable act – high versus petty – the fact that a woman convicted of petty treason was subject to exactly the same punishment as a woman guilty of high treason (burning at the stake) points to the erasure, in legal theory at least, of the distinction between the two kinds of treason. Therefore, for a woman, killing a king and killing a husband were not only analogous capital offences, but virtually identical ones.[91] Poole therefore subtly conflates the general masculinist fear of the

---

[88] For the gospel account see Luke 20 vv.20–26.

[89] Poole, *A Vision*, p. 4.

[90] Frances E. Dolan, 'Home-Rebels and Home-Traitors: Murderous Wives in Early Modern England', *Yale Journal of Law and the Humanities* 4:1 (1992), pp. 1–31; idem., 'The Subordinate('s) Plot: Petty Treason and the Forms of Domestic Rebellion', *Shakespeare Quarterly*, 43:3 (1992), pp. 317–40.

[91] Dolan, 'The Subordinate('s) Plot', p. 318.

anarchy inherent in domestic rebellion with a broadly consensual political point that the king's life ought to be spared. She uses the acceptable image of domestic harmony to bolster the less acceptable one of a spared Charles, all of which is ratified by her vision of heavenly patriarchy where all are 'Subordinate' to 'the everlasting Father'.[92]

If violence is withheld here, Poole appears to displace it into the domestic realm:

> You never heard that a wife might put away her husband, as he is the head of her body, but for the Lord's sake suffereth his terror to her flesh, though she be free in the spirit of the Lord; and he being incapable to act as her husband, she acteth in his stead; ... accordingly you may hold the hands of your husband, that he pierce not your bowels with a knife or a sword to take your life.[93]

Due to the paucity of biographical information, it is impossible to assess whether or not this is an image drawn from Poole's own personal experience, whether this is one of those rare occasions when what Laura Gowing has termed 'the drama of marital violence' becomes visible. In revealing the feminine oppression inherent in the marriage system Gowing demonstrates how a man could attest to the unfitness of his wife with some proof of her sexual promiscuity. By contrast, the unfitness of a husband in marriage could only be proved by evidence of extensive periods of life-threatening violence.[94] Whilst ballads could actually recommend wife-beating as the surest way to achieve household discipline, domestic violence against women, if not always officially sanctioned, remained a largely unpunishable offence in seventeenth-century England. Poole's use of arresting images of such violence is, however, much less masochistically quietistic than might initially appear. It is only through her apparent endorsement of violent female subjugation that she herself can press her public message, a message wherein Charles's offences against the parliamentarian side during the civil wars are accorded a legality equivalent to man's supposedly 'natural' physical dominance over his wife. The corresponding patriarchal logic is that those same offences ought not to be punishable by death.

Yet Poole does not simply leave her envisioned female General Council prey to the whims and cruelty of its violent spouse. It seems likely that Poole assented to the Particular Baptist condemnation of a husband's use of physical force over his

---

92   Poole, *A Vision*, p. 5.

93   Ibid., pp. 5–6.

94   Gowing also contrasts the invisibility of the drama of marital violence with 'the drama of adultery and its consequences [which] was played out at almost every level of early modern culture'; Gowing, *Domestic Dangers*, p. 206. For further work on early modern domestic violence, see S. D. Amussen, '"Being Stirred to Much Unquietness": Violence and Domestic Violence in Early Modern England', *Journal of Women's History* 6:2 (1994), pp. 70–89; Margaret Hunt, 'Wife Beating, Domesticity and Women's Independence in Eighteenth Century London', *Gender and History* 4:1 (1992), pp. 10–29.

wife as she offers a form of providentialist female resistance in quiescence, a form of agency which is self-effacing.[95] Thus she invokes the biblical figures of Abigail, Nabal and David:

> Wherefore put your swords into his hands for your defence, and feare not to act the part of *Abigail*, seeing *Nabal* hath refused it (by Appropriating his goods to himselfe) in relieving *David* and his men in their distress; it was to her praise, it shall be to yours, feare it not: Onely consider, that as she lifted not her hand against her husband to take his life, no more doe yee against yours.[96]

The incident she alludes to is from I Samuel 25 where David sends his men from the wilderness of Paran to Nabal (the nearest landowner whose property and livestock they had been protecting) requesting food. Yet, despite their polite civility, Nabal refuses their request, slights the soon-to-be king David, stating that he will hoard his goods for himself. When David hears of this treatment he gathers his armed forces and makes for Nabal's land with the sole purpose of destroying all in sight. However, before the slaughter can commence, Nabal's wife Abigail (who has heard of her husband's churlish response via a servant) intercepts David and his men and presents them with more food than they had requested. After an eloquent speech in which she presents her husband as foolish rather than evil, David is convinced to call off his assault; all are reconciled after divine retributive justice has brought about Nabal's death ten days later, and Abigail and David are married. The story was a favourite one in the seventeenth century (in the 1640s Milton considered it a fitting topic for pastoral) and interpretations tended to focus on the status of Abigail as the good wife.[97] Thus in 1683 Matthew Poole was especially keen to stress the humility of Abigail's address to David, the fact that she was the 'humble suppliant' *par excellence*.[98] Yet, just as Rachel Falconer has

---

[95] For one such condemnation of domestic violence see the following summary of an exchange at a Particular Baptist general meeting at Tiverton in Devon on 15th and 16th September 1657: 'Query 1: Whether a man in any case ruling over his wife may lawfully strike her? Answer: he ought so to rule over his wife in wisdom as that the ordinance of God in point of ruling may be preserved and if it may be by any means without striking of her such a proceeding being without any pretext or example that we read of in the holy spirit.' Reprinted in B. R. White (ed.), *Association Records of the Particular Baptists of England, Wales and Ireland to 1660*, 3 vols (Didcot, 1971–77), vol. 3, p. 69.

[96] Poole, *A Vision*, p. 5.

[97] For Milton's use of the story see Rachel Falconer, *Orpheus Dis(re)membered: Milton and the Myth of the Poet-Hero* (Sheffield, 1996), pp. 166–70. Abigail's speech is usefully compared to Eve's reconciliation speech in *Paradise Lost* (X, ll. 910–36) whose verbal and rhetorical similarities are seen to provide both women with 'loopholes', in the Bakhtinian sense, through which a female subjectivity may be attained. For further feminist interpretation of the Samuel narrative see Alice Bach, 'The Pleasure of her Text', *The Pleasure of her Text: Feminist Readings of Biblical and Historical Texts* (Philadelphia, 1990), pp. 25–44.

[98] Matthew Poole, *A Commentary on the Holy Bible by Matthew Poole*, 3 vols (London, 1962), vol. 1, p. 575.

demonstrated that Abigail's humility was not the straightforward token of female meekness that so many seventeenth-century male exegetes would have prized, Matthew Poole continues:

> this whole speech of Abigail's is *done with great artifice*; and she doth here, by an absolute submitting to mercy without any pretence of justification of what was done (but rather with aggravation of it) endeavour to work upon David's generosity and good nature to pardon it; and *with great art*, first would divert the punishment from her husband to herself, because she had much more to say why David should spare her than why he should spare Nabal. And there was hardly any head of argument whence the greatest orator might argue in this case which she doth not manage to the best advantage.[99]

Abigail's consummate rhetorical skill, her ability to craft an elevated position for herself among 'the greatest orator[s]' and future kings, comes through despite her 'absolute submitting' to patriarchal power.

Elizabeth Poole draws on the problematic meekness of the figure of Abigail that her male namesake later describes in a manner which enables her simultaneously to act as advisor on matters of state and apparently erase herself from the political economy. Thus her pervasively providentialist and anti-regicidal vision allies Abigail and the General Council, Nabal and Charles I, David and 'the everlasting Father'. This is perfectly tailored to the exigency of the current political situation so that Charles appears less evil tyrant than merely sottish and wilful (one who had also, through excessive taxation, attempted to 'Appropriat[e] his goods to himselfe') and God is viewed as the sole arbiter of retributive justice. The General Council is once again represented as female and features as the perspicacious pacifist. That this represents a utopian vision is beyond contention (how pacifistic did Poole expect the radical saints of the army to be in January 1649?), but it is a utopianism which, politically speaking, is always in danger of imminent collapse. Through the adjacency of the unambiguous championing of a problematic female heroism and a thorough-going act of female self-effacement (where does Poole figure in this new biblical utopia?) the vision is accordingly riddled with tensions and instabilities.[100] These are resolved however through cursory attention to the illocutionary force of Poole's prophecy. As she uttered and presented her words to the General Council, Poole herself was engaging in a pacifistic disruption of the army's movement towards the king's execution. If her visionary economy is thus

---

[99]   Ibid; emphasis added.
[100]   I am not suggesting here that Abigail's heroism is entirely unrelated to her own form of self-effacement through the apportionment of self-blame or the assumption of a supplicatory role, but merely that her feminine presence is, initially, more visible than that of Poole.

historically constituted, does not she, in effect, become the Abigail she so fervently projected onto an army who are now transfigured into a wrathful David?[101]

Whilst the effect of such a transfiguration was to transfer the potential weight of blood-guilt from Charles's shoulders to those of the army, Poole's strategy possibly draws upon her knowledge of an earlier transfiguration of the Abigail-David relationship. As had already been mentioned Poole was outlawed, in the mid-1640s, from William Kiffin's Particular Baptist congregation for committing some supposedly 'scandalous evils'. However, on hearing news of this 'a friend' of Poole's, one styled T. P., wrote an open letter to Kiffin's congregation requesting 'mercy ... towards our sister'. In calling for this mercy T. P. hoped 'I may prove to you as *Abigail* did to *David*'.[102] Here it is Poole's, rather than Charles's, supposed evil which is implicitly recast as Nabal-like folly whilst T. P's female supplicatory role is foregrounded.[103] In either case, women's actions arise through the problematic meekness and subtle self-effacement of Abigail.[104]

It is depressingly telling, therefore, that after the delivery of her pamphlet, Poole entirely disappears from the General Council's official records of their proceedings. She is last seen being interrogated by Colonel Nathaniel Rich who, vigorously maintaining the legality of the High Court, asks her what she would advise in the face of the King's refusal to plead at his own trial, in the all-too-likely event that 'he stands mute and will nott answer'.[105] Poole's last recorded words could not be set in greater contrast against the rhetorical complexity of her own texts: 'I understand itt nott'.[106] Herein lies the reason why historians have generally failed to attend to Poole's contribution to seventeenth-century regicidal discourse; officially, Poole fails to understand and then falls silent. Yet, as already mentioned, such an interpretation conspicuously fails to recognize that at a time when a king could refuse to answer treasonous charges only to be convicted *pro confesso*,

---

[101] This analysis is indebted to Norbook's discussion of speech act theory in relation to the literature and history of the seventeenth century in *Writing the English Republic*, pp. 1–22.

[102] Poole, *An Alarum* (1st ed.) pp. 13–14.

[103] On the identity of T. P., who it has been suggested is either Thomasina Pendarves or the wife of the Abingdon governor George Payne, see Richard Greaves and Robert S. Zaller, *A Biographical Dictionary of British Radicals in the Seventeenth Century*, 3 vols (Brighton, 1982), vol. 3, p. 49; Elaine Hobby, *Virtue of Necessity*, p. 211.

[104] Poole is not the only early modern woman writer to use the figure of Abigail to justify her sortie into the male realms of politics and print. Similarly, the Leveller women led by Katherine Chidley who petitioned parliament for John Lilburne's release from prison in 1653 cited Abigail as fit precedent. They criticized parliament for distinctly un-Davidic behaviour in their treatment of the Leveller leader: 'David himselfe was prevented, by the timely address of a weak woman, from a most resolved purpose of shedding of Blood ... [It is to be considered] whether the sparing of blood be not more suitable to the work before you, it being denied unto David, because his hands had been dipt in blood'; *To the Parliament of the Commonwealth of England, The Humble Petition of Diuers Afflicted Women in Behalf of Mr John Lilburne Prisoner in Newgate* (London, 1653), no sig.

[105] *Clarke Papers*, vol. 2, p. 169.

[106] Ibid.

silences were especially problematic. It is only through studying texts like Poole's and Pope's alongside the official records of oral testimony at the High Court of Justice, that we can begin to get a sense of just how problematic those silences were. Attention to such texts enables us to see that anti-regicide pamphlet complaint was a form – in spite of the intense patriarchal policing of this masculinist arena – in which the woman writer could re-negotiate the restrictions and oppressions of her own condition and claim public-sphere space to comment on the state of the political nation. Yet, as the century progressed and as republican culture gradually began to accommodate the feminine, the king's cause was less explicitly feminized and women began writing on regicide from all sides of the political spectrum. However, such a position was only tenable *after* the turbulent middle decades of the seventeenth century when the agency of God's earthly representative was itself extensively questioned.

Chapter 3

A Woman in the Business of Revolutionary News: Elizabeth Alkin, 'Parliament Joan', and the Commonwealth Newsbook

If agency is more than simply a matter of the pen – a manifestation of women's consummate rhetorical artistry in revolutionary pamphlet culture – it must also be traced in the deeper material structures of that culture. Accordingly, this chapter endeavours to explore some of the roles that women could play in making and shaping revolutionary news, a phenomenon that numerous critics have posited as instrumental in the formation of a public sphere and the expansion of political literacy in the early modern period.[1] As a result of the important work of a number of historians and literary scholars, the full extent of the manner in which newsbooks came to swamp and redefine the pamphlet culture of revolutionary England, following their first appearance in 1641, is at last beginning to emerge. Over forty years ago, in a seminal study, Joseph Frank alerted his readers to the way in which the newsbook was one of the 'more revolutionary' textual forms of the tumultuous middle decades of the seventeenth century; in the most thorough account to date, Joad Raymond has persuasively argued that 'the newsbook was the central feature' of revolutionary Britain's 'culture of the pamphlet'. Michael Mendle has endorsed this view: 'From any perspective, by any definition, news was the hub of the pamphlet culture'.[2] However, according to another narrative of seventeenth-century literary history, which has only begun to be contested

---

[1]   See, for instance, Raymond, 'The Newspaper, Public Opinion, and the Public Sphere'; Pincus, '"Coffee Politicians Does Create"'; Norbrook, 'Areopagitica, Censorship, and the Early Modern Public Sphere'; Zaret, 'Religion, Science, and Printing in the Public Spheres of Seventeenth-Century England'; Michael Mendle, 'News and the Pamphlet Culture of Mid Seventeenth-Century England', in Brendan Dooley and Sabrina A. Brown (eds.), The Politics of Information in Early Modern Europe (London and New York, 2001), pp. 57–79.
[2]   Frank, Beginnings, p. 272; Raymond, Invention, p. 13; Mendle, 'News and the pamphlet culture', p. 58.

recently, women played little part in the news trade until after the Restoration.[3] This chapter seeks to disturb that assumption and maintains that its durability rests upon a misreading of women's silences and the complex interconnections between effacement and agency in the mid-seventeenth century. In what follows, therefore, I shall interrogate the relationship between gender and modes of news production by foregrounding the collative and collective nature of the news trade. Focusing on the overlooked work of one of the foremost 'she-Intelligencers' of this period, Elizabeth Alkin, I will argue that some women eschewed individualistic modes of agency in their engagement with the collective material practices of newsbook publication. This ought not to be read as the etiolation of agency, as providing evidence that women played little or no part in the business of revolutionary news, but should instead be located within a similar hermeneutical framework as the rhetorical strategies and public negotiations examined elsewhere in this book.

The story that women only became actively involved in the material production of news after the Restoration is one that has been re-run, re-spun, and re-edited by feminist historians and literary critics for the last twenty years. In her early, eloquent attempt to reclaim the culture of the periodical press from exclusively male hands, Alison Adburgham sought to recover:

> pre-Victorian periodicals from the limbo of forgotten publications, and exhume from long undisturbed sources a curious collection of women who, at a time when it was considered humiliating for a gentlewoman to earn money, contrived to support themselves by writing, editing or publishing.[4]

Nonetheless, Adburgham's rediscovery of curious collections of pre-Victorian women and texts is somewhat limited by her imposition of a chronology which only begins with the eighteenth century and which centres around groups of exclusively 'gentle' female readers and writers. Kathryn Shevelow follows Adburgham's lead; however her enquiry into the relationship between 'femininity and the early periodical' also confines itself to such parameters by concluding that it was only with 'the eighteenth century, [that] upper- and middle-class Englishwomen increasingly began to participate in the public realm of print culture'.[5] In another illuminating study, Paula McDowell has alerted us to the ways in which, further down the social scale, groups of non-aristocratic women did actually play a part in shaping the news and the public sphere. Her work:

---

[3]   See in particular Raymond, *Pamphlets and Pamphleteering*, pp. 312–15; Freist, *Governed by Opinion*, *passim*.

[4]   Alison Adburgham, *Women in Print: Writing and Women's Magazines From the Restoration to the Accession of Victoria* (London, 1972), p. 9.

[5]   Kathryn Shevelow, *Women and Print Culture: The Construction of Femininity in the Early Periodical* (London and New York, 1989), p. 1.

demonstrates that women ... at work in the London book trades were among the first to seize ... new opportunities for public, political expression. At this time of enduring significance in English political life, women of the widest variety of socio-economic backgrounds in fact played so prominent a role in the production and transmission of political and religio-political ideas through print as to belie simultaneous powerful claims that women had no place in civic life.[6]

Despite the major advances afforded by McDowell's research, her focus on the period between 1678 and 1730 has meant that the image of late-seventeenth-century women attending their news presses for the first time has largely remained unchallenged.

Such an image is intensified by much revolutionary newsbook historiography which, despite the occasional paragraph or footnoted reference, has offered little attention to the possible material involvement of women in the civil war news trade.[7] This is undoubtedly related to the fact that images of women and femininity were appropriated by male newsbook writers for use and circulation in the symbolic economies of their texts. It is no news that women featured regularly in the civil war newsbooks, whose trade in highly gendered and misogynistic language secured both editorial notoriety and a paying audience. For both sides, the dishonesty of the times was most adequately expressed alongside the index of moral bankruptcy affixed to illicit sex, which, more often than not, featured as a female vice. Thus is it that the royalist *Mercurius Aulicus* reports of the 'zealous young Maids in the Citie of Norwich who covenanted together to raise Troope of Horse for the Rebels service'. That five of them were to become pregnant 'by whom it is not yet signified' is of no surprise whatsoever to the writer who subsequently implores 'all Virgins [to] looke to it, for people hereafter will scarce think them honest, who are so bold and shamelesse as to joyne in a Rebellion against their own Sovereign.'[8] It also seems unlikely, in a market where claims to truth and fact were made in tandem with the right to govern the English people, that people would have bought any of John Crouch's royalist newsbooks for their

---

[6]   Paula McDowell, *The Women of Grub Street: Press, Politics, and Gender in the London Literary Marketplace* (Oxford and New York, 1998), p. 6.

[7]   For instance, see Raymond, *Invention,* pp. 151, 161, 241–2, 250–51; idem., *Making the News*, pp. 122–68; Frank, *Beginnings*, pp. 146, 305, 301, 356; William M. Clyde, *The Struggle for Freedom of the Press from Caxton to Cromwell* (London, 1934), pp. 178, 200; J. B. Williams, *A History of Journalism to the Foundation of the Gazette* (London, 1908), pp. 131–42, 152–4. There are however some important discussions of women's material involvement in pamphlet culture more broadly in this period. See Freist, *Governed by Opinion*; Maureen Bell, 'Hannah Allen and the Development of a Puritan Publishing Business 1646–1651', *Publishing History* 26 (1989), pp. 5–66; idem., 'Mary Westwood, Quaker Publisher', *Publishing History* 23 (1988), pp. 5–66; idem., 'Women Publishers of Puritan Literature in the Mid-Seventeenth Century: Three Case Studies', unpublished Ph.D. thesis (Loughborough, 1987).

[8]   *Mercurius Aulicus* 2, 7–13 Jan. 1644, cited in Raymond, *Making the News*, p. 132.

informative news content. One of his publications peddled a lurid vision of a sectarian 'sisterhood of Tumblers' who 'exercise on their backs in many obscure alleys'.[9] This would probably not have prompted Thomas Edwards to undertake an alley-to-alley search of the city of London. Another Crouch title took the time to alert its readers to 'Three Nurceries of Sodomy, Lust and Uncleanness' which had sprung up as a result of the new-found liberty of the recently established Commonwealth. The first of these is:

> My Lord *Gorings* house, or the *Mulbery-Garden*, called the *Whipping-School*, erected by the Worshipful Colonel *Martin* for the encrease of the Saints in the *Iuncto*: None is to enter here except a *Parliament man*, and not he neither without the *Word*, which is *Freedom*: At the Door (when he enters) he gives five shillings the first time, and he is after free: So soon as he is come in ... he is presented with a *naked wench* lying upon a Bed, to whom he approached with bowing himself three times, and offers a Crown in Gold, and layes it upon her Chin, which she by a dexterious [sic] trick gives a toss and flings it into her *Tinder-box of Lust* ... and so they go to their exercise.[10]

Degeneracy is endemic following the collapse of the king's cause. As a libidinous radical republican converts the home of a famously debauched royalist commander (who had recently fled into exile on the continent) into a sadomasochistic pleasure dome, the sight of a woman doing 'trick[s]' for money most adequately suggests the corrupted 'Freedom' of the times. It was this combination of pornography, misogyny and titillative fiction, never for Crouch without political implications, which ensured the survival of his newsbooks in hostile times.[11]

If women figured prominently in the image-stocks revolutionary newsbooks, there is also ample evidence that they were actively and intelligently reading these same publications. Although by its very nature evidence of readership is elusive, women from all points on the social spectrum are known to have read them. Lady Brilliana Harley regularly included 'a booke of news' with her correspondence to her son Edward because she 'would willingly haue your minde keep awake in the knowedg of things abroode.'[12] Sir Thomas Knyvett also wrote to his wife Katherine discussing early newsbook reports of the war.[13] Margaret Eure kept

---

[9] *Mercurius Democritus* 17, 21–8 July 1652, pp. 129–130.

[10] *The Man in the Moon* 21, 5–12 Sept. 1649, p. 172.

[11] On Crouch see David Underdown, *A Freeborn People* (Oxford, 1996), pp. 90–111; Williams, *History*, pp. 145–8; Frank, *Beginnings*, pp. 195–231; Raymond, *Invention*, pp. 180–83. For further examples of women featuring in newsbooks see Raymond, *Making the News*, pp. 122–68.

[12] Thomas Taylor Lewis (ed.), *The Letters of Lady Brilliana Harley, Wife of Sir Robert Harley* (London, 1854), p. 32.

[13] See Bertram Schofield (ed.), *The Knyvett Letters, 1620–1644* (Norwich, 1949), pp. 109–110.

abreast of her nephew Ralph Verney's military exploits early in the civil war as much through 'the diurnals' he sent her as his own letters. When he stopped sending her these cheaply printed chronicles she declares herself 'sory for it, for we was glad to know what you dide.'[14] Dorothy Osborne, by contrast, was apparently unimpressed by the journalism of the 1650s. Her denigratory remarks, however, ought to be qualified by her awareness of the manner in which the mid-seventeenth-century newsbooks interleaved foreign and domestic news, alongside the political and the sexual in arresting, attention-grabbing detail:

> I know not how I stumbled upon a new's book [sic] this week, and for want of something Else to doe read it. It mention my L[ord] L[isle]'s Embassage againe, is there any such thing towards? I mett with something else in't, that may concerne any body that has a minde to marry, 'tis a new forme for it, that sure will fright the Country people Extreamly, for they aprehend nothing like goeing before a Justice.[15]

If Osborne affected to be bored by newsbooks, other women were clearly rather excited by them. Lady Rachael Bourchier, the Countess of Bath, regularly received copies of the latest London serials from her husband who claimed they might 'serue to informe poor Country Gossips how the business of the time goe[s]'. He envisaged his wife reading them to her family and friends 'by the fireside', and saw the newsbook as a means of communication which also enabled him to 'furnishe' his female relatives 'with knowledge stuffe' at the same time as it could 'saue [his] labour of writinge'.[16]

However, it was not merely women of royalist inclination who had an eye on the news. Lucy Hutchinson disdainfully referred to newsbook writers as 'scribblers' and recalled the way in which her husband 'scorned [their] mercenary pen'.[17] Further down the social scale, Katherine Chidley, who was, as we have already seen, sensitively attuned to the dynamics of revolutionary pamphlet culture, offered a novel insight into and critique of contemporary newsbooks. Engaged in her dispute with Thomas Edwards, she sought to discredit him by alleging the utter fictionality of all his sources in his anti-Independent writings, and vilified him for his recycling of:

---

[14] Frances Parthenope Verney (ed.), *Memoirs of the Verney Family During the Civil War* (London, 1892), vol. 2, p. 82.

[15] G. C. Moore Smith (ed.), *The Letters of Dorothy Osborne to William Temple* (Oxford, 1928), p. 76. The 'new forme' of marriage that Osborne refers to here is the 1653 Act which instituted civil marriage before a Justice of the Peace.

[16] Quoted in Catherine F. Boorman, 'Royalism and Female Authorship in the English Civil War Period: Contexts, Literary Strategies and Rewards' (unpublished Ph.D. thesis, University of Sheffield, 2004), p. 148.

[17] Lucy Hutchinson, *Memoirs*, p. 93, cited in Raymond, *Invention*, p. 251.

some lying popish stories (made by some Trencher poets) for Prelates, like the stories made by *Mercurius Alicus* [sic.] at Oxford, and some of those stories (by those who are best informed) taken to be like this booke of yours.[18]

Her attack on *Aulicus* is especially innovatory and demonstrates an acute perception of mid-seventeenth-century news culture. She, in effect, turns the stock criticism of London newsbooks on its head. Whilst charges of unreliability and fictionality were frequently levelled against the latter, the word of *Aulicus* was seen by many as gospel; indeed some clergymen were reported to have used it instead of the Bible as the text for some of their sermons.[19] *The Weekly Account*, though committed to refuting *Aulicus*, went so far as to suggest that 'as the intelligence of the West is somewhat uncertaine, by reason of the Cavalier's partie, ranging from place to place to stop roads and bypaths' all those who desired 'truly to be informed' should 'take a view of *Mercurius Aulicus*'.[20] Hence Chidley, for political ends, conflates the 'lying popish stories' of a royalist Oxford newsbook with the perceived untruths of a staunch Presbyterian. This is an extremely subtle line to take in this context given that Edwards himself had represented all newsbooks as being in the pay of the Independents when he suggested that the newsbooks were 'the pensioners of the sectaries'.[21] Chidley is ever alive to the importance and vitality of cheap print; just as she had engaged Edwards in pamphlet exchange by exploiting the dialogic potential of animadversion, she also sought to counter him by demonstrating that she was a more discerning newsbook reader.

Women were, then, both lurid symbols in and astute consumers of the newsbooks which helped define the early modern public sphere; they were also involved at various levels in its formulation. Whether petitioning parliament collectively, prophesying to and about the head of state, or contributing innumerable paper bullets to the succession of seventeenth-century pamphlet wars, women played an important role in early modern politico-religious activism and

---

[18] Katherine Chidley, *A New Yeares Gift*, p.7.
[19] The principal opponent of *Aulicus* claimed that 'The countrey-carrier buyes it for the vicar, and he expounds it instead of the Bible', *Mercurius Britanicus* 70, 10–17 Feb. 1645, p. 551. The best discussions of *Aulicus* are in Raymond, *Invention, passim*; Keith Thomas, *Sir John Berkenhead, 1617–1679: A Royalist Career in Politics and Polemics* (Oxford, 1969), pp. 28–98.
[20] Cited in Anthony Cotton's 'London Newsbooks in the Civil War: Their Political Attitudes and Sources of Information' unpublished D.Phil. thesis (Oxford University, 1971), p. 92. The partisan *Mercurius Britanicus* compared Charles I's epistolary style with *Aulicus*'s editorial matter and claimed that the king dictated the substance and style of the newsbook: 'this is part of the very same stuffe and language'; *Mercurius Britanicus* 92, 28 July–4 Aug. 1645, p. 1022.
[21] Edwards, *Gangraena*, vol. 1 (1646), p. 44.

the formation of public opinion.[22] This is not to assert that they achieved any real degree of participatory parity, but rather to contend that transhistorical patriarchal politics have – for a variety of self-perpetuative and/or sexist ends – obscured crucial and historically specific moments of women's agency.[23] A sense of that agency as self-effacing, multiple and continually misread begins to emerge when we examine the actual means of production of seventeenth-century newsbooks. Paula McDowell has shown that in post-Restoration newsbook culture if there were distinct roles, such as 'author', 'editor', 'printer' or 'publisher', these were frequently undercut by the existence of 'editor/publishers' and 'printer/publishers' so that via an elision of roles, individual agency could be seen to be subsumed within the wider structures of a collective activity.[24] This overlap between authorship, publishing and printing had certain economic and strategic advantages for contemporary workers in the news trade so that whilst costs could be cut, it also made the job of the censor or licenser more difficult. How was a seditious intention to be traced amid such a complex network of creative activity, when even hawkers selling the newsbooks at street level could be found politicizing the texts they sold in radical and seditious ways?[25] Paying attention to such collective endeavour is obviously at odds with the dominant trends of literary criticism, as McDowell explains:

twentieth-century literary critics' interest in bourgeois subjectivity and the rise of individualism has meant that dominant literary critical models emphasize individuals (especially authors). But traditional 'man-and-his-work' approaches,

---

[22] The literature on these topics is extensive. The best overview is still Hobby, *Virtue of Necessity*. For more recent work with extensive bibliographies see Megan Matchinske, *Writing, Gender, and the State in Early Modern England: Identity Formation and the Female Subject* (Cambridge, 1998); Hinds, *God's Englishwomen*; Crawford, *Women and Religion*.

[23] For a feminist critique of the classic Habermasian public sphere see Nancy Fraser, 'Rethinking the Public Sphere: A Contribution to the Critique of Actually Existing Democracy', in Calhoun (ed.), *Habermas and the Public Sphere*, pp. 109–42; idem., *Unruly Practices: Power, Discourse and Gender in Contemporary Social Theory* (Cambridge: Polity, 1989); Joan B. Landes, *Women and the Public Sphere in the Age of the French Revolution* (Ithaca, NY, 1988). For the argument that women did actually achieve participatory parity in the public sphere at a later stage in the seventeenth century see Steve Pincus, '"Coffee Politicians Does Create"'.

[24] McDowell, *The Women of Grub Street*, pp. 1–121. Contemporary seditious libel cases suggest that as it was the printer who often affixed his/her name to frequently anonymous works, and was accordingly punished, it was printers who were frequently tarred with the brush of originative agency. See Joseph F. Lowenstein, 'Legal Proofs and Corrected Readings: Press Agency and the New Bibliography', in D. L. Miller, S. O'Dair and Harold Weber (eds.), *The Production of English Renaissance Culture* (Ithaca, NY, 1994), pp. 93–122.

[25] McDowell, *The Women of Grub Street*, pp. 84–5.

with their post Romantic emphasis on individual authors, are not the most useful models for the study of non-élite men's and women's involvement in the print marketplace. This is especially true of literature in politically tumultuous periods, when authors, publishers, and other printworkers often worked closely together.[26]

Thus there is a crucial feminist imperative behind the decision to attend to the collective act of making a text, so that specific moments of female agency can be reassessed outside a patriarchal, competitively individualistic scheme of literary history. Indeed, in the recent attempt to explode this myth and counterbalance the canon, an attention to collectivity has served feminist literary historians well. Whether it be through studies of Leveller or Quaker women's strategies of collective petitioning or through attention to early modern scribal culture, where women played an integral role in the circulation, transcription and amending of manuscript compilations, the benefits of the eschewal of limited individualistic models of authorship has been widely felt.[27] However, the pre-Restoration newsbook has yet to receive the benefits of these new readings. Hence, due to a misleading over-attention to 'editors', and a reluctance to explore the profundity of silences, a select band of six men (Samuel Sheppard, Marchamont Nedham, Samuel Pecke, John Crouch, Daniel Border and Henry Walker) presides over the civil war newsbook, to the obvious detriment of the women in and around Grub Street.[28] It is ironic, but unavoidable, that the methodology involved in attempting to offer a corrective to this unsatisfactory picture of an all-male, mid-seventeenth-century news press will involve a reconfiguration of the very processes of individuation it ultimately seeks to displace. A vision of the collective enterprise and self-effacing agencies behind newsbook culture can only come into focus once historically specific moments of individual agency have been unearthed.[29]

---

[26] Ibid., p.12.

[27] Women petitioners are considered in chapter 5. On the narrative strategies deployed by women petitioners see Ann Hughes, 'Gender and Politics in Leveller Literature'; Catie Gill, *Women in the Seventeenth-Century Quaker Community* (forthcoming). On manuscript culture and women's involvement therein see Arthur F. Marotti, *Manuscript, Print, and the English Renaissance Lyric* (Ithaca and London, 1995), pp. 39–61; Harold Love, *Scribal Publication in Seventeenth-Century England* (Oxford, 1993); Wendy Wall, *The Imprint of Gender: Authorship and Publication in the English Renaissance* (Ithaca and London, 1993).

[28] See Blair Worden, 'Marchamont Nedham and the Beginnings of English Republicanism, 1649–1656', in David Wootton (ed.), *Republicanism, Liberty and Commercial Society, 1649–1776* (Stanford, 1994), pp. 45–81; Raymond, *Invention*, pp. 371–4.; idem., *Making the News*, pp. 332-79; Joseph Frank, *Cromwell's Press Agent: A Critical Biography of Marchamont Nedham 1620–1678* (Lanham, MD, 1980); idem., *Beginnings*, pp. 379–83; J. B. Williams, 'Henry Walker, Journalist of the Commonwealth', *The Nineteenth Century* (March, 1908), pp. 454–64.

[29] For a more theoretical perspective on the general, premature tendency in literary criticism to reify the author see Michel Foucault, 'What is an author?' in Josué V. Harari (ed.), *Textual Strategies: Perspectives in Post-Structuralist Criticism* (London, 1980), pp.

'In a Commonwealth, Joan is as Good as My Lady even by Daylight'

Elizabeth Alkin, or 'Parliament Joan' as she was frequently labelled by male contemporaries, is one woman who significantly problematizes the prevalent notion of an all-male civil war news press.[30] As with so many of her non-aristocratic female contemporaries, concrete biographical information about her is sparse. However, it would appear that she was born at the turn of the seventeenth century and died some time late in 1654.[31] Interestingly, some of the patriarchal force behind the obscuration of so many women's records is visible in the very process of naming and the conference of an alias. Alkin never once referred to herself as 'Parliament Joan' or 'Jone' preferring instead in the letters, petitions and newsbooks she worked on to use her full name or initials. However, from her very first appearance in the State Papers in March 1645 she features as 'Joan'. It is her alias who receives her first payment from the Committee for the Advancement of Money. Thus 'Elizabeth, alias Joan Alkyn' received payment of two pounds in the first week of March for 'severall discoveries' and in the next week it was ordered that she received '40s more, as she avers by petition that she discovered [Geo.] Mynnes wire'.[32] The naming process deserves special attention here. It would appear that although the payment was made, it was done so grudgingly, and the service or activity that Alkin performed to make that payment necessary is left ambiguous and of dubious authenticity. That she 'avers' her service is apparently insufficient, although the fact that the payment is actually made surely militates against the supposed dubiety of her testimony.

What renders her words untrustworthy is not only the well-worn trope of the unreliability of all women, but, more specifically, her name. The royalist author of *The Character of a Rebellion*, writing after the Restoration, was eager to expose the evils of the Commonwealth regime and, when addressing some of his readers, sought to express the perils inherent in non-monarchical government in particularly revealing terms:

> And here with all due respects and differences I must address my Discourse to these Noble Persons of the Delicate Sex; 'tis an ungrateful Complement to accost them

---

141–60; Lowenstein, 'Legal Proofs and Corrected Readings', pp. 93–122; Seán Burke, *The Death and Return of the Author: Criticism and Subjectivity in Bathes, Foucault and Derrida* (Edinburgh, 1992).

[30] The only extensive treatments of Alkin to date are Isabel MacDonald, *Elizabeth Alkin: A Florence Nightingale of the Commonwealth* (Keighley, 1935); G. E. Manwaring, 'Parliament Joan: The Florence Nightingale of the Commonwealth', *The United Service Magazine*, 57 (1918), pp. 301–310; J. B. Williams, *History*, pp. 131–54.

[31] In February 1650 the less than impartial John Crouch records her age as 'about fifty', *The Man in the Moon* 43, 13–20 Feb. 1650, p. 342. Her last surviving letter, detailing chronic illness, is dated 27 February 1654.

[32] SP 19/4/72; SP 19/4/77.

with, to tell them their Honours will be lost; but credit me, Illustrious Ladies, neither your Beauties, nor other most Attractive Charms, will be able to secure you from the Insolence of Common-wealth Ravishers: England can be no longer the Paradice of Women than it continues a Monarchy: My Lord cannot suffer, but my Lady will have a share; the Widows of Barons, by the Curiality and Curtesie of England, enjoy the Titles and Priviledges of Peerage, and the Daughters of Dukes, Earls, and Barons, do by the Favour of the same Custom enjoy the Honour and Title of Ladies; these too much fall with the Monarchy; and in a Common-wealth Joan is as good as my Lady even by day-light.[33]

With the privilege of rank removed, England as 'the Paradice of Women' suddenly descends into a Hobbesian state of nature with hoards of appetitive, apparently egalitarian 'Ravishers' violating everything from rank to beauty.[34] Courtesy of this rabid social and sexual levelling, a 'Lady' appears no better than her diametrically opposed inferior, a 'Joan'. This was something of a commonplace in the more ribald verse of the seventeenth century. The speaker of one of Robert Herrick's less sophisticated lyrics maintained that:

> Night hides all our thefts; all faults then pardoned be;
> All are alike faire, when no spots we see.
> Lais and Lucrece, in the night time are
> Pleasing alike; alike both singular:
> Jone and my Lady have at that time one,
> One and the self-same priz'd complexion.[35]

An entire system of constituting binaries (virgin/whore, high/low, vice/virtue, beauty/plainness) disappears under the cover of darkness. However, for the author of *The Character of a Rebellion*, the fact that these structuring identities can be mistaken 'even by daylight' reveals the full extent of the horror of republican government at the same time, of course, as it reveals the antifeministic stance of the political posturing. Early modern women's bodies had long been considered the same in the dark – the popularity of the bed trick as a device in the drama of the period amply illustrates this point – but the nightmare of the Commonwealth regime is that it fails to illuminate the critical differences between those women once they have stepped from the shadows of the bed chamber. For this author, the violations of republicanism (including, perhaps, that of sartorial distinction as an

---

[33] *The Character of a Rebellion* (1681), p.11.

[34] For the author (perhaps John Nalson), the 'Common-wealth Ravisher' *par excellence* was the republican Henry Marten.

[35] Lais was an infamous Corinthian prostitute; Robert Herrick, *Hesperides: Or the Works Both Human and Divine of Robert Herrick Esq* (London, 1648), p. 245. Herrick makes a similar epigrammatic point elsewhere in the collection: 'Night makes no difference 'twixt the Priest and Clark; / Jone as my Lady is as good in the dark'; ibid., p. 329.

index of strictly variegated hierarchy) are counterpoised to those legitimate heterosexual ones which monarchy would either sublimate or conceal.

A similar note is sounded by an earlier anonymous royalist ballad which mused 'from the Rout who can expect / Ought but confusion, / Since Unity with good Monarchy / Begin and end in one?'[36] It renders the political uncertainty of the civil war as a cacophony of dissonant voices which become most alarming in a discussion about the best principles for stable government:

> Then let's have King Charles sayes George,
> Nay we'll have his Son, sayes, Hugh;
> Nay, then let's have none, sayes jabbering Jone,
> Nay, wee'l all be Kings sayes Prue.[37]

It is women's voices that jar in this debate. As men reveal their adherence to monarchy in measured terms, declarations of egalitarian principles are made to sound as ridiculous as 'jabbering' in the mouths of lower-class women, most particularly 'Jone' whose disturbing presence is emphasized through the single use of the alliterative adjective.[38] The sexism and classism lurking behind the name surely, therefore, inform the reason why the Committee for the Advancement of Money chose to doubt Alkin's claim that she had effected her 'discoveries'. However it is important to remember that it was the Committee and their male contemporaries who first bestowed the alias in this instance. The issue of re-naming becomes even more interesting once we discover the nature of Alkin's 'discoveries'. Elizabeth Alkin was a spy, and was involved in providing intelligence, the lifeblood of both state security and the newsbooks of the period.

Her involvement in the discovery of George Mynne again earned her two pounds in September 1647 when the Order Book for the Committee for the Advancement of Money records '40s to be paid to Joan —, she pretending to have made a discovery of Mynne's delinquency'.[39] What was earlier rather vaguely termed the 'discovery of Geo Mynne's wyre', now re-termed his 'delinquency', was a crucial piece of parliamentary intelligence. Mynne, a prominent iron master

---

[36] *Rump: Or an Exact Collection of the Choycest Poems and Songs Relating to the Late Times* (London, 1662), p. 293.

[37] Ibid., p. 292.

[38] That Joans were low-born was axiomatic in the early modern period. J. B. Williams glosses the name as being 'given to any ill mannered or ill kept rustic woman, or scullery maid, who had to do dirty work', *History*, p. 131. A notable exception is the fabled female 'Pope Joan' of the ninth century, famed not only for her supposed licentiousness, but also for her untrustworthy words and capacity to prevaricate and deceive. See C. A. Patrides, *Premises and Motifs in Renaissance Thought and Literature* (Princeton, 1982), pp. 152–81; Sarah Lawson, 'From Latin Pun to English Puzzle: An Elizabethan Translation Problem', *The Sixteenth Century Journal* 9 (1978), p. 27.

[39] SP 19/5/284.

of Surrey, was engaged in supplying the king with the raw materials for warfare; he supplied royalist forces with four hundred tonnes of iron and the start of the war, and had iron and wire secreted in various parts of the country amounting to some £40,000.[40] What is as significant as the meagre sum Alkin was paid for her work in March 1647 (some spies are known to have been paid up to £200 a month for their intelligence, whereas Alkin's immediate superior, Gualter Frost, earned a more modest £400 per year) is the fact that in a profession that was so reliant on singly sourced auricular and written testimony, her word should still remain 'pretended' or untrustworthy.[41] Indeed, there is a sense that through the conference of her denigratory alias, the very authorities who were paying her for the veracity of her intelligence were simultaneously denying its validity, equating it with the mere gossip of a very different kind of hired help. This complex attempt to deny Alkin any agency whilst using her as an agent exemplifies the precarious position of a woman venturing forth into the early modern public sphere. This position is crystallized in her name itself; the epithet bespeaks the patriarchal dilemma whereby Alkin can only ever be located on the cusp between private and public, in the strangest of contact zones between kitchen and parliament.

The name of 'Joan' placed another woman in precisely such a zone. Elizabeth Cromwell, wife of the Lord Protector, was vilified throughout the 1650s and 1660s by both republicans and royalists for the way in which she was perceived to have usurped the authority of her social and sexual betters (see figure 7). In fact, as Katharine Gillespie has argued, she came to represent a 'compelling icon for the Protectorate itself as tenuous middle way'.[42] As the Protectorate strove to define itself between the competing claims and loyalties of monarchy and radical republicanism, the wife of the nation's leader was figured as presiding over a 'paradoxical kitchen court' in the satirical cheap print of the period. Appropriately enough, this 'oxymoronic plebeian queen' was given a series of peculiar names.[43] John Tatham in his Restoration play *The Rump* has Cromwell herself recall these as 'Old Joan, Old Bess, Old Bedlam, Old Witch, Old Hagg, the Commonwealths Night Mare'.[44] The most popular by far, however, was Protectorate or 'Protectress Joan'. Another writer outlines the reasons for the durability of this sobriquet in *The Court and Kitchin of Elizabeth, Commonly Called Joan Cromwell*, published some

---

[40]   G. E. Manwaring, 'Parliament Joan', p. 302.

[41]   It was Sir Edward Nicholas, the royal Secretary of State, who was paid this astonishing sum for his work. See, Alan Marshall, *Intelligence and Espionage in the Reign of Charles II, 1660–1685* (Cambridge, 1994), pp. 1–19; the figure for Frost's 1653 salary is from D. L. Hobman, *Cromwell's Master Spy: A Study of John Thurloe* (London, 1961), p. 23.

[42]   See Katharine Gillespie, 'Elizabeth Cromwell's Kitchen Court: Republicanism and the Consort', *Genders* 33 (2001), <http://www.genders.org/g33/g33_gillespie.html>.

[43]   Ibid., section 5.

[44]   John Tatham, *The Rump* (London, 1660), p. 21; cited in Gillespie, 'Elizabeth Cromwell's Kitchen Court', section 4.

half a dozen years after the Lord Protector's death. In this recipe book cum anti-Cromwellian invective, readers are given detailed instructions on how to make such delicacies as 'white Quince cakes', 'a rare Dutch pudding', or 'a Turkish dish of meat' at the same time as they are taught to savour the wholesome flavour of monarchs instead of the unpalatable harshness of illegitimate tyrants.[45] In this imaginative attempt to cultivate Restoration taste, the boundless plenitude of the king's table is contrasted with Cromwell's penchant for abstinence which, he suggests, can be traced back to:

> The sordid frugality and thrifty baseness of his wife, Elizabeth Bowcher [sic], Daughter of Sir James Bowcher, commonly called Protectress Joan and vulgarly known of latter years by no other Christian name, even in the great Heighth of her Husbands power, and that chiefly out of Derision and contemptuous indignation that such a person durst presume to take upon her self such a Soveraign Estate, when she was an hundred times fitter for a Barn than a Palace.[46]

Whereas Elizabeth Cromwell was given 'that Sarcastic ... nickname' by her husband's politico-religious opponents, Elizabeth Alkin was described thus by her own employers.[47] Her negotiation of the restrictions such a label placed upon her – restrictions intensified by the fact that her position, as far as the authorities were concerned, must remain unacknowledged – is instructive. In the early to mid 1640s her husband was discovered as belonging to a parliamentarian spy network; when he was caught by royalist forces at Oxford he was duly hanged.[48] Alkin chooses to mobilize his legitimate image with the Cromwellian authorities in order to gain financial recompense, and thereby official recognition, for her more problematic sorties into the public sphere. The following petition is particularly revealing:

> To the right Honourable Committee for Compositions sitting at Goldsmiths Hall
> The humble petition of Elizabeth Alkin Widdowe,
> Sheweth,

> That for her many faythfull and hazardous services she hath done for the Parliament they were favourably pleased to recommend her to the Comittee of Examinations, that she might have a Sequestered house of one Stephen Fosett that was in actuall Warr against the Parliament and Chirurgeon to Sir Arthur Ashton, whoe most cruelly caused her husband to bee hanged in Oxford for doeing service for the State, in which house she yet remaynes.

---

[45] *The Court and Kitchin of Elizabeth, Commonly Called Joan Cromwell* (London, 1664), pp. 47, 71, 131.
[46] Ibid., sig. B3r.
[47] Ibid., sig. B3v.
[48] SP 19/98/80; SP 23/62/228; SP 23/62/232; *The Kingdomes Faithfull and Impartiall Scout* 19, 1–8 June 1649, p. 2014; *A Perfect Diurnall of Some Passages in Parliament* 310, 2–9 July 1649, p. 2635.

Figure 7: *The Court and Kitchin of Elizabeth, Commonly Called Joan Cromwell* **(1664), title page**

As the daughter of Sir James Bourchier, Elizabeth Cromwell was of nobler birth than Alkin. She became a low-born 'Joan', or domestic servant, because her gender rendered her alleged interference in matters of state trangressive. The inscription reads: 'From feigned glory and Vsurped Throne / And all the Greatnesse to me falsly shown / And from the Arts of Government set free / See how Protectress and Drudge agree'.

But for it is that the said Fossett by some meanes haveing compounded her doth now goe about to imprison your poore petitioner and to that purpose hath entred actions against her and endeavours nothing lesse than to ruyne her and her many Fatherless Children.

Her humble suite unto this honourable Committee is that you will take her into consideration who hath neither spared estate nor paines to doe the State service, as is evidently knowne to the Members of both houses of Parliament and to Order that she may continue still in the said house without any molestation.

And she shall pray &c. [49]

Alkin's husband appears as the guiding spirit of this petition; he, or at least the remembrance of his loyal activities, initiates all the action and proceedings. Thus Alkin offers herself as the loyal member of the commonwealth, which in gender terms means playing the part of the dutiful wife and mournful 'Widdowe'; she is a 'poore petitioner' beset not only by the vengeful royalist Fossett but by 'many Fatherless Children'. Patriarchally speaking, she registers herself as the comforting, conformable presence of the fecund woman who desires only to remain in a domestic realm 'without molestation'. Yet such ostensibly quietistic purpose is undercut by the very public form of the manuscript petition itself, and furthermore by the fact that whilst eschewing publicity she is actually offering more intelligence to the authorities by revealing the continued presence of yet another disaffected royalist in the commonwealth. That Fossett was called in 'to answer' on the day the petition was read is testament to Alkin's skill as a petitioner.[50] Whether or not she retained the house is unclear, but by October that year the Committee had granted Alkin a further fifty pounds and 'a fit house to dwell in'.[51]

Wherever she was living, it is clear that Alkin did not opt for a widow's retirement indoors, and in fact over the next two years continued to remember that she had 'lost her husbands life in the service of the Parliament' in public petitions, and thereby succeeded in gaining more payments, improved accommodation (eventually at Whitehall itself), and protection from counter-petitioners.[52] All of this time she was still providing intelligence to the state. The significantly underacknowledged high point of her involvement came in 1653. On 22 November the brother of the Portuguese ambassador, Don Pantaleon de Sá, and some Portuguese and Maltese friends, were engaged in a fierce dispute at the New Exchange with a group of Londoners.[53] A fight ensued in which men from either

---

[49]   SP 23/62/228.
[50]   Ibid. The order is scrawled in a different hand at the bottom of the manuscript of the petition
[51]   SP 23/62/233.
[52]   SP 25/87/61; SP 25/63/16; SP 23/62/235; SP 23/62/232; SP 23/8/151; SP 25/65/238.
[53]   There are a number of narratives of the incident at the Exchange. Official versions can be found in: *Calendar of State Papers Domestic Series 1653–1654*, pp. 360, 427; *CSPD*

side were injured. On the following evening, the Portuguese returned to the Exchange and yet more violence erupted. On this occasion, a passerby, one Mr Greneway, was caught up in the disturbance and was fatally shot. Sá was eventually apprehended and incarcerated in Newgate by July the following year; after an attempted escape, he was moved to the Tower to be eventually tried and executed. The incident was sensational, prompting an intense legal wrangle involving Lord Chief Justice Rolle himself, about whether it was possible for the family of a foreign diplomat to be tried by English law, and if so, whether it was to be before a jury. It also prompted a welter of pamphlet and newsbook literature. In the second week of December both Pantaleon de Sá himself and the sister of the murdered Greneway published pamphlets which condemned the other party's actions and exonerated their own.[54] Similarly, from the last weeks of November to the first week of December, the newsbooks picked up on the incident for a variety of nationalistic ends. The most detailed of these was published in the *Severall Proceedings of State Affairs* which claimed that Sá and his compatriots returned to the Exchange to wage a well-planned, lavishly resourced guerrilla war which would bring about the wholesale slaughter of English subjects:

> They had ... two or three coaches that brought ammunition for them in which were hand-Granadoes, and bottles, and some little barrels of power, and bullets and other necessaries ... They had also some boats ready to attend them at the water side ... Thus they came with a resolution to fall upon every English Gentleman they should find in or about the Exchange ... they intended to kill every body they met with, that stood before them.[55]

Sá refuted these claims in his own published account of the incident, but some newsbooks even went so far as to stress that the situation had strained diplomatic relations between England and Portugal to such a pitch that an alliance with the Spanish was imminent.[56] Amid the welter of competing narratives the truth of the matter became elusive and it was difficult for the authorities to decide upon appropriate action. Although none of the newsbooks mention her presence on the Exchange, Elizabeth Alkin played an integral role in that decision since it was solely because of her advice, intelligence and 'Information ... concerning the murder committed by the Portugalls upon the Exchange' that the Council of State

---

1654, pp. 151, 156, 169, 214; *Calendar of State Papers Venetian Series 1653–1654*, pp. 153, 162, 166, 180, 236–8.

[54] Don Pantaleon de Sá, *A Narration of the Late Accident in the New Exchange*, (London, 1653); Frances Clarke, *A Brief Reply to the Narration of Don Pantaleon Sá* (London, 1653).

[55] *Severall Proceedings of State Affairs* 217, 17 Nov.– 4 Nov. 1653, p. 3436.

[56] For newsbook accounts of the incident see *The Moderate Publisher* 6, 19 Nov.–2 Dec. 1653, p. 49; *Severall Proceedings of State Affairs* 218, 24 Nov.–1 Dec. 1653, p. 3443; *The Perfect Diurnall* 207, 21–28 Nov. 1653, sig. 9Z3r–9Z3v; *The Faithful Scout* 139, 18–25 Nov. 1653, pp. 1096–7, 1200.

set up a committee to consider the nature of the facts.[57] The relevant entry in the Council's order book shows that on this occasion (in marked contrast to the Mynne case) her word went undoubted. This time, as she delivered her intelligence, the Whitehall-based Alkin was transfigured from a 'Joan' to the infinitely more respectable, economically independent 'Eliz: Alkin Widdow'.[58]

'Good Service': Women and Intelligence Networks

In the climactic year of 1649, at about the same time as Elizabeth Poole was making her appearances before the General Council of the Army, Alkin consolidated her relationship with intelligence. She became a book trade informant, searching out unlicensed or seditious presses for the authorities.[59] In July of that year, *A Perfect Diurnall* makes reference to 'one Jone (a clamerous woman) whose husband was hang'd at Oxford for a spie, & she sometimes imployed in finding out the presses of scandalous pamphlets'.[60] A year later, John Crouch was complaining of the intrusive activities of parliamentarian press informants and singled two out for particular attention:

> Gentlemen pray have care of a fat woman, aged about fifty, her name I know not, she is called by many Parliament Jone, and one Smith, Printer, a tall thin chapt Knave, if any such persons come pretending to search, looke to yourselves and money, and say Towzer gave you warning.[61]

Whether Crouch knew Alkin's name or not, he was eager to assist in both the circulation of her denigratory alias and in the allegation that her activities were nothing more than a kind of legitimized robbery.[62] About a year earlier, another royalist news writer, Samuel Sheppard, had bewailed the fact that he had been 'Routed out of my lodgings and acquaintance by *Parliament Beagles* and whole

---

[57] SP 25/72/174.

[58] Ibid.

[59] J. B. Williams claims that Alkin was involved in the capture and committal of Thomas Budd, editor of *Mercurius Catholicus*, in 1648; *History*, p.152. For a discussion of the role of 'female trade informants' after the Restoration, see Paula McDowell, *The Women of Grub Street*, pp. 90–118.

[60] *A Perfect Diurnall* 310, 2–9 July 1649, p. 2623.

[61] *The Man in the Moon* 43, 13–20 Feb. 1650, p. 342.

[62] Alkin is easily recognizable from Crouch's comments, however the identity of the 'Smith' he refers to is far from certain. Henry Plomer has demonstrated that there were at least eight different Smiths registered as printers and booksellers in London in the 1640s and 1650s, however, there are no extant records which prove that any of them were employed as press informants. H. R. Plomer, *A Dictionary of the Booksellers and Printers Who Were at Work in England, Scotland and Ireland from 1641–1667* (London, 1907), pp. 166–8.

squadrons of *rebellious Mermidions* & forc't to build my nest in another angle where now I am, and (God willing) doe intend to satisfie the Kingdome weekly of the wicked *Consultations* of Parliament'.[63] Whilst news trade informants were undoubtedly viewed with disdain, a less sensationalized view of their day-to-day operations comes from the pen of Alkin herself. Ever the skilled petitioner, she appeals to Parliament to recoup some of the money she has spent in their 'service':

To the Right Honourable the Comittee of Haberdashers Hall for Advance of Money

The Humble Petition of Elizabeth Alkin, a poore distressed widdow.

Sheweth,

That your petitioner at the beginning of the warre, and for divers yeares since was imployed as a spye by the Earle of Essex, Sr Wm Waller, and the now Lord Generall Fairfax, hath performed much service for the State in that kind, to the hazard of her life, had her husband hanged at Oxford by the late Kings party.

That your petitioner hath of late done good service for the State by discovery of printing and publishing of Scandalous books, and but the last weeke your petitioner discovered fouwre presses in one Dugards Custody, in Mearchant Taylor School, weare all seized upon, and the said Dugard committed to Newgate, for which, nor any other service of the like nature, your petitioner never receaved any recompense, Albeit shee hath expended all that ever shee was worthe in the world, in the pursuance of your service.

That more particularly your petitioner did discover the delinquency of Mr Minnes and divers others, to one William Mills late a collector at Cambden House, the whole benefit of which discovery the said Mills received to his owne use, to the value of 2 or 300 *l*, and never allowed your petitioner one penny for the same. That now your petitioner understanding yet there is about 40 *l* belonging to the said Mills, in the hands of the Treasurer belonging to this honourable Comittee.

Your petitioner most humbly prays that this Honourable Comittee wilbee pleased (in consideration of her former good services, your petitioner being ready to bee cast into prison for debt, to the utter ruine of her 3 children) to order her the said 40*l* remayning in the said Treasurers hands, for the releife of her.[64]

---

[63] *Mercurius Pragmaticus* 43 [sic], 20–27 Feb. 1649, sig. Gggr.

[64] SP 19/98/80. There is a problem with the dating of this manuscript petition. It is currently dated at September 1647 and is archived with a number of other manuscripts from that period. However the specific historical details of the petition suggest a later date of early February 1650. Specifically, the petition refers to 'last weeke your petitioner discovered fouwre presses in one Dugards Custody, in Mearchant Taylor School' and that 'the said Dugard [was] committed too Newgate'. This is the same William Dugard who began editing and printing the French newsbook *Nouvelles Ordinaires de Londres* in July 1650, and to many students of early modern culture he is remembered as the first printer of Milton's *Eikonoklastes*. Less well known is the fact that in January 1649 he also published Salmasius's *Defensio Regia*, the French scholar's famous attack on the regicides, and in March of that year also published an expanded edition of *Eikon Basilike*. These offences had

The importance of this manuscript petition for any reassessment of the role of women in the seventeenth-century news trade, indeed for early modern women's agency more generally, ought not to be underestimated. To find a woman publicly declaring that she was 'for divers yeares since employed as a spye' and then going on to detail the names of her employers, activities and requested rates of pay is unprecedented. Close attention to the rhetorical structures of the petition also reveals that Alkin is exploring the limits of the concept of 'good service', subtly counterbalancing the image of the 'poore distressed widdow' fending off jail and the 'utter ruine of her three children' (that is, according to the terms of patriarchy, the comforting image of the caring, vigilant mother) with that of the 'spye' 'hazard[ing]...her life' for the benefit of the commonwealth. Motherhood and espionage are thereby accorded a certain equivalence, so that as the boundaries between public and private are breached, spying is presented, not as alien, exclusively masculine terrain, but as an activity that is particularly suited to the feminine.[65]

This is clearly at odds with both modern and early modern views of the world of espionage. Historians have long been sensitive to the ways in which both sides in the civil war sought to make symbolic capital out of the bodies of male spies captured during the conflict.[66] Richard Symonds recalled an occasion when the royalist army was deliberately marched under a gallows so that they could see the body of a parliamentarian spy above. Similarly, one David Kniverton, a royalist spy, was publicly hanged outside the Royal Exchange, and copies of parliamentary ordinances forbidding unlicensed travel were stuck to various parts of his body.[67] However, women's involvement in civil war intelligence networks has been largely overlooked by modern commentators. This is in marked contrast to parliamentarian newsbook writers who seized upon the rumoured activities of royalist women spies as a potent symbol of the unstrustworthiness of the king and

---

him committed to Newgate on 20 February 1650. As this was Dugard's only period of incarceration whilst he was headmaster of the Merchant Taylor's School, and Alkin was handsomely rewarded in March of that year with Whitehall lodgings, it seems most likely that Alkin's petition actually dates from the third week of February 1650, the same week in which Crouch was vilifying her in *The Man in the Moon*. On Dugard, see *Dictionary of National Biography* XV, pp. 133–4; W. R. Parker, *Milton: A Biography* (Oxford, 1996), pp. 263–4; Leona Rostenberg, *Literary, Scientific, Religious and Legal Publishing, Printing and Bookselling in England, 1551–1700: Twelve Studies* (New York, 1965), pp. 130–160.

[65] Alkin's activities as a trade informant continued until November 1651, when she was paid £13 8*s* by the Council of State 'in consideration of the good service done by her in the discoverie of the booke *manus testium, lingua testium*'. This was Edward Hall's pro-royalist *Manus Testium Movens* which appeared in July of that year. See SP 25/24/68; SP 25/24/71.

[66] See C. Carlton, *Going to the Wars: The Experiences of the British Civil Wars 1638–1651* (London and New York, 1992) pp. 263–4; Alan Marshall, *Intelligence and Espionage*, p. 1–18.

[67] Carlton, *Going to the Wars*, p. 264.

his cause. One such serial was exultant when a 'Mrs Leveston ... said to be a constant conveyer of dangerous Intelligence betwixt Oxford and London' was caught with 'many papers and letters of consequence'.[68] The London-based *Mercurius Civicus* was particularly keen on such stories and ran an exposé of the 'wife of one Penyall' who:

> give[s] information to the Lords at Oxford, she carries letters constantly of information of all the businesses of London, and againe brings Letters from Oxford hither, and to some other parts ... Also Mistris Guy, a Proctors wife, now at Oxford, is another great Informer of news from London. This Mistris Guy and Penyals wife be chiefe confederates.[69]

In a later issue, *Civicus* began speculating as to the full extent of female involvement in the royalist intelligence trade, and toyed with the terrifying possibility of a nationwide alliance of such 'confederates':

> There was this week apprehended in London, a woman who is suspected to be a spie or she-Intelligencer for Oxford and other the enemies quarters, shee is wife to an Episcopall man of no small note in Ireland, and lay at the Swan in Houndsditch ... If strict enquiry were made I doubt not *but there might be many of these Female-Intelligencers found about London*, and in the Lines of Communication, who are capable as doing as much mischief in that kind as any man whatsoever.[70]

Civicus was originally set up to refute Oxford's *Mercurius Aulicus*, and it used its penchant for stories about women spies in an attempt to tarnish the *Aulicus*'s reputation for professionalism and accuracy by associating its reportage with the words of female intelligence agents. In one issue it alleged that its editor, Sir John Berkenhead, relied on the words of bands of 'shee-informers' for the vast majority of his stories.[71] Whether or not this was the case, the link between spies and newsbooks, between very different uses of intelligence, was not a particularly difficult one to make. Those 'Lines of Communication' that *Civicus* so exercised itself about need not, of course, merely hint at a system of strategic spy networks or secretive espionage communities but could also extend along the more public routes and cheaply printed pages of the mid-seventeenth-century news trade. Serials such as *The Moderate Intelligencer*, *The Compleate Intelligencer*, *The Armies Intelligencer*, *The Impartial Intelligencer*, *The Daily Intelligencer*, *The Scotch Intelligencer*, *The Colchester Spie*, *The Dutch Spy* and *The Spie Communicating Intelligence from Oxford* advertised this very point on their title pages. Intelligencers were thus pamphlets as well as people, intelligence the stuff

---

[68] *A Diary or Exact Journal* 20, 19–26 Sept. 1644, p. 139.
[69] *Mercurius Civicus* 79, 21–8 Nov. 1644, p. 729.
[70] Ibid., 26, 26 June–3 July 1645, p. 980; emphasis added.
[71] Ibid., 4, 25 May–1 June 1643, p. 32.

of both the newshound and the spy. As we have seen that intelligence sustained Alkin and her children throughout the economically depressed 1640s and 1650s, it need be no surprise, therefore, to find her eventually turning to the publication of newsbooks herself. It is to an analysis of these texts, and in particular Alkin's eschewal of individualistic modes of agency, that this chapter now turns.

From Spy to *Scout*

Between 21 June 1650 and 30 September 1651 Alkin involved herself in the publication of ten issues of different newsbooks.[72] The first occasion she puts her name to a newsbook is in 1650 with *The Impartial Scout*, a title which once again fuses the worlds of espionage and reportage, and which was primarily concerned with supplying naval and military news. Hitherto it had been associated almost exclusively with Daniel Border and his printer Robert Wood.[73] Border was one of the more resilient and prolific journalists of the Commonwealth and Protectorate, having some 14 different serials to his name. Whilst he was certainly no Marchamont Nedham and will never be remembered for any pioneering work at journalistic frontiers, he was a competent newsman perhaps best remembered for his polemical skirmishes with Henry Walker.[74] These began in March 1649 and tended to focus upon Walker's disdain for Border's unimaginative journalistic style, his replication both of the former's extravagant use of Hebrew and his habit of printing the London bills of mortality.[75] Border responded with a vitriolic personal attack ridiculing Walker's ginger hair, calling him 'the Judas bearded iron monger', at the same time as he criticized his news writing as 'pernicious and destructive'.[76] Walker's counter is especially interesting; it includes an attack by the deputy censor Theodore Jennings:

> I desire all people to take notice that I denie to give any authority to a pamphlet called *The Kingdomes Scout*, because the Commonwealth hath been so abused by it, by Robert Wood of Grub Street who contrives false invectives at an Alehouse to add to it what he fancies as news after M.Border the author hath write it [sic], ... and the author doth now disclaim it refusing any more to write it for him; if he be so

---

[72] Carolyn Nelson and Matthew Seccombe, *British Newspapers and Periodicals, 1641–1700: A Short Title Catalogue of Serials Printed in England, Scotland, Ireland, and British America* (New York, 1987), p. 705.

[73] For Border see Frank, *Beginnings*, pp. 211–28.

[74] Ibid., pp. 176–8.

[75] The arguments continued until around the end of the year; ibid., p. 178.

[76] *The Kingdomes Faithfull and Impartiall Scout* 20, 8–15 June 1649, pp. 154, 160.

impudent still to publish it, I desire all those whom it concerns to suppress it that the people may not be cheated by it.[77]

Border is berated for his inability to subscribe to individualistic models of authorship; for allowing the text to slip from his exclusive, privileged grasp to be pawed, sullied and altered by others in 'an Alehouse'. The terms of Walker's and Jennings's critique are fascinating for a number of reasons. Firstly, they provide an interesting nuance to Steve Pincus's study of the emergence of the public sphere in the later seventeenth century with the discussion and circulation of news in English coffeehouses.[78] Secondly, they show the difficulties and limitations of effective censorship and licensing at a time when both practices were rather haphazard or careless.[79] Thirdly, and more importantly for the consideration of women's involvement in the civil war news trade, the newsbook features as a collective enterprise: one in which a text can be politicized and re-authored in a variety of different, and frequently contradictory, ways, by a number of different, and frequently untraceable, authors. In the face of such a melee of intentions and narratives, the strategy of the deputy licenser was to attempt to define the roles within the newsbook more clearly, and in the process promote a divisive acrimony amongst the team that produced the *Scout*. Jennings's tactic was unsuccessful as the newsbook continued to be approved, and Border and Wood worked together until the mid-1650s.

It is difficult to ascertain whether Border's and Wood's working relationship is representative, but the fact that they produced runs of seven different titles between them suggests that, Jennings's criticism notwithstanding, it was an effective one. For four weeks in June and July of 1650 their relationship was altered by the presence of Elizabeth Alkin on the team of *The Impartial Scout*. There is little concrete evidence of the reasons for Alkin's joining the *Scout*; the serial represented a new journalistic enterprise for both Border and Wood following the closure of their *The Faithful and Impartial Scout* in the preceding autumn and Alkin replaced the printer/publisher George Horton who had been involved with the *Scout* since its fifth issue.[80] The two men had certainly known of her for over a year, since in the first week of June 1649 they reprinted the following 'Order' from the Council of State:

---

[77] *Perfect Occurences of Every Daies iournall in Parliament* 129, 15–22 June 1649, pp. 1128.

[78] Pincus, '"Coffee Politicians Does Create"', p. 811.

[79] Frank, *Beginnings*, p. 178.

[80] Border had also been involved in the publication of a second weekly serial at this time, producing *The Perfect Weekly Account* every Wednesday with the highly skilled printer Bernard Alsop.

Saturday June 2. Ordered that it be referred to the Councel of State to bestow a house upon Mrs Alkeen (a Widdow) whose Husband dyed in the Parliament's service, and consider of some competent maintenance for her and her children, which is ... needful, for they are in a very low condition until relieved.[81]

What is striking about this item is that it is perhaps the first non-derogatory reference to 'Mrs Alkeen' (not 'Parliament Joan') in a newsbook. That its obvious un-newsworthiness had become newsworthy attests to one of two things: either Alkin had achieved such celebrity status by mid-1649 that details of her life were deemed significant, or the item became news because Alkin was the personal acquaintance of one or both of the parties involved in the *Scout*. All information points to the latter suggestion since no other newsbook that week reprints the order, an odd fact if Alkin's name had indeed accrued an immense cultural capital, and even odder once we remember that neither Border nor Wood were the sharpest news-hounds.[82]

Whatever her relationship with the two men, it seems unlikely that she was brought in to give the venture financial backing since just three days before the appearance of the first issue of *The Impartial Scout* Alkin was once again petitioning parliament for money and accommodation. She protested, as 'an aged woman ... having three children to maintain' that she had 'no meanes of subsistence but what she is faine to take great paines for'.[83] We should perhaps treat these claims to impoverishment with some circumspection since, as we have already seen, Alkin was the consummate parliamentary petitioner and was adept at deploying poverty and weakness topoi in a variety of ways. Nonetheless, when the first issue of the *Scout* appeared, it was printed 'for' her 'by Robert Wood'. This indicates that Alkin was the newsbook's publisher, an important entrepreneurial role which meant that she had significant input into the *Scout*'s journalistic policy and that she had financed, or at least part-financed, the new venture.[84] Even if her petition is taken at face value and Alkin was indeed indigent at this time, the costs involved in the publication of a newsbook were not necessarily prohibitive. In 1642, the printer Robert White charged Francis Coles and Thomas Bates 18*s* for printing 1,500 sheets of Roger Pike's *A True Relation of the Proceedings of the Scots and English Forces in the North of Ireland*. Joad Raymond has adapted this 'improbably low' figure to demonstrate that if a newsbook print run was the

---

[81] *The Kingdomes Faithfull and Impartiall Scout* 19, 1–8 June 1649, p. 147.

[82] Border's promise in the first issue of *The Kingdomes Weekly Post* that it would print news that the other newsbooks missed was, like the majority of his predictions, unfulfilled.

[83] SP 23/62/232/.

[84] *The Impartial Scout* 53, 21–8 June 1650, p. 217. Frank describes the role of the newsbook publisher thus: 'since 1642 the publisher had been responsible for hiring the editor and establishing a paper's policy, and he [sic] would have been the one to bear the losses and reap the profits', *Beginnings*, p. 234. For a view that intimates at a more creative involvement, see Paula McDowell, *The Women of Grub Street*, pp. 30–45, 60–71.

'plausible minimum' of 250 copies, the print cost would probably be no more than 9*s* which, if the newsbook were sold for a penny, would provide a profit of 11*s* 10*d* to be divided amongst the publisher, the editor and the distributing hawker or mercury woman.[85] It seems likely therefore that for a penurious Alkin, all too aware of the erratic nature of state payment to petitioners, the publication of a newsbook represented a way in which she could make a small but immediately realizable profit in an industry of which, as we have seen, she had considerable knowledge.[86] That there is no record of Alkin petitioning for relief when she was involved in the publication of her newsbooks serves to reaffirm this.

Irrespective of costs, it is probable that Alkin's reputation as an 'Intelligencer' preceded her and that she joined with Border and Wood in order to inject some much-needed life and information into a rather unspectacular publication.[87] At another level Alkin's incorporation represents a broad political, as well as editorial, alliance. All three were anti-royalist, although the mild opposition to monarchy expressed in Border's and Wood's earlier publications looks much less perilous than Alkin's long involvement in the exposure of dissident royalists.[88] Despite these broad political sympathies, Alkin's arrival also heralded a change in the news writing of the *Scout* enterprise. The earlier *Faithful and Impartial Scout* had been peppered with platitudinous editorial comments and asides which served to provide the reader with a lens through which to view the events of the week. The following is representative:

> Necessity is not ruled by Law, the force is so great; through many dangers she finds out the way, but it sufficeth not to the strength of armes, to have flesh, blood, and bones, unless they have also sinews to stretch out, or pull in for defence of the body: so an Army consisting of many men, and furnished with war-like habilements is but lame and unserviceable if God give not a blessing of their undertakings.[89]

---

[85] In his *Glossographia* (1656), Thomas Blount clarifies the distinction between hawkers and mercury women: 'Those people which go up and down the streets crying News-books, and selling them by retail, are also called Hawkers and those Women that sell them wholesale from the Press, are called Mercury Women', cited in D. F. McKenzie, 'The London Book Trade in the Later Seventeenth Century' (Unpublished Sandars Lectures, 1976), p. 25.

[86] See Cotton, 'London Newsbooks in the Civil War', p. 8; Raymond, *Invention*, pp. 233–4. Although Raymond's figures are for the early 1640s, the fact that *The Impartial Scout* did not procure any advertising revenues during Alkin's involvement makes his calculations applicable.

[87] On the unoriginal, 'facile', and 'noncommittal' nature of the Border/Wood newsbook see Frank, *Beginnings*, p. 128.

[88] Frank offers the most interesting discussion of Border and Wood's anti-royalism; ibid., pp. 91–2.

[89] *The Kingdomes Faithful and Impartial Scout* 36, 28 Sept.–5 Oct. 1649, p. 257.

However, once Alkin becomes involved in the enterprise, passages of such florid prose all but disappear. Instead of an editorial comment, the first words of the newsbook Alkin is involved with are the rhetorical commonplace of 'This day we received Intelligence'.[90] The contrast with what Border and Wood had produced earlier is stark. Instead of being forced to read the news from a particular interpretive perspective (which may or may not co-extend with an editorial position), the reader's attention is immediately drawn to the fact that this text is a collative and collective speech act.[91] Indeed, there is a sense in which the distinction between author and reader is reconfigured so that instead of any privileged, self-reflexive acts of authority or authorship, what we are faced with is the realization that the writing, reading and discussion of newsbooks are, in fact, part of the same process; all are equally vital moments in the circulation and renewal of intelligence. This is entirely concordant with, and received its most dangerous expression in, Alkin's activities as a trade informant. Intelligence gathering demanded exemplary acts of reading which prompted the discussion and discovery of seditious literature and presses; these acts in turn became the material of future newsbooks. Throughout her career, therefore, Alkin can be seen impressing the pre-eminence of intelligence above 'information'. George Smith, the editor of *The Scottish Dove*, was just one newsman who reflected upon the importance of this relationship. Responding to criticism of his flamboyant editorial style he contends:

> It may be some will tell me ... that I digress from the way of intelligence ... to them I answer; That I digress not from the way of information, which I have ever propounded to my selfe to mix with my intelligence; information to cleare the judgement, is better then intelligence to please the fancie; and by such information the evil causes may be removed, from whence flow evill effects and sad intelligences.[92]

It was the 'mix' of a newsbook's intelligence and its apparently digressive yet pleasing informational qualities which gave each seventeenth-century serial its particular style and appeal. As Raymond has pointed out, if 'information referred to editorial matter informing the judgement of the readers', then intelligence stressed a much more collective approach to news writing. Intelligence was the gathered raw material of the newsbook, and was 'a relationship, a footing of intercourse', which implicated all in the communicative circuit; everyone from

---

[90] *The Impartial Scout* 53, 21–8 June 1650, p. 217.
[91] Border had also regularly dropped editorial comments and asides from his collaboration with Bernard Alsop. See Freist, *Governed by Opinion*, pp. 104–7.
[92] *The Scottish Dove* 92, 25 July 1645, p. 723, cited in Raymond, *Invention*, pp. 162–3. Joseph Frank refers to Smith's editorials as 'tangles of purple prose'; *Beginnings*, p. 55.

[217] P.P. London.   Numb. 53. 16

The Impartial

SCOUT:

FAITHFULLY

Communicating the moſt remarkable Paſſages of
the Armies, in England, Scotland, and Ireland ; With
the Proceedings of the ſeveral Navies at Sea, and other
choiſe Intelligence from Forreign-parts, both Civil
and Military.

From Friday the 21 of June, to Friday the 28 of June,
1 6 5 0.

LONDON, Printed by *Robert Wood*, for *E. Alkin*, and are to
be ſold in *Corn-hil*, near the *Royal Exchange.*

Beginning, *FRIDAY June* 21.

His day we received Intelligence from the Weſt
of *England*, that *James* (ſecond ſon to the late
King of *England*) is preparing for a Voyage
from the Iſle of *Scilly*, to the City of *Paris* in
France, being invited thither by the Queen his
Mother, who hath prevailed with the *French*
King, both for employments and accommo-
dations for him; who hath made choiſe of him
to be Colonel of his Life-guard of *Scots :* he is
daily expected there, but is not haſty to put
forth to ſea, leſt he ſhould be met withall by
ſome of the Parliaments ſhips, who are coaſt-
ing hereabouts, to ſuppreſs the inſolencies of
Sir *Richard Greenvile* ; who is providing (as
our laſt Letters make mention) ſeveral ſmall Scuits or Veſſels, that will
hold about 50 men apiece, beſides Rowers, intending if any Fiſherboats, or
other ſmall ſhips paſſe near that Iſland, to ſeize upon them.

Ggg   By

Figure 8: *The Impartial Scout* 53, 21–28 June 1650, title page
The first issue, 'printed for E. Alkin', eschewed editorial flamboyance.

editor to reader, printer and publisher.[93]

The material of *The Impartial Scout* itself reaffirms this notion of the circular and collative nature of news. Through the almost total absence of any ostensible 'authorial comment', the newsbook itself privileges the act of collation by reprinting its sources wholesale. This strategy is perhaps a later manifestation of John Dillingham's first professed editorial commitment to 'represent an exact weekly of such things as come to knowledge, and are fit for publike view ... which shall ever be according to intelligence, and without invectives.'[94] Thus the first three issues Alkin worked on were replete with 'official' parliamentary news, Acts and innumerable newsletters from around the country, continuing to reprint the London bills of mortality, despite the fact that Henry Walker, the originator of the practice, had ceased to do so in his concurrent *Severall Proceedings in Parliament* and *Perfect Passages of Everie Daies Intelligence*. Whilst this may prove unspectacular journalism, as in an instance where over half of the second issue of *The Impartial Scout* is given over to the slavish reprinting of the act passed on 28 June 'for the better preventing of prophane Swearing and Cursing', the increased stress on collectivity that such wholesale collation necessarily entailed opened up a discursive framework which was redolent with silent presences and which women could exploit.[95] It is my contention that this apparent denial of individual agency, employed in a way which surreptitiously and paradoxically reintroduces it, ought to be viewed as a less immediately readable counterpart to the rhetorical strategies analysed in the opening chapters.

It is therefore arresting to find the sudden emergence of a distinct editorial voice at the opening of the fourth issue of *The Impartial Scout*:

> It is a Princely Alchumy, out of necessary War to extract an honourable peace; and more beseeming the Majesty of a Prince, to thirst after Peace, than Conquest:

---

[93]   Raymond, *Invention*, p. 162. An interesting contrast to Alkin and her negotiation of relationship between intelligence and information is perhaps the period's most famous newsman, Marchamont Nedham. Nedham's newsbooks are amongst the most individualistic and floridly written pamphlet publications of the period, yet in 1653 he too was the foremost undercover agent in the Cromwellian secret service. See Frank, *Cromwell's Press Agent*, pp. 107–110.

[94]   *The Moderate Intelligencer* 1, 6–13 March 1645, p. 1.

[95]   *The Impartial Scout* 2 (54), 28 June–5 July 1650, pp. 225–8. Tantalizingly, another woman, Jane Coe, who was involved in the printing of pamphlets and newsbooks (but does not appear to have had as thorough-going a relationship with intelligence as Alkin) was systematically denied these benefits of collectivity. Her involvement between June 1644 and November 1647 in the production of *The Kingdomes Scout, Mr Peters Report, The Moderate Messenger,* and *Perfect Occurrences* is obscured not only by the obtrusive editorial voices of a younger Daniel Border and Hugh Peters but by the fact that she was frequently working in tandem with, and was introduced to the printing industry by her husband, Andrew Coe. On the Coes see Henry R. Plomer, *Dictionary,* p. 471; D. F. Mckenzie, *Stationer's Company Apprentices, 1605–1640* (Charlottesville, 1961), p. 22.

Blessedness is promised to the peace-maker, not to the conqueror: That is a happy
State, which hath a peaceful hand, and a martial heart; able both to use peace and
manage War: Even so it is with the Parlament of *England*, who have not been
wanting in the offer of all fair and amicable means, for composing the differences
and obtaining due satisfaction.[96]

The florid rhetoric, the ungainly martial versions of body politic imagery set rather
precariously alongside pacifistic biblical echoes, alerts us to the fact that we are
back in the realms of Border's and Wood's *Kingdomes Faithfull and Impartiall
Scout*. If this were not sufficiently unlike Alkin's journalistic method, then the noncommittal, moderate nature of the political rhetoric, pandering at once to expectant
royalists and parliamentarians alike, makes the point more clearly. For a woman
who had had her husband and the father of her three children hanged by the
royalists at Oxford, and who had spent the majority of her life exposing dissident
royalists, references to 'Princely Alchumy' and the 'honourable peace' and
'Majesty of a Prince' were surely anathema.[97] It is telling therefore that this is the
last involvement that Alkin was ever to have with a Border/Wood newsbook, so
that when the next issue opened with similar militaristic metaphors of the body
politic it did not bear her name. It is simply 'Printed by Robert Wood', implying
that Alkin left the two men to their own devices in search of a journalistic vehicle
more suited to her resolutely anti-royalist temperament.[98]

From *Intelligencer* to Nurse

The suggestion that Alkin did indeed leave the *Scout* enterprise because of its
political neutralism or because she was at odds with the direction its journalism
had once again taken, is strengthened by the fact that most of her remaining forays
into newsbook publication were made in direct opposition to Border and Wood.
Between September 1650 and September 1651 Alkin was involved in the
production of single issues of *The Moderne Intelligencer, Mercurius Anglicus* and
The Modern Intelligencer, all newsbooks closely associated with Border's old
adversary Henry Walker. Walker's brand of anti-royalism was much more

---

96   *The Impartial Scout* 4 (56), 12–19 July 1650, p. 241.
97   Border's attitude to royalism had always been complexly neutral. For instance, *The
Weekly Account* refused either to praise or condemn 'the number of people that resorted to
his Majesty for cure of the Evill'. *The Weekly Account* 8, 17–24 February 1647; see also *The
Weekly Account* 46, 28 Oct.–4 Nov. 1646 and *The Weekly Account* 13, 24–30 March 1647;
cited in Frank, *Beginnings*, p. 128.
98   *The Impartial Scout* 5 (57), 19–25 July 1650, p. 249.

committed than that of Border and Wood, and was thus more allied to Alkin's.[99] He frequently worked with politico-religious radicals in the news trade, gave more space to the Levellers than any other contemporary editor and had been an excited onlooker at Charles I's trial. Walker had been in trouble with the authorities as early as 1641 when he was arrested for hurling a copy of his pamphlet *To Your Tents O Israel* into the king's coach, and throughout the mid-1640s his newsbooks continually stressed the need for local vigilance against royalist plots.[100] Politically and religiously Independent, he was an accomplished pamphleteer and had probably been publishing newsbooks since the autumn of 1644. By September 1650 he had developed into a skilled, relatively even-handed, newsman and had acquired a reputation as a rather showy classicist who persistently and ostentatiously revealed his authorial hand through Greek, Latin and Hebrew quotations and etymological word play.[101]

However, none of the newsbooks that Alkin published with Walker contain any of these supposedly stock traits. When the first of the two issues of *The Moderne Intelligencer* appeared in September 1650 it was remarkable only in its likeness to *The Impartial Scout*.[102] Once again, the focus was on naval and military news and the first issue began with a less than eye-catching opening sentence:

> From abroad, the Resolution in the Bay of Lisborn the 15 of August came intelligence under the hands of the Admirals Blake and Popham concerning the state and condition of their Fleet, and also of *Ruperts* endeavors to get out to his old Trade of robbing, sayling forth of the Bay of *Weres* with 26 ships and 18 Carrels.[103]

The reader is thrown unceremoniously in *media res* as the first sentence of the first issue of this new publication strives to conceal its distinctive status. 'From abroad' sound less like nervous inaugural words than those of anticipated continuation, which are doing their utmost to stress their openness to dialogue or the interanimation of different discourses. As a result, this serial seems less a platform for an individual editor than a threshold to the words and worlds of others. At such moments Elizabeth Alkin's newsbooks sound curiously like Katherine Chidley's

---

99 Between January 1644 and October 1649 he collaborated on the *Perfect Occurences* with the antinomian John Saltmarsh; Nelson and Seccombe, *British Newspapers*, pp. 308–314, 702; Raymond, *Invention*, p. 199.

100 Henry Walker, *Collections of Notes taken at the Kings Tryall, at Westminster Halls* (1649); Ernest Sirluck, 'To Your Tents, O Israel': A Lost Pamphlet', *Huntingdon Library Quarterly* 19, (1955–56), pp. 301–5; Frank, *Beginnings*, pp. 108–9; Raymond, *Invention*, pp. 199, 217.

101 See, for instance, *Perfect Occurences* 63, 10–17 March 1648, p. 516. For a discussion of Walker's classicism see Frank, *Beginnings*, pp. 81, 109, 150.

102 Nelson and Seccombe do not venture an attribution of *The Moderne Intelligencer*. However both Joseph Frank and J. B. Williams positively identify Walker as its editor.

103 *The Moderne Intelligencer* 1, 10–18 Sept. 1650, p. 1.

revolutionary animadversions; 'information' is downgraded and editorial intrusions and asides are forced out by a new attention to the effaced agencies and collective processes of intelligence gathering.

There is a sense, however, that this imbalance between intelligence and information did not particularly suit Walker (he had tried it briefly in an earlier, short-lived newsbook) and that with Alkin involved, *The Moderne Intelligencer* was decidedly too unspectacular for this showy newsman.[104] Hence, the following postscript is hastily appended at the end of the newsbook:

> Courteous Reader,
> I thought it convenient (as formerly) to give you a brief account of the most modern and material proceedings in several parts. And though at present, (by reason of the slackness of Intelligence this Week) I am forced to break off abruptly; yet I thought good to divulge these few lines as a caution to my future intentions; not doubting but to give you satisfaction next Tuesday for my neglect in this.[105]

Walker himself here presents the newsbook as atypical of his work. As is intimated, the postscript replaces the functional summary that Walker had introduced to his newsbooks some years earlier. He implies that in this issue readerly 'satisfaction' will be low because 'Intelligence is slack'. However, to some extent this is disingenuous as the newsbook contains extremely detailed information about the activities and engagements of the parliamentarian and royalist armies in Scotland, a similarly precise account of the movements of the naval fleet, five items of foreign news, three letters, a reprint of a letter of 'pious advice' by Fairfax and an item on the death of 'Lady Elizabeth Stuart Daughter of the late king'.[106] If it is difficult to make a case for this newsbook as the most news-crammed of the week, it is similarly difficult to substantiate Walker's claim that it was under-informed. Yet it *was* under-informed in a more specific respect, in the sense that it was of a low informational quality, due to the paucity of editorial matter. The terms in which Walker accounts for this are noteworthy: he has been 'forced to break of abruptly', that is coerced by some external agent to resist punctuating the newsbook with his familiar, florid editorial rhetoric and classical references. The external agent is, I would aver, less a quiet news week – this was, after all, the week after the battle of Dunbar – than the publisher, Elizabeth Alkin, pressing as ever for the collative nature of intelligence. In contrast

---

[104] Between March and November 1648 Walker was probably, though by no means certainly, involved in the production of *Packets of Letters ... to members of the House of Commons*. These too had no editorial content. See Nelson and Seccombe, *British Newspapers*, p. 415.

[105] *The Moderne Intelligencer* 1, 11–18 Sept. 1650, p. 8.

[106] The only other newsbook to pick up on this last item at this time was Walker's other journalistic enterprise. See *Perfect Passages* 10, 9–13 Sept. 1650, p. 78.

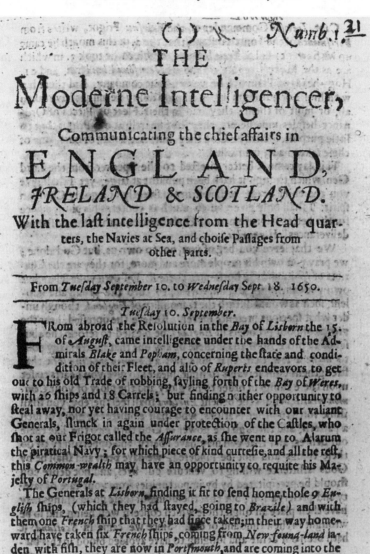

Figure 9: *The Moderne Intelligencer* 1, 10–18 Sept. 1650, title page
The Moderne Intelligencer, published by Alkin and edited by Henry Walker, was remarkably similar in tone and content to *The Impartial Scout*.

to the present issue, Walker promises his readers 'satisfaction next Tuesday', and, sure enough, when the second issue appeared published this time by Jane Coe, not only had the concluding news-summary returned, but so had the intrusive editorials, larded with classical allusion.[107]

Nonetheless Alkin and Walker persevered with each other, publishing another two issues of different newsbooks after their collaboration on *The Moderne Intelligencer*, the former doubtless needing the money, the latter perhaps aware of the benefits of working with a well-connected intelligencer. The anti-royalist *Mercurius Anglicus* appeared nine days later, perhaps representing a compromise between Alkin's and Walker's preferred working methods. The single issue they produced in collaboration opens with a short paragraph of recherché editorial invoking Pindarus, Pythagoras and Apolonius after which the collative process of newsgathering is foregrounded through unimaginative reprinting of letters and intelligence; there are no editorial asides and Walker's penchant for recondite word play is abandoned.[108] The title of this uninspired venture is much more significant than its content. When *Mercurius Anglicus* appeared for the very first time for two weeks in 1644 it set itself the unenviable task of being London's and parliament's *Mercurius Aulicus*.[109] It is unsuccessful in this attempt, but some four years later the title was revived, this time as a royalist serial bent on persuading 'the besotted City ... to rescue his Majesty from his base Imprisonment, to restore him to his just Rights, and the people to their lost Religion, Laws, and Liberties'.[110] Its news content was, by its own admission, questionable, but it did devote plenty of space to criticizing Walker, the *'Hebrew Ironmonger, Judas-bearded Harrunney'* and his anti-Scottish writings.[111] In effect, then, Walker's and Alkin's latest enterprise represents an attempt to re-appropriate the name of *Anglicus* for a parliamentarian, anti-royalist, and anti-Scottish position. In the process they were reassociating it with trustworthy intelligence, an urgent cause which allied both news workers. Whilst the new *Anglicus* certainly outdid its predecessors on all these counts, it was an unspectacular production, relying heavily on official documents, letters and items that could largely be found in most other newsbooks of the time.

---

[107] In marked contrast to the first, the second issue begins: 'It is a fiction, That Tiresias of Thebes, striking two Adders (through their conjunction) became a *Woman*, till (long after) by bruising two Serpents he was turned into a man again.'; *The Moderne Intelligencer* 2, 18–25 Sept. 1650, p. 9. As has already been mentioned Jane Coe appears to be an interesting contrast to Alkin in that she continually allowed her influence on the newsbooks she published to be utterly obscured. She worked on the *Perfect Occurences* with Walker and Saltmarsh for the entire period between June 1644 and November 1647.

[108] *Mercurius Anglicus* 1, 24 Sept.–1 Oct. 1650, p. 1.

[109] *Mercurius Anglicus* 1, 31 Jan.–7 Feb., 1644. On other London-based newsbooks which set themselves up in opposition to *Aulicus*, see Raymond, *Invention*, pp. 26–36.

[110] *Mercurius Anglicus* 1, 27 July–3 Aug. 1648, p. 1.

[111] Ibid. 'Luke Harruney' was the, not entirely successful, anagram Walker used to mask himself when working on *Perfect Occurences*.

Nonetheless, the collective nature of this endeavour perhaps allowed Alkin, with her expert knowledge of contemporary book trade intelligence networks, to show her journalistic hand that week. When the Ranter Lawrence Clarkson's book *The Single Eye* had been published, seized, burnt in public and its readers forced to report to their Justice of the Peace, *Anglicus* offered an account of the event which surpassed all of its competitors. It reprinted, like most of the other newsbooks, the report from the Commons Journal of the day when the report was presented to parliament. Yet it went further, attempting to offer brief descriptions of both the pamphlet and Clarkson himself, and actually went so far as to offer this as the sole important news item of the day.[112]

As no other issue of *Anglicus* appeared from the stable of Alkin and Walker, one can only assume that it proved as unsuccessful as its predecessors. Nonetheless, this did not signal the end of the Alkin/Walker collaboration, which announced itself once again the following year with several issues of a revamped, re-spelled *The Modern Intelligencer*.[113] Like so many other Alkin productions, the serial begins with an understated 'This day we received intelligence', but once again this seems to have proved a failure. It seems likely that the removal of all editorial intervention and the strict privileging of intelligence over information proved to be no great selling point for a newsbook associated with Walker, used as the public was to his flamboyantly obtrusive editorial style.

The Modern Intelligencer heralded the end of Alkin and Walker's journalistic relationship, but it did not signal the end of Alkin's involvement in the material production of newsbooks since less than three weeks after *The Modern Intelligencer*, *Mercurius Scoticus* or the *Royal Messenger* appeared bearing Alkin's imprint as publisher. The content of this publication tallied with that of all of Alkin's other serials in that it was concerned primarily with naval and military news and espoused a strongly anti-royalist position. J. B. Williams has speculated that the title was intended solely to flush out contemporary royalist newsbook readers. Alkin was apparently:

Able to approach any persons noted as strangers and royalists, get them into conversation extract all she knew from them, and afterwards utilise the information thus gained. Naturally the unlucky royalist, thus stealthily approached, would at once hide in his pocket a copy of this newsbook which he had purchased ... and his conference gained by this attractive title would hold a whispering conversation with

---

[112] Lawrence Clarkson, *A Single Eye: All Light, no Darkness; or Light and Darkness One* (London, 1650); *Mercurius Anglicus* 1, 24 Sept.–1 Oct. 1650, pp. 6–7; *Perfect Diurnall* 42, 23–30 Sept. 1650, pp. 553–4; *Mercurius Politicus* 17, 26 Sept.–3 Oct. 1650, p. 286; *Severall Proceedings of Parliament* 53, 23 Sept–3 Oct. 1650, p. 790.

[113] *The Modern Intelligencer* V, 26 Aug.–3 Sept. 1651. Nelson and Seccombe list four issues of this serial. George Thomason, however, only managed to collect one.

the hawker, and not until reaching home and drawing out his little newsbook would he discover that he had been swindled.[114]

It is difficult simply to dismiss this account because there is a lack of substantiating evidence either way. Such speculation well accords with Alkin's history as an informer for the authorities. However, it seems equally plausible that the number of readers who considered a 1651 newsbook 'Examined by the Originalls, published by Authority' to be royalist were few and far between.[115] That said, what is most striking about the final newsbook Alkin published is its style. It is crammed with editorial comments and classical allusion, even going so far as to include Latin encomia by Francis Nelson on Cromwell and the recent victory at Worcester.[116] Perhaps Alkin was trying to learn the lessons of more successful, individualistic Henry Walker. She allows a new editor complete license because she had gathered, too late in the day, that turning the effaced agency of the intelligence gatherer into the founding principle of a newsbook's journalistic style was doomed to failure in the hyper-competitive news market of the 1650s. Not to individuate could lead to the promotion of the styles of one's competitors; this is egalitarian, certainly, but must also sound the death knell for any business venture.

If *Scoticus* intimates that Alkin was lessening her direct involvement in London newsbook culture, official records confirm this. After discovering Edward Hall's *Manus Testium* two months after publishing her final newsbook, she moved to Dover to become a naval nurse, no doubt drawing on the intricate knowledge of the Fleet she had acquired in her journalistic endeavours. When tending to the sick and wounded, here she once again began petitioning parliament for maintenance and lodgings and the various letters and petitions that survive attest that the career of the nurse was not as renumerative as that of the newswoman.[117] Her last letter, dated February 1654, is to Robert Blackbourne, a member of the Council for the Navy, and is a heartfelt plea for assistance in illness. It concludes:

> my sickness & manie infirmities being procured by my continuall watchings night and day to do service for this Commonwealth ... I have beene inforced to sell my bed and other goodes to make ... satisfaction & to prevent ... clamor, I therefore humbly request I maie [have] a little monie or else be put in some Hospitall my daies being but short & to prevent a miserable ending of them my charge being very great for Physick and necessarie attendance for my preservation.

---

[114] Williams, *History*, p. 142.

[115] *Mercurius Scoticus*, 23–30 Sept. 1651, title page.

[116] This has led Nelson and Seccombe to attribute *Scoticus* to Francis Nelson; *British Newspapers*, p. 388. This *Scoticus* survived for only one issue and is not to be confused with Scotland's first newspaper of the same name which also appeared that year.

[117] The best discussion of nursing in the early modern period is Margaret Pelling, *The Common Lot: Sickness, Medical Occupations and the Urban Poor in Early Modern Britain* (London and New York, 1998), pp. 179–202.

And Sir I shall think my selfe ever bound to you for all your favours hoping I shall be no more troublesome to you, but shall while I live pray for you and yours & rest

your poore servant in distress,
Elizabeth Alkin.[118]

Just as she had in her spying days, Alkin reworks the notion of good 'service' in an attempt to obtain relief, and, as previously, she was successful, receiving £40 that year for her 'reliefe' and 'services', and a further 'twenty markes' in the next.[119] After these payments we hear nothing more of her for over two hundred years, when J. B. Williams offers his study of the newsbook complete with his claim that there is an undated petition in which Alkin asks to be 'buried in the cloisters of Westminster Abbey without charge'.[120] Whether or not this is the case, the fact that there is no record of her name in the Abbey registers reveals that just as during her lifetime there was an agency-denying counter-measure for every one of her various acts of Intelligence-gathering, so too, posthumously, Elizabeth Alkin's body and memory are forcefully denied any place in the public sphere. However, by placing the silences that have engulfed Alkin in a context of multiple and self-effacing agencies inherent in both the news trade and the proximate worlds of espionage, we can at least begin to sketch one woman's intelligent, if finally unrenumerative, manipulation of the interpersonal networks of intelligence.

---

[118] SP 18/66/74.

[119] SP 25/75/258; 25/75/545; 25/76/73.

[120] Williams, *History*, p. 154. However, I have not been able to locate this petition.

Chapter 4

Clothing the Naked Woman: Writing Women's Agency in Revolutionary England

In previous chapters we have scrutinized a variety of rhetorical and material methods through which women managed to engage in the prodigious pamphlet production of the revolutionary decades. Despite significant obstacles to women's involvement in this thriving culture of cheap print, we have seen how agency might be achieved through a careful manipulation of both discursive formulations and existing book trade practices. Our attention turns now to the ways in which a group of male pamphlet writers responded to the political intervention of a single woman in Whitehall. Unlike Trapnel, Chidley, Poole, Pope or Alkin, however, the name of this woman was never recorded; nor did she, seemingly, ever write a single word. Her intervention is instructive, however, in that it amply demonstrates the lengths to which some male contemporaries would go to deny the very possibility of women's goal-oriented action.

'A Mad-Woman Onely'?

On the Sunday morning of 17 July 1652 at a chapel in Whitehall not far from the tavern which was the scene for Anna Trapnel's *The Cry of a Stone*, Oliver Cromwell's chaplain, Peter Sterry, ascended the pulpit to begin his weekly sermon before a congregation packed with dignitaries, soldiers and statesmen.[1] His subject

---

[1] The principal sources for what follows are David Brown, *The Naked Woman, Or a Rare Epistle Sent to Mr Peter Sterry, Minister at Whitehall* (London, 1652); *Perfect Passages of Every Daies Intelligence from the Parliaments Army* 57, 16–23 July 1652, pp. 438–9; *The Faithful Scout* 80, 23–30 July 1652, p. 629; *Mercurius Britannicus* 19–26 July, 1652, p. 15; *A Perfect Account of the Daily Intelligence from the Armies of England, Scotland and Ireland*, 21–28 July 1652, p. 649; *French Occurences*, 26 July–27 Aug. 1652, p. 76. The most recent analyses of the incident are in Hilda L. Smith, *All Men and Both Sexes: Gender, Politics and the False Universal in England, 1640–1832* (Philadelphia, 2002), pp. 123–4; Susan Wiseman, 'Margaret Cavendish among the Prophets: performance ideologies and gender in and after the English Civil War', *Women's Writing* 6:1 (1999), pp. 95–112; Sharon Achinstein, 'Women on Top', pp. 149–51. A much less sensitive reading of the

was the Resurrection and his deliberations proceeded smoothly enough until the minister arrived at a point about half way through the sermon. Sterry continues the story:

> I was in the midst of my sermon, when I saw at one end of the Chappell a great disturbance among the people, with a sudden fear. I cast my eye on the other end, where I saw in the midst of a crowd a Woman, as I guest by her head, bare to the middle of her back, the rest of her being hid from my sight in the throng: Hereupon I turned to the disturbed people to quiet them, by telling them that there was no danger, that it was a mad-woman onely that occasioned the Stir ... Before I could again turn my eye towards that place, the Woman was suddenly carried out by the Souldiers, who alwayes keep a court of Guard close by the door of the Chappel: It was when I came out of the Pulpit that I first was acquainted with the Truth of this Story, which for the monstrousness of it seemed incredible to me.[2]

The minister is keen to cultivate a sense of the collective 'fear' the incident engenders in his congregation, and accordingly refrains from offending the delicate sensibilities of his readers by refusing to reveal the final, dreadful 'Truth of this Story'. He continually withholds the unspeakable horror, the 'monstrousness' of the ultimate actions of a solitary, semi-naked 'mad' woman in a chapel full of armed guards. The newsbooks of the following week were quick to recycle the incident. Despite the fact that this was an extremely busy news week (the first Anglo-Dutch war was claiming more and more victims at sea) several editors found the time and space to cover the story at the chapel in Whitehall in lurid, if conflicting, detail. Thus one inveighs against the general corruption of the times and finds the Whitehall episode particularly emblematic:

> There be many unto whom the Sun of Truth is declined, and with the Clouds of vice their minds are darkened ... And surely that floodgate of wickedness is open where immodesty hath deprived Reason of her due; a strange example whereof was this week acted by a woman, who prosterated [sic] herself stark naked in a Church at the time of publick exercise.[3]

Sterry's awful, withheld 'Truth' is simply, it would seem, the naked one. All other newsbook accounts corroborate the woman's nudity but flesh it out with various other details. *A Perfect Account* therefore informed its readers not only that a woman 'stripped herself quite out of her cloathes in a Church' but also that she 'cried out, *Resurrection I am ready for thee*' and was accordingly 'committed to

---

event is provided in Vivian de Sola Pinto, *Peter Sterry: Platonist and Puritan, 1613–1672* (Cambridge, 1934), pp. 26–7.

[2]   Sterry's version of events is to be found in the reprint of a letter written to David Brown and appended to Brown's *The Naked Woman*, pp. 16–17.

[3]   *Perfect Passages* 57, 16–23 July 1652, pp. 438–9.

custody'.[4] The woman's direct speech and the authorities' 'examination and exemplary punishment' of her are also recorded in the version of the story run by *The Faithful Scout*, and *Mercurius Britannicus* confirms the woman's words but concludes its coverage of the event with a lamentation of the fact that the woman escaped 'without any known Mulct [punishment]'.[5]

The central fact (or character) may well be bare, but the story these pamphlets and newsbooks tell is far from clear. What did this woman's intervention ultimately mean? Did she speak as well as strip? Was she punished for her actions or did she escape? Such conflicting reports are never resolved by the pamphlet press as they undoubtedly contributed to the incident's notoriety, provided it with a titillative and sensationalist energy, allowing fact and fiction to collide and produce further narratives for larger paying audiences. These continued to circulate and alarm for many months, and eventually passed under the eye of a London-based, Scottish writing master called David Brown. Brown, outraged at the possibility that the incident might have gone unpunished, penned a scurrilous pamphlet inveighing against the actions of the woman and any who might be inclined to sympathize or support her.[6] His *The Naked Woman* is a 22-page pamphlet written as an *'Epistle sent to Mr Peter Sterry'* (it also includes Sterry's reply), which expands upon the information supplied in the newsbooks and supplements it with fragments of auricular testimony from 'both eye and ear witnesses' present at Whitehall in July.[7] However, in fact, the only further clues that the pamphlet provides as to the woman's identity is the single statement that she is 'a bold woman of about thirty years old, sober in her speech'.[8] Brown is more certain than *Mercurius Britannicus*, and even more profoundly anxious, that she escaped following the confrontation and is now at large, beyond the scope of law, punishment and knowledge. He is desperate to find answers to the following questions:

> What were the reasons and intentions of that her so presumptuous, impudent and barbarous attempt? ... Whether such kind of lasciviousness and licentious carriage, be the custom of the company where she useth to walk? ... With what company she walketh? ... How long? ... Whether or no[t] she was sent by them? ... If not, then by

---

[4] *A Perfect Account*, 21–28 July 1652, p. 649.

[5] *The Faithful Scout* 80, 23–30 July 1652, p. 629; *Mercurius Britannicus*, 19–26 July 1652, p. 15.

[6] For biographical details of David Brown, see Murray Tolmie, *The Triumph of the Saints: The Separate Churches of London 1616–1649* (Cambridge, 1977), pp. 13, 17, 22, 47, 49, 111, 147, 178. Brown himself confirms that he neither saw the woman's actions nor was ever a member of Sterry's congregation. Addressing Cromwell's chaplain in his Epistle Dedicatory he states 'I neither know you, nor, I suppose, you me by face', *The Naked Woman*, sig. A3r–A3v.

[7] In particular Brown is keen to acknowledge that much of his detail comes from 'a discreet Military Officer, who ... commanded the guard, when the impudent woman before that High Assembly appeared'; *The Naked Woman*, sig. A3r, p. 18.

[8] Ibid., p. 9.

whom? ... If by none at all, they did she not run unsent? ... What her name was? ... Is she hath a husband? ... If yea, what his name was? ... Where he dwelleth? ... And if he and she live together? So that by knowing these or most of these particulars, both the neighbours where they dwell, and others who would have visited her in her imprisonment, might possibly in short time [have] declared divers things which her self would have alwayes obscured.[9]

Brown registers a patriarchal fear of the socially mobile woman tied to neither household nor community, neither husband nor name. He gives interrogative voice to the anxieties provoked by the transgressive woman who escapes exemplary punishment. His account is also expressive of a sense of the complexities of female agency in the period, for Brown realizes that it is precisely at that moment when name, place and status are 'obscured' that this woman becomes her most potent and active.

We will return to the naked woman's agency in due course, but what is noteworthy at this point of male ignorance is the manner in which Brown turns his attention from female indiscipline to male misbehaviour. For the most striking feature of Brown's pamphlet is not so much his treatment of the naked woman herself, but rather his excoriation of the conduct of Cromwell's chaplain. Doubtless aware of the possibility that the naked woman's protest was not merely spectacular action but also discursive work (*'Resurrection I am ready for thee'*), Brown is horrified at Sterry's apparent failure to offer any public words (spoken or written) in response to a 'most presumptuous and impudent act ... by one of the female sex whose duty it was to have been most shamefac'd'.[10] He can barely conceal his disbelief that a woman's activity has been 'smoothed over by your *silence'*, and acerbically reminds Sterry that 'neither King Solomon, the wisest of mankind, nor any other writer of the Scripture, did ever forbid any wise or discreet man, to speak in time or place convenient'.[11] It is not just the case, however, that male words are deemed more important than (or necessary correctives to) female words at this point, but rather that 'shameless', dissident female behaviour and male public silence are deemed commensurately shameful. Brown's furious incredulity is directed at:

> *both* that shameless woman's presumption (of whom we speak) and your silent beholding of her ... and being also in the Pulpit and middle of your Sermon, yea and none other then having authority to speak, how you in your conscience could both in so needful a time, so eminent a place, and upon so urgent an occasion be so negligent in the discharge of your duty as well as your delivery of the Sermon itself, which you being forced to forbear, during that time and presence of that shamefull

---

[9]   Ibid., p. 8.
[10] Ibid., p. 5.
[11] Ibid., pp. 1, 2.; emphasis added.

spectacle, was the more free to have expressed your mind concerning her misbehaviour.[12]

Transgression here is constructed around the male inaction which follows female agency, around a man's dereliction of a masculine 'duty' to speak and act when 'place and urgent ... occasion' dictate.[13] Brown is troubled not so much by a woman's unsanctioned violation of the tranquillity of chapel and service (as one might expect given the Pauline injunction that women 'keep silence in ... churches') as a more profoundly destabilizing breach of speech, an uncomfortable moment of *discursus interruptus*, which leaves the assembled statesmen and soldiers alike prey to a resounding *male* silence.[14] Even if, as Christina Luckyj has shown, there was a longstanding tradition that construed silence as both eloquence and impotence, the 'insolent and presumptuous act' which so infuriates the Scottish writing master is one in which naked woman and taciturn minister are equally implicated.[15]

Brown's outrage in part stems from what he perceives to be both parties' refusal to govern their tongues in accordance with the codes through which speech and silence were gendered during the early modern period.[16] Since the late fifteenth century there was a growing body of devotional literature and practical guidebooks in English which defined silence, in one formulation, as a

---

[12] Ibid., p. 6; emphasis added.

[13] Brown expands upon this point earlier in the pamphlet: 'I am confident that it is a greater and more inexcusable fault for a wise and discreet man to be silent, when in the dutifull charge of his office ... than for a simple fool when he should hold his peace, even freely to deliver his mind'. He also reminds Sterry that '[your silence] doth greatly endanger your reputation in that you was [sic] the only man then appointed to be the mouth ... of that honourable assembly'; ibid., pp. 1, 3.

[14] For the Pauline injunction against women speaking in churches see I Corinthians 14 v. 34: 'let your women keep silence in the churches: for it is not permitted unto them to speak; but they are commanded to be under silence.'

[15] Brown, *The Naked Woman*, p. 6. He further emphasizes this by informing Sterry that 'your silence and negligence [are] the instrumental cause that all of her mind ... are not only waxed both more audacious, outrageous and numerous, but likewise do think themselves to be more confirmed and allowed, thus by outfacing Authority, to proceed in their wickednesse, then ever since we heard that there was any such miscreants in the valley of tears.'; ibid., p. 10. For a fascinating study of the ways in which silence was described in the period see Christina Luckyj, *'A Moving Rhetoricke': Gender and Silence in Early Modern England* (Manchester and New York, 2002).

[16] On this topic see Luckyj, *'A Moving Rhetoricke'*, pp. 42–77; Jane Kamensky, *Governing the Tongue: The Politics of Speech in Early New England* (New York and Oxford, 1997); Laura Gowing, *Domestic Dangers Women, Words and Sex in Early Modern London* (Oxford: Oxford University Press, 1996); Suzanne W. Hull, *Chaste, Silent and Obedient: English Books for Women 1475–1640* (San Marino, 1982); Ruth Kelso, *Doctrine for the Lady of the Renaissance* (Chicago and London, 1978).

characteristically female virtue.[17] Thus in 1529, when Catherine of Aragon's adviser Joanne Ludovicus Vives's *The Instruction of a Christian Woman* was translated from Latin into English for the first time by Richard Hyrde, 'All maydes, & all women' were notified that there was an abundance of sacred and secular texts which decreed that:

> Silence [is] the noblest ornament of a woman. And Sophocles is of the same opinyon: for with silence both wysedom and chastite be swetely poudered. Thou art none atturney of the lawe good doughter, nor pleadeste nat in the courte, that thou shalt nede to quayle either thyn owne or thy clyentes matter ... Holde thou thy peace as boldly as others speke in courte: and so shalt thou better defende the matter of thy chastite, which afore iust iudges shal be stronger with silence than with speche ... I had leuer a mayde shulde loue to lytle talke than to moche: For ... women be commaunded to holde theyr peace of holy matter in ye churche, and ask theyr husbands at home.[18]

Vives extends the Pauline injunction concerning female silence from the 'churche' to the 'courte[s]' of sixteenth-century rulers and lawyers. Public discourse is a distinctly male office, the privilege of a homosocial community of 'atturneys' and 'husbands'; women's strength and their best defence, however, resides with those male figure heads and their own silence. Vives's text was popular in England well into the seventeenth century and English authors were quick to echo his message.[19] Some forty years after the first English edition, the Protestant divine Thomas Becon confirmed that:

> This also must honest maides provide, that they be not full of tonge, and of much babling, nor use many wordes, but as fewe as they may, yea & those wisely and discreetely, soberly and modestly spoken, ever remembring this common proverbe: A maid shuld be seene and not h[e]ard. Except the gravity of some matter do require, that she shuld speake: or else an answer is to be made to such thinges as are demaunded of her: let her kepe silence.[20]

---

[17] On other formulations, such as the frequently overlooked relationship between masculinity and inscrutable silences in the period, see Luckyj, *'A Moving Rhetoricke'*, pp. 45–9.

[18] Joannes Ludovicus Vives, *A very frutefull and pleasant boke called the instruction of a Christian women* [sic], *made fyrst in Laten, and dedicated unto the quenes good grace, by the right famous clerke mayster Lewes Vives, and turned out of Laten into Englysshe by Richarde Hyrd* (London, 1529), sig. Diiiv –Divv.

[19] On Vives's reception in the seventeenth century see Kamensky, *Governing the Tongue*, pp. 26–7.

[20] Thomas Becon, *The Worckes of Thomas Becon, which he hath hytherto made and published with diuerse other newe Bookes*, 3 vols (London, 1560–64), vol. 1, sig. BBb.iir.

Female honesty and virtue once again reside in an unspoken, private realm whilst men are free to be as full of public 'tonge' as 'proverbe'-framing or shrew-taming dictate.

Such views persisted well into the seventeenth century. Richard Brathwait wrote his female conduct manual, *The English Gentlewoman* (1631), in terms strikingly reminiscent of Thomas Becon. Brathwait maintained that for women:

> To enter into much discourse or familiarity with strangers, argues lightnesse or indiscretion: what is spoken of Maids may be properly applyed by an usefull consequence to all women: *They should be seene and not heard*: A Traueller sets himselfe best out by discourse, whereas their best setting out is silence ... It will beseeme you, *Gentlewomen* ... in publike consorts to obserue rather than discourse. It suites [sic] not with her honour, for a young woman to be prolocutor. But especially, when either men are in presence, or ancient Matrons, to whom shee owes a ciuil reverence, it will become her to tip her tongue with silence.[21]

In a world where male travellers are constituted as much by their public narratives as their physical shapes, we find 'Gentlewomen' confined to positions of mute spectatorship. Such spectatorship had not, of course, attained the kind of empowered status which Luce Irigaray would give it in the twentieth century, but was rather an unambiguous mark of 'ciuil reverence' which placed young gentlewomen further down the social and acoustic hierarchies than men or 'ancient Matrons'.[22] If the only thing that 'Gentlewomen' were supposed to have at the tips of their tongues was silence, it also seems unlikely in this period that women from lower points on the social scale were encouraged to enter into the male world of public speech.

This becomes apparent when we interrogate the popular scrutiny given to such debates in early seventeenth-century pamphlet culture itself. The controversy which enveloped the publication of Joseph Swetnam's *The Arraignment of Lewde, idle, froward and unconstant women* in 1615 is instructive here. Swetnam's pamphlet peddles antifeminist invective alongside a series of exhortations on the dangers and pleasures of marriage, but is perhaps best read as a provocative collage of misogynistic aphorisms and texts concerning female conduct.[23] *The Arraignment*'s relationship with this discourse is complicated since its collusion in misogynistic argument is compromised and satirized by moments of contradictory

---

[21] Richard Brathwait, *The English Gentlewoman* (London, 1631), pp. 41, 89.

[22] Irigaray's theories about spectatorship, specularity and the 'trap' of visibility are most comprehensively outlined in *Speculum of the Other Woman*, trans. G. C. Gill (Ithaca, 1985); *This Sex Which Is Not One*, trans. Catherine Porter (Ithaca, 1985).

[23] For a suggestive reading which uncovers the effects of ludic misogyny in Swetnam's tract see Diane Purkiss, 'Material Girls: The Seventeenth-Century Woman Debate', in Clare Brant and Diane Purkiss (eds.), *Women, Texts and Histories 1575–1760* (London and New York, 1992), pp. 69–101.

logic, dubious source citation and the flagrant travestying of classical authorities.[24]
As such, it probably represents an attempt by the English fencing master to
capitalize on the plethora of contemporary moral discourses surrounding women's
speech and prompt a lucrative pamphlet war.[25] In this at least Swetnam was
successful; his own pamphlet was reprinted ten times in twelve years and by 1617
there were three printed responses to it. Later that year the controversy itself
became the subject of a stage play.[26] However it is the manner in which Swetnam
attempts to initiate pamphlet dialogue that is most noteworthy for our purposes.
Before he advises 'the ordinary sort of giddy headed young men' that 'the answer
of a wise woman is silence', indulging them in a fantasy of homosocial interpretive
community ('I thinke it were not amisse to driue all the women out of my
hearing'), he opens his pamphlet by addressing the 'common sort of women' he
actually assumes to be reading his work:

> Let me whisper privately one word in your ears, and that is this: whatsoever you
> think privately, I wish to conceal it with silence, lest in starting up to find fault you
> prove yourself guilty of those monstrous accusations which are here following
> against some women.[27]

Swetnam thus constructs a double-bind for his women pamphlet readers; either
they remain silent at this misogynistic *Arraignment,* a silence which apparently
registers assent, or they respond publicly and prove themselves as lewd, froward,
idle or unconstant as the countless, nameless women who fill his pages. His female
readers are represented, then, as just so many Vittorias. John Webster famously
used his heroine in *The White Devil* (1612) to explore the early modern gendering

---

[24]   Thus Swetnam's offensive injunction to domestic violence 'as a sharpe bit curbes a
froward horse, euen so a curst woman must be roughly used' is soon tempered by the
reminder that 'a man ought to be comforter of his wife, but then he ought not to be a
tormentor of her, for with what face can a man imbrace that body which his hands have
battered and bruised'. Satiric distance is more obviously interposed with an allusion to a
two-headed Cerberus and the assessment of Agamemnon's sacrifice of Iphigenia as a 'small
injury' to her mother Clytemnestra; Joseph Swetnam, *The Arraignment of Lewd, idle,
froward and unconstant women* (London, 1615), sig.A4r, Cv, F4v, H4r.

[25]   This is an argument advanced by Ann Rosalind Jones, 'From polemical prose to the Red
Bull: The Swetnam controversy in women voiced pamphlets and the public theater' in
Elizabeth Fowler and Roland Greene (eds.), *The Project of Prose in Early Modern Europe
and the New World* (Cambridge, 1997), pp. 122–37. Swetnam himself clearly anticipated
offering another sally in this pamphlet war when he compared his *Arraignment* with 'a
bulrush, in respect of a second booke, which is almost ready'. No such pamphlet appears to
have been published however; Swetnam, *The Arraignment*, sig. A4r.

[26]   The responses to Swetnam were Rachel Speght, *A Mouzell for Melastomus* (London,
1617); Ester Sowernam, *Ester hath hang'd Haman* (London, 1617) and Constantia Munda,
The Worming of a mad Dogge (London, 1617). The play, *Swetnam the Woman-hater
Arraigned by Women*, was performed at the Red Bull in the same year.

[27]   Swetnam, *The Arraignment*, sig. A2v.

of silence by demonstrating that her conviction results as much from her eloquent speech acts as her crimes.[28] However, Swetnam denies the women who refused to be subjected to or silenced by his antifeminism, the problematic heroism of Webster's Vittoria, because he styles the discursive exchange initiated by his pamphlet as a 'Bearbaiting of women'. The female pamphleteer who would not be silent is therefore less an author capable of writing acute, penetrating argument than an animal. Swetnam thus opens his pamphlet with the jocular prediction that he 'shall be bitten' rather than confuted by any number of women respondents.[29] In a moment that perhaps foretells the way in which male readers wrote about Katherine Chidley's revolutionary animadversions, women's pamphlet writings are sensed rather than read.

Faced with the assumptions governing this gendering of silence, David Brown was anxious to correct the error of what he perceived as a prominent minister's ill-advised strategy of giving an unquiet, disobedient woman silent treatment. Thus he opens his pamphlet with a deliberate attempt to coax words, printable text, or even the barest of signs from Sterry:

> I am therefore the more earnest to entreat you by these lines that you will be pleased to declare unto me, by your direct answer in writing, the true causes and reasons of your silence, which is usually taken for consent, seeing you only filled up the room of your Pulpit, much worse than any meer or bare cipher, which although of it self it signifieth no value of anything, yet it maketh the most of all the figures about it, to betoken a far greater value than they would without it whiles a signifying figure is not in place of it.[30]

As if anticipating Ferdinand de Saussure, Brown is sensitively aware that meaning is relational and habitual, that a signifier or 'signifying figure' only acquires 'value' through 'the figures about it'. A naked woman's words and deeds thus loom 'greater' alongside ministerial silence, whilst the 'bare cipher' of that silence 'usually' denotes 'consent' when placed in the context of transgressive signs and deeds. Luckily, Brown was not disappointed in his desire to change the meanings of the signifying practices surrounding the incident at Whitehall; Sterry was quick to provide him with the response he required:

> Sir,
> You charge me ... with being in the Pulpit and being silent there at the time, when a very great offence was committed in the Congregation. You all along take that for granted which is altogether a Mistake ... I appeal to those who hear me in publick, how farre in a constant course upon all occasion; how far after a more particular

---

[28] Vittoria herself recognizes this when she says 'What, is my just defence / By him that is my judge called impudence?'; John Webster, *The White Devil*, III ii, 126–7 in René Weiss (ed.), *The Duchess of Malfi and Other Plays* (Oxford, 1998).

[29] Swetnam, *The Arraignment*, sig. A2v, A4r.

[30] Ibid., pp. 1–2.

manner in the first sermon which I preached after that enormous Scandall, I have declared myself against the heynous evill of such Practises, and those corrupt Principles which lead to such Practises. I doe not therefore think it needfull for me to say more in a private Letter, seeing I say so much, so frequently in Publique.[31]

For Brown and Sterry alike, the 'enormous Scandall' of female misconduct can only emerge through a narrative comprised of 'Publique' male words. Whether that narrative is addressed to the members of Sterry's Whitehall congregation or to the less definable group of Brown's anonymized pamphlet readers, the implication seems to be that if neither of them fulfils a masculine duty to 'say so much' then the naked woman's agency remains a potent, disruptive force. Thus figured, male silence speaks of the possibilities of female subversion. However, as soon as men begin to speak, write and publish pamphlets the dangers of female agency are curtailed and the female voice that might declaim 'Resurrection, I am ready for thee' is muted. It is therefore telling that Brown's pamphlet text only begins to circulate once Sterry's (apparently private) epistolary discourse has been appended and publicized and the naked woman's alleged (and spectacularly public) prophetic discourse has been edited out.[32]

The Politics of Nudity

When Brown received Sterry's reply to his pamphlet, he published it declaring 'for my own part, as one honest man should trust another, I am sufficiently satisfied'.[33] Satisfaction comes with the homosocial relations that are forged when a woman's voice is silenced and public discourse (written and spoken) is left in the hands and mouths of men. By refusing to attend to the possibility that the naked woman might have spoken before the Whitehall congregation, Brown diverts his readers' attention towards the more strictly spectacular aspects of the woman's appearance:

> And for any thing I could ever hear (for I was never to see) the like shamelesse spectacle hath not been so publikely and impudently shewed nor acted in all the vile shews and whorish masks (where many thousands of pounds have been spent in one night) even to provoke God to wrath, and mankind to wickednesse ... not a little at Whitehall Palace before these Wars, even where this vile act came to passe, which would be a great shame to expresse.[34]

---

[31] Ibid., p. 16.
[32] The naked woman's alleged words are only reprinted in the sensational accounts of the newsbooks.
[33] Brown, *The Naked Woman*, p. 18.
[34] Ibid., p. 9.

Uninhibited by the fact that he 'was never [there] to see' the incident, Brown construes the naked woman's actions as a purely visual event.[35] In much the same way that Anna Trapnel's Whitehall protest was frequently re-scripted by newsmen and intelligence agents as a spectacularly theatrical act, Brown constructs the naked woman's work as a 'shamelesse spectacle' which might have taken place in a chapel but which could easily have been set in the more famous banqueting house at Whitehall, the setting for so many lavish state revels throughout the early modern period. Whilst his deployment of a stock Puritan anti-theatricality *topos* might, as Sterry's biographer maintains, be due to Sterry's renowned love of all arts (a position which the Puritan minister often had to defend), Brown's vision of a naked woman outmasquing the 'mask' allows him to equate a woman's agency in public with what many Puritans vilified as the worst excesses of royalist court culture.[36] What is striking about Brown's description of the naked woman's appearance as a 'shamelesse spectacle' whose 'wickednesse' exceeds that of the 'whorish mask', is both the way in which it consigns her action to a purely visual level and, like Gaywood's engraving of Trapnel (figure 1), the manner in which it resignifies and repoliticizes it. By stating that stripping during a church service and performing publicly in inordinately extravagant court masques are equivalent or proximate female vices, Brown is implicitly assigning the naked woman's deeds a crypto-royalist or anti-Puritan agenda. When queens masque and other women go naked, it is the duty of every God-fearing man to protest.[37]

This concern with the theatrical or public display of the female body is not, of course, an exclusively mid-seventeenth-century preoccupation. A particularly pertinent example, which relates back directly to the socio-political developments of the 1640s and 1650s, appeared in 1755 with the publication of a satirical, pseudonymous pamphlet that lamented the moral laxity of eighteenth-century London society. The author, Adam Eden, laments the fact that 'the Fair Sex have

---

[35] For an interesting interrogation of the ways in which positions of spectatorship, spectacle and performance ideologies intersect in the naked woman's Whitehall appearance see Wiseman, 'Margaret Cavendish among the prophets', pp. 102–4.

[36] Vivian de Sola Pinto, *Peter Sterry*, p. 27. For further biographical details see N. I. Matar, *Peter Sterry: Selected Writings* (New York, 1994); idem., '"Oyle of Joy": The Early Prose of Peter Sterry', *Philosophy Quarterly* 71:1 (1992), pp. 31–46; idem., 'Peter Sterry and the Ranters', *Notes and Queries* 29 227:6 (1982), pp. 504–6. It was famously, of course, the appearance of another theatrical woman (Henrietta Maria) in a masque at Whitehall some twenty years or so earlier which prompted the Puritan anti-theatricalist William Prynne to refer to all actresses as 'notorious whores'. For recent discussions of the masque in the early modern period see D. Bevington and P. Hobrook (eds.), *The Politics of the Stuart Court Masque* (Cambridge, 1998); David Lindley (ed.), *The Court Masque* (Manchester, 1984).

[37] Susan Wiseman is therefore surely correct to aver that Brown's protest is a result of the Puritan anxiety over a perceived increase in 'lascivious, unruly and theatrical behaviour under the new post-monarchical state'; Wiseman, 'Margaret Cavendish among the Prophets', p. 103.

laid aside rigid Notions of Modesty' to show 'snowy Bosom', 'well made Leg', 'beautiful thin Heel' and 'go stark naked' and deems this a specific attempt 'among the Ladies, to abolish modesty and chastity, and Restore the native simplicity of Going naked'.[38] Like David Brown, he believes that the practice has its origins in the middle decades of the seventeenth century. He confidently asserts that 'it began so long ago as the Reign of King Charles I.'[39] However, unlike Brown, who laid his charges of immorality at the door of royalist or anti-Puritan excess, Eden politicizes sartorial shamelessness in a strikingly different fashion. For him this 'State of Anarchy' has its origin in that 'Glorious ... Spirit of Liberty' which brought about 'the Beheading of our King'. Towards the end of the pamphlet, Eden goes on to lay bare both authorial intention and political allegiance:

> I hope to convince my Reader that ... while men were plotting to strip the Prerogative, their Wives and Daughters were contriving to *strip themselves*, and labour'd as much to Free themselves from the Incumbrances and Restraints imposed on them by the coy and modest Queen Elizabeth, as the Men did to remove the Ill-Conveniences they *thought* themselves subject to, from the Prerogative under King Charles I and if the Reformers in Politicks designed totally to abolish the Prerogative, our *Reformers* were contriving as utterly to get rid of all Dress.[40]

Monarchs' heads and women's clothes come off at the same time as divestiture and regicide become curiously indistinguishable, and equally horrific, spectacles. Though the coyness and modesty of a virgin queen who presented herself in later life bare-breasted at numerous public pageants may well be contestable, Eden's prizing of 'Restraint' in dress and political activity is unmistakable.[41] Furthermore, his masculinization of the realm of political action was an all too familiar strategy which, as we have seen, early modern women had long faced.

Eden's scotching of Brown's equation of female nudity and courtly excess is disarmingly similar to the manner in which the vast majority of seventeenth-century pamphleteers wrote about public nakedness. Despite David Brown's

---

[38]   Adam Eden (Esq.) *A Vindication of the Reformation on Foot, among the Ladies, To Abolish Modesty and Chastity, and Restore the Native Simplicity of going Naked. And An Attempt to reconcile all Opposers to it, And Make them join in a speedy Completion of this Glorious Design* (London, 1755), p. 9.

[39]   Ibid., p. 10.

[40]   Ibid., pp. 12–13.

[41]   Elizabeth is reported as wearing her necklines 'passing low' in her later years. In 1597, the ambassador extraordinary of the French King Henri IV recorded the queen's appearance in his journal. She was 'attired in a dress of silver cloth, white and crimson ... She kept the front of her dress open, and one could see the whole of her bossom, and passing low, and often she would open the front of this robe with her hands ... Her bosom is somewhat wrinkled ... but lower down her flesh is exceeding white and delicate'; quoted in Louis Montrose '"Shaping Fantasies": Configurations of Gender and Power in Elizabethan Culture', *Representations* 1:2 (1983), pp. 61–94; p. 62.

protestations to the contrary, by the early 1650s, the act of going naked in public had acquired radical (rather than anti-) Puritan connotations.[42] From the very start of the revolutionary decades conservative pamphleteers, worried by London's rapidly burgeoning sectarian population, had sought to caricature what they perceived to be the worst excesses of the proliferating radical Puritan congregations by creating a sect known as the Adamites. The Adamites first appeared in the pages of a number of pamphlets published in 1641, all of which claim to be the eye witness reports of orthodox, pious writers who have managed to infiltrate Adamite conventicles. All tell tales of piety gone awry, of the debauchery of shamelessly naked congregations who commune in both spirit and body, and are transported to heights of spiritual and sexual ecstasy. In an attempt to detail the full extent of sectarian depravity, many of the pamphlets were accompanied by graphic woodcuts which showed male and female Adamites at varying stages of sexual arousal. Thus the title page to the 1641 *A Nest of Serpents Discovered Or a Knot of Old Heretiques Revived, Called the Adamites* (see figure 10) foregrounds a naked Adamite woman whipping a male member of the congregation whilst declaiming 'Downe Lust' to his erect penis.[43] Even though the Adamites disappeared from print following the publication of Ephraim Pagitt's *Heresiography* in 1645, the relationship between radical Puritanism and public nakedness was indelibly marked. When the Ranters first took their notorious place in London's radical milieu in 1650, the pamphlet press abounded in tales and images of their blasphemy, licentiousness and public nudity.[44] Alongside lengthy discussions of the body of heterodox Ranter belief (hell as a figment of the

---

[42] On the political significance of nakedness in early modern England see David Cressy, *Agnes Bowker's Cat: Travesties and Transgressions in Tudor and Stuart England* (Oxford, 2000), pp. 251–80; Kristen Poole, *Radical Religion From Shakespeare to Milton* (Cambridge, 2000); pp. 147–81; Judy Kronenfeld, *King Lear and the Naked Truth: Rethinking the Language of Religion and Resistance* (Durham and London, 1998); Richard Bauman, *Let Your Words Be Few: Symbolism of Speaking and Silence Among Seventeenth-Century Quakers* (Cambridge, 1983), pp. 84–94; Kenneth Carroll, 'Early Quakers and "Going Naked as a Sign"', *Quaker History* 67 (1978), pp. 69–87; W. C. Braithwaite, *The Beginnings of Quakerism* (Cambridge, 1955), pp. 148–50, 192.

[43] David Cressy has recently speculated that this pamphlet 'contains perhaps the first depiction of an erect penis in English popular print'. Samoth Yarb's (or Thomas Bray's), *A New Sect of Religion Descryed* was published in the same year with a similar title page depicting a female Adamite looking on as a male Adamite strikes another co-celebrant's erect penis with a stick saying 'Downe Proud Flesh Downe'. See Cressy, *Agnes Bowker's Cat*, p. 261. For a reproduction of the Bray title page see Poole, *Radical Religion*, p. 153.

[44] I take as read that the Ranters *did* exist as a group of radical antinomians who congregated around the charismatic prophets Laurence Clarkson, Abiezer Coppe, Jacob Bauthumley and Joseph Salmon. On the Ranters see Clement Hawes, *Mania and Literary Style: The Rhetoric of Enthusiasm from the Ranters to Christopher Smart* (Cambridge, 1996); J. F. McGregor, Bernard Capp, Nigel Smith, B. J. Gibbons and J. C. Davis, 'Debate: Fear, Myth and Furore: Reappraising the Ranters', *Past and Present* 140 (1993), pp. 155–210; Christopher Hill, *A Nation of Change and Novelty: Radical Politics, Religion and*

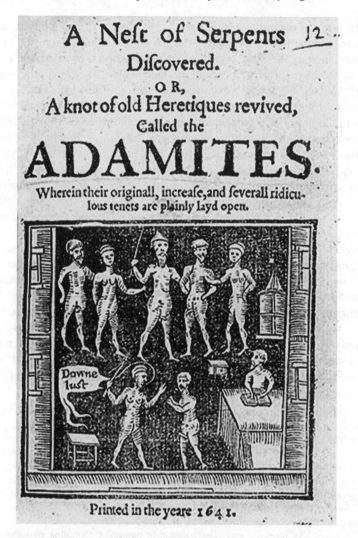

Figure 10: *A Nest of Serpents* (London, 1641), title page

Literature in Seventeenth-Century England (London, 1993), pp. 172–218; J. C. Davis, 'Fear, Myth and Furore: Reappraising the Ranters', *Past and Present* 129 (1990), pp. 79–103; J. F. McGregor and B. Reay (eds.), *Radical Religion in the English Revolution* (Oxford, 1986), pp. 121–40; J. C. Davis, *Fear Myth and History: The Ranters and the Historians* (Cambridge, 1986); Christopher Hill, *The World Turned Upside Down: Radical Ideas During the English Revolution* (Harmondsworth, 1984), pp. 184–258; Nigel Smith (ed.), *A Collection of Ranter Writings from the Seventeenth Century* (London, 1983). All are indebted to A. L. Morton's *The World of the Ranters: Radicalism in the English Revolution* (London, 1970).

The Ranters Religion.
※ OR,

A faithfull and infallible Narrative of their damnable and
diabolical opinions, with their deteſtable lives & actions.

With a true diſcovery of ſome of their late prodigious
pranks, and unparalleld deportments; with a paper of
moſt blaſphemous Verſes found in one of their pockets,
againſt the Majeſty of Almighty God, and the moſt ſa-
cred Scriptures, rendred *verbatim.*

Publiſhed by Authority.

Behold theſe
are Ranters.

London, Printed for *R. H.* 1650.

Figure 11: *The Ranters Religion* (1650), title pageThe link between nakedness and radical Puritanism was remembered throughout the revolutionary decades.

imagination, God as the author of all sin, the elect's freedom from sin), the pamphlets also lingered over innumerable naked or semi-naked Ranter bodies. *The Ranters Recantation* (1650) describes a Ranter congregation in typical terms:

> On Tuesday last being the 17th of this instant December, a great company of Ranters had a meeting neer the Horns in White-Chappel, where they began to put in practice several Christmas Gambols, and amongst the rest, one Mrs Hull led them a dance ... And calling to one of her fellow creatures to sit on her knee, she bid him take up her coats and smock, which he did ... and so in the presence of about 60 persons, [they] entered into venial exercise.[45]

The Ranter pamphlets continually paraded such venial exercises before a paying audience by carefully exploiting the titillative equation of radical religion and public nudity set up by the Adamite literature of the early 1640s. Thus, when another Ranter pamphlet, *The Ranters Religion*, appeared in 1650 it was sold bearing a barely modified version of the title page woodcut from *The Nest of Serpents* (see figure 11). Whereas the earlier female Adamite had whipped up sexual and textual interest declaiming 'Downe lust', some nine years later she has been transformed into a speechless Ranter flagellant, with the text instead endeavouring to prick the conscience of its readers by adding the voyeuristic admonition 'Behold these are Ranters'. David Cressy is thus surely correct to infer that throughout this period Adamites and Ranters were in fact 'iconographically ... interchangeable'.[46]

However, at the time when the naked woman was making her appearance in Whitehall in 1652, the relationship between radical religion and public nudity was being freshly intensified. As the Quakers began exploring and communicating the mysteries of the revealed Word, a number of prominent Friends sought to issue their testimony of the light of Christ in more extreme and radical ways. In 1652, some Quakers therefore followed the biblical example of Isaiah and started to strip off their clothes in public in order to go 'naked as a sign'.[47] The act itself could signify in a number of different and complicated ways. It could, for example, refer to the union of body and spirit in the godly; it could act as a metaphorical vehicle expressive of the glory of the Word made flesh; otherwise, it could operate as a

---

[45] *The Ranters Recantation: And their Sermon Delivered at a Meeting on Tuesday last, in White-Chappel, being the 17 of this instant December* (London, 1650), p. 1.

[46] Cressy, *Agnes Bowker's Cat*, p. 272. Similarly, as Kristen Poole has demonstrated 'in the 1650s many of the attributes of the Adamites were shifted onto accounts of the Ranters. The full title of *Bloudy News from the North* refers to "the Ranting Adamites" and tells of their resolution to "murther all those that will not turn Ranters"'; *Radical Religion*, p. 155.

[47] The biblical precedent of Isaiah going 'naked and barefoot three yeares, as a sign and wonder upon Egypt and Ethiopia' [Isaiah 20] was one on which the Quakers frequently drew. See Thomas Ellwood, *The History of the life of Thomas Ellwood, Written by his own hand* (London, 1906), p. 38; Solomon Eccles, *Signes are from the Lord to a People or Nation to Forewarn them of some Eminent Judgment near at hand* (London, 1663), no sig.

trenchant reminder to the ungodly of the naked truth of their need for Christ, of their need to be stripped of the corrupt trappings of the world of the flesh.[48] Whatever the case, the action always bore with it a weight of historically and geographically specific politico-religious import. Thus, when William Simpson left Lancashire for Oxford in the early 1650s, he passed through the streets 'naked and in sackcloth in the days of Oliver and his Parliament, as a sign to them and the priests showing how God would strip them of their power, and that they should be as naked as he was, and should be stripped of their benefices'.[49] Quaker women also engaged in such radically politicized nakedness in the early 1650s. In Oxford, for instance:

> Elizabeth ffletcher [sic] was a very modest, grave young woman, yet Contrary to her own will or inclination, in obedience to ye Lord, [she] went naked through ye Streets of that Citty, as a signe against that Hippocreticall profession they then made there, being then Presbeterians & Independents, w[hi]ch profession she told them the Lord would strip them of, so that theire Nakedness should Appear, w[hi]ch shortly after, at ye Return of King Charles ye 2d, was fulfilled upon them, they being turned out or made Hippocretically to Conforme.[50]

Radical nudity was therefore carefully tailored to suit the politico-religious exigencies of a given situation and, as deliberately dissident political expression, the authorities were not slow to respond. The magistrates at Oxford ordered Elizabeth Fletcher to be 'severaly whip[p]ed' following her appearance; the ordeal left her so 'weake and bruised' that she died from her injuries in 1658. More famously, Solomon Eccles began appearing naked throughout London in the late 1650s and early 1660s.[51] When he stripped as a sign against the dissolute ways of the ungodly, he was so savagely beaten that he 'had much a-doe to come off with [his] Life', as was Richard Simpson, whose public nakedness resulted in his 'being often Cruelly beaten and Sorely Bruised at Severall Places'.[52] The political implications of radical nudism also provoked a heavy-handed response by administrations on the other side of the Atlantic. When Lydia Wardel went naked as a sign in Newbury, Massachusetts the local authorities:

> Soon laid Hands on her, and to the next Court at Ipswich had her; where, without law, they condemned her to be tyed to the fence-Post of the Tavern where they sat,

---

[48] The best general discussions of this particular Quaker practice are to be found in Bauman, *Let Your Words be Few*, pp. 84–94; Carroll, 'Early Quakers'; Braithwaite, *Beginnings*, pp. 148–50.
[49] Cited in Norman Penney (ed.), *The First Publishers of Truth* (London, 1907), p. 365.
[50] Ibid., p. 259.
[51] Pepys mentions his 'extraordinary' activities in his diary. See Robert Latham and William Matthews (eds.), *The Diary of Samuel Pepys*, 11 vols (London, 1974), vol. 8, p. 360.
[52] Eccles, *Signes are from the Lord*, no sig.; Penney, *The First Publishers of Truth*, p. 308.

which is usually their Court-place ... whereunto she was tyed, stripp'd from the Waste upwards, with her naked Breasts to the Splinters of the Post, and there sorely lashed, with twenty or thirty cruel Stripes; which tho' [sic] it miserably tore and bruised her tender Body, yet, to the Joy of her Husband and Friends that were Spectators, she was carried through all these inhuman Cruelties ... This is the Discipline of the Church of Newbury in New England.[53]

The radical energy of public nakedness, coupled with the spectacular 'Discipline' it provokes, must surely come as a surprise to anyone who first encounters the practice as mediated by David Brown's 1652 pamphlet about the incident in Whitehall. Neither there nor in the newsbook reports that followed that week do we get any real and sustained sense that this solitary woman's act might have a coherently organized politico-religious motivation or that it might belong to a body of contemporary popular dissent.[54] At best, her stance is projected to silhouette the masquing women of Stuart court culture rather than those shadowy figures who skirted London's radical milieu as Ranters, Quakers or Adamites. At worst, Brown, Sterry and the newsbook writers collude in rendering her protest as lunacy or infernal possession: the naked woman is either 'a mad-woman onely' or one who works 'by the means of Sathan'.[55]

Re-Writing Protest: The Naked Woman as *The Naked Woman*

It is possible to read past the allegations of lunacy, monarchism and infernal possession to recover a sharper sense of the naked woman's agency in Whitehall. As with the work of every other woman in this study, this necessitates a carefully sustained analysis of women's textual traces, a repositioning of their work to the interpretive centre rather than a contextual periphery where it must ever operate as a marginal gloss upon male-authored texts and actions. Importantly, this re-siting does not entail the creation of a room which female pamphleteers of the early modern period might properly call their own, a separate, homosocial discursive environment annexed to a hall of women's authorial fame. Instead it involves a recognition that the praxis undertaken by some seventeenth-century women emerged through productive dialogue with the (frequently hostile) texts and actions

---

[53] George Bishop, *New-England Judged, By the Spirit of the Lord* (London, 1703), 3rd edn.

[54] Brown does actually on one occasion refer to 'a diabolical sect' but he clouds the issue when he reprimands Sterry for doing little to prevent this 'absurd act' by an orthodox 'member of your own Church'; Brown, *The Naked Woman*, pp. 7, 9.

[55] Brown, *The Naked Woman*, pp. 9, 16. Such quotations lead me to believe that Achinstein overstates the case in her otherwise superb assessment of the incident: 'For Brown, the woman was not mad; rather she was making a sincere and coherent gesture of protest. David Brown wanted the minister to be sure to address this woman as a self-motivated agent, in control of her actions, not mad.'; 'Women on Top', p. 150.

of their male contemporaries. We have already seen how Katherine Chidley wrote against religious intolerance in the 1640s: she did so not with a wink and a glance to the sufferings and texts of any number of medieval anchoresses, fifteenth-century prophetesses or sixteenth-century female controversialists, than an ear and an eye to the all-male pamphlet war provoked by the recent publication of Thomas Edwards's anti-tolerationist tracts. Similarly, the radicalism of the naked woman's actions in Whitehall in 1652 can only be ascertained by viewing those acts in central dialogic interaction with a number of other female and male cultural interventions throughout this period. Thus, when viewed alongside the politicized public nudity of those numerous Quaker women and men who began taking their clothes off in 1652 (and who were so spectacularly punished for it in the following years), her actions seem to stem more from an awareness of contemporary popular protest than from the apparently motiveless outpourings of insanity or the hidden forces of satanic association. This sense that her appearance is part of a specific politico-religious agenda is heightened if one considers the party to whom her performance is addressed, rather than simply dwelling on the fact of her naked body in isolation. Her imputed words, 'Resurrection I am ready for thee', are not only an (admittedly oblique) dialogue with a public sermon on the subject of the Resurrection, but are also specifically placed to interrupt the discourse of Cromwell's chaplain in particular. As one of the most eminent Puritan ministers of the Commonwealth and a renowned tolerationist, Peter Sterry was centrally concerned with the rapid growth of radical sectarianism in London throughout the 1640s and 1650s.[56] More specifically, Sterry was preoccupied with the rise of the Ranters in the capital's radical milieu and he published the earliest extant public refutation of (broadly) Ranter principles in 1649.[57] Such principles continued to concern Sterry until the end of his life, so much so that in a posthumously published pamphlet he worried that his protracted engagement with these issues might have lead his readers to think that he himself adhered to the Ranters' 'licentious principles'.[58] On one occasion in the late 1640s, the Ranter Laurence Clarkson claimed to have preached 'at Bow in Mr Sterry's place'. As a result, Christopher Hill has maintained that throughout his controversial life Sterry, like another Independent divine William Erbury, came under increasing pressure to dissociate himself from the Ranter movement.[59] Whether or not this was the case, the fact that Ranter doctrine and Cromwell's chaplain were never far apart at least points to the possibility that the naked woman's appearance in the chapel at Whitehall was more calculated than either Sterry or Brown allowed. For in a symbolic economy where public nakedness was equated with the radical activities

[56] For Sterry's tolerationism see De Sola Pinto, *Peter Sterry*, pp. 19–20.
[57] See Peter Sterry, *The Commings Forth of Christ* (London, 1649); N. I. Matar, 'Peter Sterry and the Ranters', p. 504.
[58] See Peter Sterry, *A Discourse of the Freedom of the Will* (London, 1675), pp. 155–6.
[59] Christopher Hill, *Milton and the English Revolution* (London, 1977), pp. 301, 315.

of interchangeable Ranters and Adamites, confronting a minister concerned with the relationship between himself and the Ranters with the starkest, most familiar image of Ranterism bespeaks the reasoned agency of an activist rather than the ravings of a lunatic or the devil.

If we shift our attention from the cultural significance of male anxiety and place the naked woman's agency at the interpretive centre of this incident, a very different picture begins to emerge. This is because taking one's clothes off in public in early modern England was not necessarily regarded as a 'shamelesse' or exhibitionist assertion of self-hood. In fact stripping could, in a Renaissance context, also betoken a form of self-abnegation. Thus, Ann Rosalind Jones and Peter Stallybrass, in their landmark study of clothing in Renaissance culture, remind us that:

> To understand the significance of clothes in the Renaissance, we need to undo our own social categories, in which subjects are prior to objects, wearers to what is worn. We need to understand the animatedness of clothes, their ability to 'pick up' subjects, to mold and shape them both physically and socially, to constitute subjects through their power as material memories. Memories of subordination (of the livery servant to the household to which she belongs); memories of collegiality (of the member of a livery company with his or her guild); memories of love (of the lover for the beloved from whom he or she receives a garment or a ring); memories of identity itself.[60]

If clothing thus made both the woman and the man, situated them as subjects within a history and a finely woven social fabric, then what did it mean to go unclothed? Did it indicate a rejection of the past and the traces or threads of time? Did it merely place you at the bottom of a series of material social relations, as King Lear clearly felt in his naked affinity with the dispossessed on the heath? Or did it (more disturbingly) place you beyond the scope of material culture's identity-shaping force?[61] If clothes were, as Jones and Stallybrass suggest, material mnemonics of social relations, then surely to go without them represented less lunacy or devilish impudence than a radical suppression of memory, a spectacular instance of forgetting one's place or indeed a wholesale disregard of notions of place, degree and difference.[62] This need not seem far-fetched in a seventeenth-

---

[60] Ann Rosalind Jones and Peter Stallybrass, *Renaissance Clothing and the Materials of Memory* (Cambridge, 2000), pp. 2–3.

[61] For Lear's naked ´egalitarianism on the heath see William Shakepeare, *King Lear* (London and New York, 1989), III iv, ll. 26–36.

[62] For the Puritan Arthur Dent (amongst many others), clothing was the surest index of social identity. Constant innovations in fashion however made things less certain. 'All is out of joint' he lamented, as 'nowadays few will keep within compass, few will know their places; but the most part run beyond their bounds, and quite leap out of their sockets ... For now we cannot, by their apparel, discern the maid from the mistress, nor the waiting woman

century radical culture where Quakers, in their famed refusal of hat honour, were just one sect manipulating the materiality of social relations for egalitarian ends.[63] Yet the radicalism of a woman who went naked in public is surely more striking than this since women's bodies have always been more significantly marked than men's by the clothes they wear – more rigorously policed by the sartorial codes of patriarchal cultures. The naked woman who refuses to be constituted by patriarchal dress codes (of class, age or marital status) and who accordingly escapes codifying punishment, is a disturbingly radical agent indeed.

However, were one to interrogate the significance of the naked woman's agency through the male-authored pamphlet literature immediately surrounding the incident, as we have seen, an altogether different narrative would come into focus. There she is repeatedly stripped of sane political and religious motivation. The most extensive printed response to Brown's and Sterry's account of what happened at Whitehall appeared nearly three weeks after the controversy had subsided and is, I would argue, representative of the way in which much of the male-authored pamphlet literature of the period engages with female agency. Samuel Chidley, son of Katherine Chidley, penned a pamphlet entitled *Cloathing for the Naked Woman* as a 'Correction of Mr David Brown His errors [and] frivolous discourses'.[64] Eminently placed in both the Leveller movement and the radical sectarian culture of 1650s London, Chidley was (like his mother) well versed in the tactics of popular dissent; with the benefit of this and three weeks' worth of reflective distance, he refrained from co-opting the naked woman's actions to a lunatic's or devil's agenda. For Chidley, her appearance obviously came straight from 'The Dunghill of the Ranters ... those wretched, miserable, poore, blind, *naked*, deluded and bewitched people who are conceited of the Raritie of their Ranting fooleries'.[65] However, instead of proceeding to inveigh against the woman for her lack of modesty, or interrogate the radical significance of her actions within London's radical subculture, Chidley rounds on David Brown claiming that he:

[sh]ould have taken a better course, and instead of sounding a Trumpet about her, have been so modest as to turne away the peoples eyes from beholding vanity, and

---

from her lady'; Arthur Dent, *The Plaine Man's Path-way to Heaven*, 2nd edn (London, 1640), pp. 54–5.

[63] A useful way of distinguishing the radicalism of going naked in public might be glimpsed by contrasting it with the social conservativism of revenge tragedy's revenger who, desperate to restitute an order in which dead relatives and old social formations are remembered, is prompted to vengeful murder by acquiring surplus clothing in the form of scarves, torn garments and other mementoes. The best work on the memorialism of revenge tragedy can be found in Michael Neill, *Issues of Death: Mortality and Identity in the English Renaissance* (Oxford, 1997), pp. 243–61.

[64] Samuel Chidley, *Cloathing for the Naked Woman, Or the second part of the Dissembling Scot, Set Forth in his Colours* (London, 1652), title page, p. 3.

[65] Ibid., p. 3; emphasis added.

much more should he have sought to take away that false principle, upon which the Ranters build their carnall exercises.[66]

Whereas we saw a desire on Brown's part *not* to attend to the real presence of the naked woman's body (he preferred to counsel Peter Sterry on the evils of male silence), Chidley hears an obsessive concern with her body, 'a Trumpet about her' and her 'carnall exercises'. The above-quoted phrase, along with the title, is the only one in the entire course of his densely printed eleven-page pamphlet that he mentions the naked woman at all and, as such, he is even more successful than either Sterry or Brown in drawing attention away from her protest. Instead, Chidley spends the bulk of his pamphlet in a doctrinal meditation, a thorough confutation of a large number of the 'false principles' of Ranter theology. The effect of this is that doctrinal debate and male pamphleteering are foregrounded whilst the naked woman disappears, or is, in Chidley's words, 'cloath[ed]'. Throughout his pamphlet, Chidley draws attention to the fact that his words are little more than a textual engagement with the agency of other men, rather than (as his title appears to suggest) a reflection upon a naked woman's radical actions. He therefore signposts the argument of the second half of his pamphlet by informing his readers:

> Thus having written somewhat to convince the sect of Libertines of their abominable sinnes, and to deterre them there from I shall proceed to answer *DB* in those matters concerning my selfe wherein I referre him and the Reader, first of all to the book which I set forth in vindication of Lieutenant Col Lilburne and Mr MUSGRAVE, and others from David Brownes false aspersions.[67]

In enjoining his readers and David Brown to look away from the naked woman, to ignore her action and deny the possibility of female agency, Chidley demands that they look to his own theological excursus and supplementary texts. He asks them to avert their gaze from the radically destabilizing potential of a naked woman's body and direct their attention to the respectable rhetorical and material 'cloath[ing]' of his pamphlet. Thus patriarchal social relations (in which men are the only politico-religious agents and women remain silent, appropriately attired and marginalized) are restituted through the analogous material practices of dressing up an argument and covering up a body.

As Samuel Chidley's and David Brown's pamphlets emerge, the naked woman's body-'signe'-text, the traces of her agency, disappear. When this occurs

---

[66]   Ibid.

[67]   Ibid., p. 6. The pamphlet Chidley is advertising here is his recently published *The Dissembling Scot Set forth in his Coulours or A Vindication of Lieu Col John Lilburne and Others. From those Aspersions cast upon them by David Brown in his idle pamphlet directed to the Supream Authority of England the Parliament Assembled, and presented to curry favour with them* (London, 1652).

she is transformed from a radically naked woman to a male-authored text; the naked woman becomes *The Naked Woman* and female agency becomes a male speech act. We have already seen, though, that some interventions by women in the period were much more difficult for male writers to ignore or appropriate. Anna Trapnel's performances, for instance, close to the centre of power at Whitehall, drew large crowds from London and beyond. However, for every Anna Trapnel there were many more women, women who protested without clothes, women like Katherine Chidley, Elizabeth Poole and Elizabeth Alkin, for whom agency (and the recognition of that agency by their male contemporaries) was much more problematic. Chidley's pamphlets were anonymized and euphemized as spit; Poole disappeared from the official record the moment she drifted off the regicidal message preferred by the General Council of the Army; Alkin was given a denigratory alias which stuck precisely because it converted her engagement with the murky worlds of espionage and newsbook production into the dirty work of a domestic drudge. In the next chapter we shall scrutinize another example, both prosaic and moving, of how a group of seven thousand women tried to resist such hostile treatment through the medium of cheaply printed text.

Chapter 5

Gender Identities and Women's Agency in Early Modern Tithe Dispute

Two chapters back we traced one woman's involvement in the material culture of collective newsgathering. The image of Elizabeth Alkin as one of the foremost 'she-Intelligencers' of her generation, as a silent, active presence rather than unacknowledged absence, only emerged through reading apparently unspectacular public journalism alongside more spectacularly assertive private manuscript petitions for payment and relief. The telling irony is that these latter petitions, which also show Alkin at her most forthright, have necessarily remained her most secret and private; she has all too frequently been effaced from the historical record either by a need to keep the business and payment of espionage quiet or by the marginalization of her petitionary texts through their miscataloging in the State Papers. Yet, as David Zaret has recently demonstrated, a large number of mid-seventeenth-century writers contrived to circumvent the perils and silences of state secrecy by uniting the hierarchical, deferential world of the petition with the more democratic and, what we have seen to be, more associative realm of print.[1] Printed petitions appeared for the first time during the revolutionary decades and were, like the newsbooks which developed alongside them, instrumental in defining 'the early democratic public sphere [in] that they were the principal means by which readers and subscribers participated in public debates, whose aim was to lobby elites on behalf of a legislative agenda'.[2] The following chapter is an attempt to analyse some of the ways in which groups of women engaged in this particular variety of public sphere activity. It will show how in a discursive arena that is apparently predicated upon principles of democratization and inclusivity (namely in petitions and pamphlets disputing the right of the clergy to enforce tithe payment from the general population), an attempt was once again made by male writers to exclude women from the deliberative process. I will go on to contend that in order to participate in that process, groups of Quaker women exploited the material culture and associative nature of the printed petition to their utmost in a manner absolutely distinct from any other writers in this forum.

In order to undertake any genuine assessment of the status and potential for women's agency in the revolutionary period, simple statistics demand that Quaker

---

[1]   Zaret, *Origins of Democratic Culture*, pp. 217–65.
[2]   Ibid., p. 217.

women writers come within the purview of this study. So numerous are they that the compilers of a recent biographical dictionary of women writers in early modern England, devoted over one third of their entries to Quaker women.[3] Unsurprisingly, therefore, in recent years there has been a corresponding welter of secondary material by feminist historians and literary critics whose task has been the recovery, republication and reassessment of this overlooked and under-used cultural material.[4] It is my intention here to attend to the material culture surrounding the proliferation of Quaker women's writing. Few issues contributed more to that culture in the 1650s than that of tithes. As a method of taxation imposed to support the national church and clergy, tithes consisted of one tenth of the annual produce of land or labour levied against every household in a given parish.[5] They were an extremely durable and long-standing form of ministerial

---

[3]   M. Bell, et al., *A Biographical Dictionary of Women Writers, 1500–1800* (London, 1993), pp. 257, 295. Their inclusion of more than 200 Quaker women is, by their own admission, conservative. The reasons for this preponderance are complex. Key factors include: the movement's early acceptance of women's prophecy; the fundamental importance of print culture to the evangelical force and defence mechanisms of Quakerism; (not least) the meticulous archival skills of Friends in preserving their historical documents. See M. Bell, 'Mary Westwood, Quaker publisher', *Publishing History* 23 (1988), pp. 5–66; T. P. O'Malley, 'The press and Quakerism 1653–1659', *Journal of the Friends Historical Society* 54 (1979), pp. 169–84.

[4]   Catie Gill, 'Identities in Quaker Women's Writing', *Women's Writing* 9:2 (2002), pp. 267–84; Susan Wiseman, 'Read Within: Gender, Cultural Difference and Quaker Women's Travel Narratives', in Kate Chedgzoy, Melanie Hansen and Susan Trill (eds.), *Voicing Women: Gender and Sexuality in Early Modern Writing* (Edinburgh, 1998), pp. 153–71; Hinds, *Gods Englishwomen;* Elaine Hobby, 'Handmaids of the Lord and Mothers of Israel'; N. T. Burns, 'From Seeker to Finder: The Singular Experiences of Mary Pennington' in Corns and Loewenstein, *Emergence of Quaker Writing*, pp. 70–87; Catherine M. Wilcox, *Theology and Women's Ministry in Seventeenth-Century English Quakerism* (Lampeter, 1995); Bonnelyn Young Kunze, *Margaret Fell and the Rise of Quakerism* (London, 1994); Mack, *Visionary Women*; Elaine Hobby, 'O Oxford Thou Art Full of Filfth: The Prophetical Writings of Hester Biddle, 1629[?]–1696' in Susan Sellers (ed.), *Feminist Criticism Theory and Practice* (London and New York, 1991), pp. 157–70; Christine Trevett, *Women and Quakerism in the Seventeenth Century* (York, 1991); Hobby, *Virtue of Necessity*; E. Potts Brown and S. Mosher Stuard (eds.), *Witnesses for Change: Quaker Women Over Three Centuries* (New Brunswick and London, 1989); Moira Ferguson (ed.), *First Feminists: British Women Writers 1578–1799* (Bloomington, 1985); Beatrice Carré, 'Early Quaker Women in Lancaster and Lancashire in Michael Mullet (ed.), *Early Lancaster Friends* (Leeds, 1978), pp. 43–53. All are indebted to Mabel Brailsford, *Quaker Women, 1650–1760* (London, 1915).

[5]   For a broader discussion of the status of tithes in the early modern period see Laura Brace, *The Idea of Property in Seventeenth-Century England: Tithes and the Individual* (Manchester and New York, 1998); Edith Bershadsky, 'Politics, Erudition and Ecclesiology: John Selden's *Historie of Tithes*' (unpublished Ph.D. thesis, John Hopkins University, 1994); idem., 'Controlling the terms of the debate: John Selden and the Tithes Controversy', in G. J. Schochet, P. E. Tatspaugh and C. Brobeck (eds.), *Law, Literature and the Settlement of Regimes* (Washington, DC, 1990), pp. 187–220; Barry Reay, 'Quaker Opposition to Tithes 1652–1660', *Past & Present* 83 (1980), pp. 98–120; Christopher Hill,

maintenance whose roots in England ran from the pre-Reformation Catholic priesthood and continued until 1836 when they were commuted into a rent charge dependent on the price of grain.[6] Their defence in the early modern period rested precisely upon this longevity which was seen by many as a clear indication of their status as a ministerial divine right. William Prynne, for instance, chose to deploy Old Testament scriptural arguments in order to buttress this view of the English tithe-paying tradition and defend:

> the practice, wisedome and piety of Abraham, the Father of the Faithfull, and all the people of God in the Old Testament, before and under the Law, and of most Christian States and Churches under the Gospel in paying, prescribing Tithes, as the most equal, rational, just, convenient maintenance for the Priests and Ministers of God and all others; but likewise ... the wisdom, prudence, providence of God, who is Wisdom itself, and God only wise, whose very Folly is wiser than men, in instituting such a constant settled maintenance for them in his Word, as the best, fittest of all others.[7]

Prynne envisages the entire Judaeo-Christian tradition as a line of diligent tithe-payers whose method of payment is revealed as the primary signifier of ministerial faith, congregational piety and Godly wisdom. Similarly, Immanuel Bourne confirms the Presbyterian perspective and declares the content of his pro-tithe treatise to be that:

> Tythes are proved to be gods Reserved part, and due to the Ministers of the Gospel by Divine right; and the unsettling of this antient Right may prove (I fear) the removing of a house built upon a Rock, and setting it upon the Sand, or a sandy Foundation, which may prove the ruine of the House, and of those that inhabit it.[8]

Where Bourne contends that the erosion of the bedrock of ministers' paid maintenance is an infringement on 'Divine right', others saw the corrosive process operating throughout the secular realm as symptomatic of the breakdown of the very fabric of early capitalist society. In a world where God's will as revealed through the tithe system was apparently challenged, it was no leap of faith to perceive that rents, wages, taxes and property itself could also be under attack. Samuel Clarke saw taints of the extreme Levellerism of the Diggers in the mass of

---

Economic Problems of the Church: From Archbishop Whitgift To the Long Parliament (Oxford, 1956), pp. 77–167; Margaret James, 'The Political Importance of the Tithes Controversy in the English Revolution', *History* 26 (1941), pp. 1–18; W. Easterby, *The History of the Law of Tithes in England* (Cambridge, 1888).

[6] This rent charge was only abolished in 1936. See Bershadsky, 'Controlling the Terms', pp. 188–9; Brace, *The Idea of Property*, pp. 15–16.

[7] William Prynne, *Ten Considerable Quaeries Concerning Tithes, The Present Petitioners and Petitions for their total abolition, as Antichristian, Jewish, burdensome, oppressive to the godly, conscientious People of the Nations* (London, 1659), p. 4.

[8] Immanuel Bourne, *A Defence and Justification of Ministers Maintenance By Tythes* (London, 1659), sig. A4r.

anti-tithe protest and asked 'Whether would not these Petitioners (if Tithes were removed) cry out and complain as much of the tyrannicall oppression and burden of Rents as the Anabaptists in Germany did, and so never be quiet till they have levelled all things?'[9] The staunchly royalist Peter Heylyn saw these attacks on property as emanating from an altogether more sinister quarter; he averred that tithe-abolition was merely 'private plunder' orchestrated on a nationwide scale by 'Satan, the prince of darkness'.[10]

Whatever its form or ultimate origin, there is no doubt that the socio-religious decay perceived in tithe dispute was indeed well under way before the Restoration. Throughout the 1640s and 1650s tithes were being hotly disputed and frequently unpaid by various sections of society for numerous complex reasons. It is beyond the scope of this chapter to plot the intricacies of anti-tithe argument and consider the failure of early modern English state apparatus to implement the tithe system fully. Commentators have generally agreed, however, that the implementation and consolidation of ambiguous legislation following the Tithe Act of 1549 had not only failed to secure the church the revenue it needed but had correspondingly (and paradoxically) made the recovery of tithes more difficult.[11] Similarly, even when non-payment was proved and prosecuted, there still remained, in legal theory at least, the potential for a protracted legal wrangle over the jurisdiction of the various civil and ecclesiastical courts in tithe disputes.[12] That this remained largely inconclusive throughout the period served only to contribute more material to the barrage of anti-tithe argument and further weaken the authority with which tithes were demanded.

Nonetheless, the inefficacy of legislative power was not what generally impelled the majority of Quakers into print. Instead eminent and less well known Quakers from all around the country wrote pamphlets which contended against tithes on a basic doctrinal level.[13] For a movement whose origins are inextricably

---

[9] Samuel Clarke, *A Caution Against Sacriledge: Or Sundrie Queries Concerning Tithes* (London, 1659), p. 6. For the argument that the abolition of tithes was merely Levellerism in a different guise see Richard Culmer, *The Ministers Hue and Cry* (London, 1651), p. 6.

[10] Philip Treileinie (pseud.), *The Undeceiving of the People in the point of Tythes* (London, 1651), no sig.

[11] Hill, *Economic Problems*, p. 84; Bershadsky, 'Controlling the Terms', p. 191; Brace, *Idea of Property*, p. 20.

[12] The criminal and corrective jurisdictions of the church courts were, however, abolished during the Interregnum. On the extremely complicated issue of jurisdiction over tithes in the early modern period see Bershadsky, pp. 192–7; Craig W. Horle, *The Quakers and the English Legal System* (Philadelphia, 1988), pp. 26–38; Alfred W. Braithwaite, 'Early Tithe Prosecutions: Friends as Outlaws', *Journal of the Friends Historical Society* 49 (1959/1961), pp. 148–56.

[13] There are two main exceptions here. One is Anthony Pearson, Sir Arthur Haselrig's secretary, whose *The Great Case of Tythes Truly Stated* (London, 1659) contains extended sections of legal analysis. More developed interrogation of the jurisdiction of civil courts to try tithe cases can be found in John Crook, *Tythes No Property* (London, 1659). See also

linked to the rise of sectarianism at a time when the powers and wealth of a national church were in gradual decline, the idea of forced maintenance of a paid ministry was obviously anathema to the Quakers. The Quaker JP John Crook was far from unusual when he asserted that tithes were 'no property to nor lawful maintenance for a Gospel, powerful, preaching Ministry' and fellow Friend, John Osborne, was merely making the commonest of Quaker scriptural arguments when he did 'not finde any Warrant in the Word of God, to uphold Ministers Maintenance by Tythes'.[14] Gervase Benson agreed; he maintained with admirable clarity that 'Tyths were a Command and Ordinance of God, and the first Priesthood had a command to take Tyths of the People according to the Law ... But the first Priesthood being changed ... and the Commandments being disanulled which the first Priesthood had to take Tyths, ... Tyths must of necessity be taken away'.[15] Such positions were held by Quakers of all classes across the country throughout the period and seem to support Barry Reay's observation that 'in the 1650s abolition of tithes seemed to become a *raison d'être* of the Quaker movement'.[16]

Tithe Dispute, Masculinity and 'the unwearied pain of Gathering'

However, if tithe opposition was indeed a Quaker's *raison d'être* by the 1650s, then Quaker women must have had altogether different senses of selfhood from their male contemporaries. This is because those Quaker women who were so voluble on so many other subjects (such as the nature and extent of female ministry, the relief of the poor, the workings of God through the spirit) are scarcely heard at all in this context. When Mary Braidley reminded her readers that 'the gospel of Jesus Christ is free to all without money' and declaimed 'woe unto the hireling', she did so in a pamphlet that was aimed primarily at discrediting two local clerics rather than debating the institution of tithes *per se*. Similarly, Grace Barwick instructs her readers to 'remove the wedge of gold out of your camp even Tithes, for it brings the curse upon you' but passes up the opportunity to discuss the imposition of tithes in favour of prophesying that John Lambert's army regiment would be the true agents for godly reform of the military in 1659.[17] Such

---

Robert Winter, *The Plea and Protest of Robert Winter of Elmston in the County of Kent, for his Non Payment of Tithes* (London, 1656).

[14] Crook, *Tythes No Property*, p. 1; John Osborne, *An Indictment Against Tythes: Or Tythes No Wages for Gospel-Ministers* (London, 1659), sig. A2v.

[15] Gervase Benson, *The Cry of the Oppressed from Under Their Oppressions* (London, 1656), sig. A3v.

[16] Reay, 'Quaker Opposition to Tithes', p. 105. Reay actually posits early tithe resistance in the parish of Burnham as a statistical correlate to later Quaker membership.

[17] Christopher Taylor, *Certain Papers Which is the Word of the Lord as was moved from the Lord by his servants to several places, and persons* (London, 1654), pp. 5–6; Grace

examples are indicative of the way in which Quaker women only ever write about tithes in the context of something else and suggest that tithe debate was, for these women, rarely a discursive end in itself.[18] The causes and effects of this curious disparity are best examined through an exploration of the gendered nature of the pamphlet debates surrounding tithes and by placing the status of women within seventeenth-century tithe debate in relief against their status as seventeenth-century tithe payers. Only then will the material interventions of those Quaker women who did manage to navigate the specific prohibitions placed on them in the public arena, most notably when seven thousand of them co-authored and counter-signed a series of anti-tithe petitions presented to the restored Rump parliament in 1659, emerge as critical moments in the history of early modern women's writing.

There can be no doubt, however, that contemporaries viewed the seventeenth-century tithe debate as a peculiarly male discursive practice. The pamphlets themselves betray a near obsessive concern with finding and defining an appropriately masculine audience. Milton had long contested the issue of forced maintenance of a national clergy, and lambasted what he perceived to be the concomitant clerical abuses. In *Lycidas* (1637) he had famously inveighed against conspicuously consuming, time-serving ministry as 'Blind mouths' who 'for their bellies' sake, / Creep and intrude, and climb into the fold'.[19] By 1659, his views on this subject had hardened, and in *Considerations touching the likeliest means to remove hirelings from the church*, he once again pours scorn upon the established clergy, those 'sharking ministers with a spiritual leprosie'.[20] This time however, his anti-clericalism is less elegaic, less directed to offset the true godliness of a recently deceased close friend, than polemical, aiming to excoriate the whole system of tithe payment as the prime corrupter of the clergy. The issue is of national political importance and a matter of national shame as the English remain:

> the only people of all Protestants left undeliverd, from the oppressions of a Simonious decimating clergie; who shame not against the judgement and practice of all other churches reformd, to maintain, though very weakly, thir Popish and oft refuted positions, not in a point of conscience ... but in a point of covetousness and

---

Barwick, *To all Present Rulers, whether Parliament, or Whomsoever of England* (London, 1659), pp. 2–3.

[18] For examples of Quaker women writing briefly on tithes but in other contexts see Margaret Abbot, *A Testimony Against the False Teachers of this Generation* (London, 1659), pp. 1, 5; Sarah Blackborow, *Herein is held forth the Gift and Good-will of God* (London, 1659), p. 7; Dorothy White, *Friends You that are the Parliament, hear the Word of the Lord* (London, 1662), pp. 3–5; Theophilia Townsend, *A Word of Counsel in the Love of God* (London, 1687), p. 3. There is a rare instance of a woman devoting an entire pamphlet to tithe protest after the Restoration; see Judith Boulbie, *A Testimony for Truth Against All Hireling Priests* (London, 1665).

[19] John Milton, *Lycidas*, ll. 114–20, in John Carey (ed.) *John Milton: Complete Shorter Poems* (London and New York, 1992), p. 248.

[20] Idem., *Considerations Touching the likeliest means to remove Hirelings out of the Church* in *CPW*, vol. 7, p. 297.

unjust claim to other mens goods ... Till which grievances be remov'd and religion set free from the monopolie of hirelings, I dare affirme, that no model whatsoever of a commonwealth will prove successful or undisturbed.[21]

As Milton self-consciously positions himself in the public sphere, where tithes represent the greatest of politico-religious stakes, it is perhaps no surprise that he should style this discursive forum as an exclusively male one. Therefore in *Considerations* knowledge of and participation in tithe controversy become allied to his more general views on the nature of Christian education *per se*. Thus amid a discussion of the unjustness of the forced maintenance of ministers he digresses:

> I offer it to the reason of any man, whether he think the knowledge of Christian religion harder than any other art or science to attain. I suppose that he will grant it far easier ... since it was preached as well to the shepherds of *Bethlehem* by angels, as to the eastern Wisemen by that starr ... Hence we may conclude, if men be not all thir life time under a teacher to learn Logic, natural Philosophie, Ethics or Mathematics, which are more difficult, that certainly it is not necessarie to the attainment of Christian knowledge that men should sit all their life long at the feet of a pulpited divine; while he, a lollard indeed over his elbow-cushion, in almost the seaventh part of 40 or 50 yeares teaches them scarce half the principles of religion; and his sheep oft-times sit the while to as little purpose of benefiting as the sheep in their pues at *Smithfield* ... or if this comparison be too low, like those woemen, 1 Tim 3.7. *ever learning and never attaining*; yet not so much through their own fault, as through the unskilful and immethodical teaching of thir pastor, teaching here and there at random out of this or that text as his ease or fansie, and oft times his stealth guides him.[22]

Milton's inclusive, anti-clerical rhetoric concerning the necessary reformation of Christian knowledge and the promotion of more egalitarian pedagogical practices bear a characteristically Quaker stamp.[23] However, the fact that women are excluded from the readership of Milton's sole contribution to the pamphlet wars surrounding the payment of tithes is equally telling. The 'man' of 'reason' to whom he addresses his digression is the descendent of the 'eastern Wisemen' of the bible, and his ability to 'suppose' common knowledge with that enlightened male reader is the result of Epiphanic educative moments to which only men are permitted access. Whilst shepherds represent the lowest level to which Christian knowledge can penetrate in mankind, it is 'woemen' who symbolize those men whose ignorance places them beyond the reach of erudition. Despite the proviso that this effeminate unenlightenment is largely the result of 'immethodical

---

[21] Ibid., p. 275.

[22] Ibid., pp. 302–3.

[23] This Quaker stamp is one that has been detected by other commentators on Milton's later work. See, for instance, Corns, *John Milton*, pp. 108–15; David Loewenstein, 'The Kingdom Within: Radical Religious Culture and the Politics of *Paradise Regained*', *Literature and History* 3:2 (1994), pp. 63–89; Steven Marx, 'The Prophet Disarmed: Milton and the Quakers', *SEL* 32 (1992), pp. 111–28.

teaching' and male clerical abuse, Milton, whilst softening the misogyny of original Pauline epistle, is still only willing to accord women a symbolic status that is marginally more positive than the irrationally ovine.[24]

He was not, of course, alone in maintaining this masculinist position. We have seen in previous chapters that whatever the issue under discussion, 'learning' and erudition could be mobilized in an attempt to bar female participation in public debate. The principal writers in the tithes controversy also use their privileged access to educative opportunities to justify and consolidate their position within the controversy. Michael Beynon, for instance, addresses his treatise on tithes:

> To the Learned Readers
> Sirs,
> You may be pleased to remit the severity of that Censure which the ignorant Rudeness of my Style and the Brevity and paucity of the Arguments I have made use of (far below the merits of the Cause I have taken upon me to defend) may possibly deserve; [this is] the effect of an unlearned hand ... so naturally falling from my Pen, being yet in my Tyrocinium, and a Candidate both in the Arts and Laws.[25]

Notwithstanding the humility topoi and the rhetorical self-abasement here, Beynon still betrays a desire to be numbered amongst the ranks of exclusively male 'Learned readers' and writers to whom he is addressing himself. He wishes to locate his tract in a tradition of heroic male writing on tithes by placing it alongside 'the *immense labours* of so many Learned and Orthodox Divines, in their voluminous Tracts of Casuistical Debates'.[26] This sense of the heroism of the tithe writer is intensified when Beynon refers to his intellectual development and emergence into the public sphere in pointedly martial terms whereby publication of his tract becomes a 'Tyrocinium', or first military campaign, against the Quaker lawyer John Crook. As we shall see, in moments remarkably reminiscent of the dynamics of the toleration debates of the early 1640s, the image of the male polemicist-errant doing battle with doughty disputants was a common trope used to exclude women from tithe debate.

---

[24] The reference is not to I Timothy 3.7 but II Timothy 3.7 which recounts Paul's encounter with 'captive silly women laden with sins ... Ever learning and never able to come to knowledge of the truth.' Milton's views here are perfectly concordant with his masculinist theorizations of education elsewhere. For him the main aim of educating the young is to infuse 'into their young breasts such an ingenious and noble ardour as would not fail to make many of them renowned and matchless men'. Furthermore 'the main skill and groundwork will be, to temper them such lectures and explanations upon every opportunity, as may lead and draw them in willing obedience, enflam'd with the study of learning and the admiration of vertue, stirr'd up with high hopes of living to be brave men and worthy patriots, dear to God and famous to all ages. That they may despise and scorn all their childish and ill taught qualities, to delight in manly, and liberall exercises'. John Milton, *Of Education*, in *CPW*, vol. 2, pp. 384–5.

[25] Michael Beynon, *The Antitythe-Monger Confuted*, sig. A3r.

[26] Ibid.

It will no doubt seem strange, however, to aver that erudition should predominate in a discursive arena in which the Quakers featured so prominently. The movement was, after all, initially characterized by a conviction of the primacy of the spirit over the intellect and a fundamental belief in the egalitarian principle of the priesthood of *all* believers.[27] Yet, as the historian W. C. Braithwaite has demonstrated in his discussion of post-Restoration Quakerism, the movement gradually incorporated both legalism and the need to complement the workings of the spirit with a new, disciplined intellectual rigour.[28] It is my contention that this process actually begins earlier than Braithwaite credits – it can in fact be glimpsed in nascent form in the tithe debate of the 1650s – and that detailed attention to the intellectualism of the tithes controversy can help to provide a corrective to the view that Quakerism was a movement that uncomplicatedly championed female participation in public sphere activity. Of central importance here is Anthony Pearson's *The Great Case of Tithes Truly Stated*, a key text which helped to define the Quaker position on tithes as the controversy raged in 1659. That treatise itself is, however surprisingly, inextricably linked to the learned (and heroic) discourses of seventeenth-century juristic humanism. In particular, it owes a significant, if unacknowledged, debt to John Selden's monumental *Historie of Tithes* (1618).

John Selden holds a privileged place in many discussions of early modern thought as one of the most learned men of his age.[29] Esteemed as a jurist, legal historian, philologer and antiquary he is perhaps, alongside Samuel Hartlib and Thomas Hobbes, one of the foremost representatives of the ideal of Renaissance polymathy.[30] He was a prolific writer whose publications include some twenty-

---

[27] For a succinct assessment of the relationship between sectarianism and education in the civil war see Hill, *The World Turned Upside Down*, pp. 300-305. On the role of education in Quakerism more specifically see D. G. B. Hubbard, 'Early Quaker Education, c. 1650–1780', unpublished M.A. thesis (University of London, 1939); W. C. Braithwaite, *The Beginnings of Quakerism*, pp. 48, 293–4, 330, 370; idem., *The Second Period of Quakerism* (Cambridge, 1961), pp. 524–3.

[28] Braithwaite, *Second Period*, pp. 524–5.

[29] For details of Selden's life and work see Paul Christianson, *Discourses on History, Law and Governance in the Public Career of John Selden 1610—1635* (Toronto, 1996); Jason P. Rosenblatt, *Torah and Law in Paradise Lost* (Princeton, 1994), pp. 124–31; Richard Tuck, *Natural Rights Theories Their Origin and Development* (Cambridge and New York, 1993), pp. 82–100; A. L. Rowse, *Four Caroline Portraits: Thomas Hobbes, Henry Marten, Hugh Peters, John Selden* (London, 1993), pp. 125–55; Jonathan R. Ziskind (trans. and ed.), *John Selden on Jewish Marriage Law: The Uxor Hebraica* (London, 1991); Bershadsky, 'Politics, Erudition and Ecclesiology'; idem., 'Controlling the Terms'; Richard A. Filloy, 'The Religious and Political Views of John Selden: A Study in Early Stuart Humanism' (unpublished Ph.D. thesis, University of California at Berkeley, 1977); Eric Fletcher, *John Selden 1584-1654: Selden Society Lecture Delivered in the Old Hall of Lincoln's Inn* (London, 1969); F. Smith Fussner, *The Historical Revolution: English Historical Writing and Thought 1580-1640* (London, 1962), pp. 275–98; *DNB* 51 (1897), pp. 212–24.

[30] F. Smith Fussner eulogizes Selden as one of the foremost 'giants of erudition' whilst J. P. Rosenblatt simply states that he was 'the most learned man in the seventeenth century'; *The Historical Revolution*, p. 275; *Torah and Law in Paradise Lost*, p. 85.

seven titles, most of which were in Latin and covered topics as diverse as Anglo-Saxon history and Jewish marriage law. Whilst he is probably best remembered by modern day commentators for his *De Iure Naturali et Gentium iuxta disciplinam Ebraeorum* (1640), a work exploring the relationships between man, the natural law and the nature of moral obligation, it was his *The Historie of Tithes* that provoked most contemporary response.[31] Published in 1618 as a sally in the pamphlet war that had sprung up originally around tithe payment, but had audible detonations in wider contests (such as those between the relative powers of church, canon and civil law and those of parliament, Erastianism and the common law), the *Historie* went through four editions in less than ten months after its first appearance.[32] It provoked a flurry of printed responses, as a result of which Selden was summoned before members of the High Commission and Privy Council, and ordered to write a statement regretting the publication of the work. After James I had himself questioned Selden three times, the book was suppressed and its author bound from offering a printed response to any of his disputants.[33] The principal reason for this furore was not for anything outrightly heretical that Selden had published in his *Historie*. Instead his exhaustive philological and historical analysis of Jewish and Christian text, statute and legislation proved inflammatory because it demonstrated that tithes had been instituted throughout history as a result of historically specific custom and secular law. Selden outlined and defended his position in the preface to his tract:

> And plainly he that talks of Tithes without reference to such *positiue Law,* makes the object of his discourse rather what he would haue should be, then any thing that indeed is at all. For what State is in all Christendom wherein Tithes are paid *de facto*, otherwise then according to Human Law positiue? That is, as subject to some Customes, to Statutes, to all ciuill disposition. If they bee in truth due *Iure Divino*

---

[31]   Richard Tuck stresses the centrality of Selden's *De Iure Naturali* in the early modern English philosophical tradition, and goes so far as to suggest that one cannot get to Thomas Hobbes without it: '*De Iure Naturali* constitutes the first example of the English interest in the nature of moral obligation, and of the scepticism found in many later seventeenth-century English philosophers over whether there can be an account of obligation distinct from one of motivation', *Natural Rights Theories*, p. 90. For J. P. Rosenblatt, the work is absolutely essential to comprehending the worlds of Milton's *Paradise Lost, Areopagitica* and *The Doctrine and Discipline of Divorce*; *Torah and Law in Paradise Lost*, pp. 85–9.

[32]   For a survey of the wider implications of the tithes controversy in the early seventeenth century see Bershadsky, 'Controlling the Terms'; Eliane Glaser, '"Uncircumcised Pens": Judaizing in Print Controversies of the Long Reformation' (unpublished Ph.D. thesis, University of London, 2000).

[33]   The main protagonists here, as outlined by William Prynne in his *Ten Considerable Quaeries* (sig. A3r), are Sir James Sempill, *Sacrilege Sacredly Handled* (London, 1619); Richard Tillesley, *Animadversions upon M. Seldens History of Tithes* (London, 1619); Richard Montague, *Diatribe Upon the First Part of the Late History of Tithes* (London, 1621); William Sclater, *The Quaestion of Tithes Revised* (London, 1623); Stephen Nettles, *An Answer to the Jewish Part of Mr Selden's History of Tithes* (Oxford, 1625).

(which Diuines must determine of) they remain equally so aswel [sic.] after as before Human Laws made touching them.[34]

Few, however, were willing to concede Selden this point. William Sclater, outraged by Selden's impertinence at even probing the issue in such depth, went so far as to compare the book to 'some Gorgon's head, to affright him whosoever should cast an eye on it, retaining opinion of a Diuine law for Tything'.[35] Others claimed that the author's 'lips deserued to be sewed vp, and your mouth to bee coped, vntill you put in practice better manners'.[36] For a number of Selden's opponents the very existence of the *Historie* seemed to deny (albeit inferentially) that tithes were maintained by *jus divinium*.

If the seventeenth-century episcopal hierarchy were aghast at the potentially deleterious effects the *Historie* might have on their ability to claim the tithe by divine right, the exhaustive and expansive nature of Selden's approach to the issue of tithes has granted his *Historie* a centrality in tithe historiography which has been maintained until recently. William Esterby wrote the Yorke Prize Essay of Cambridge University in 1887 on the back of Selden's *Historie*; his own historical account of the English laws pertaining to tithes was glutted with references to Selden, to whose 'great work on the *Historie of Tithes* ... the Author is greatly indebted'.[37] Similarly, it is to the obvious detriment of the most recent published account of tithe payment and historiography in the early modern period that Selden should not figure once in its two hundred or so pages.[38] It is its sheer exhaustiveness, its unremitting, painstaking returns to original sources that makes the *Historie* loom so large in tithe discussion. As it wades through documents pertaining to tithe payment from pre-Christian to medieval period, from Hebrew manuscript to English statute, the *Historie* can be wearying for the modern reader, yet it is this humanistic copia which most commentators on the tract praise. Ben Jonson famously wondered which of Selden's qualities to laud first:

> Your skill
> Or faith in things? Or is't your wealth and will
> To instruct and teach? Or your unweary'd paine
> Of Gathering? ...

---

[34]   Selden, *Historie*, sig. c2r–c2v.

[35]   Sclater, *The Quaestion of Tythes*, p. 197. A more dispassionate voice amongst Selden's other opponents was that of Sir James Sempill who maintained 'But seeing Mr Selden, both by his Title ... and by his Preface fully disclaimeth it to be written to prooue that Tithes are not due by the law of God, &c. I haue no reason to suspect, much lesse to account him as an aduersarie of my Position'; *Sacrilege Sacredly Handled*, sig. Sv.

[36]   Montague, *Diatribe*, p. 33.

[37]   William Esterby, *The History of the Law of Tithes in England. Being the Yorke Prize Essay of the University of Cambridge for 1887* (Cambridge, 1888), p. viii.

[38]   The work referred to here is Laura Brace, *The Idea of Property in Seventeenth-Century England: Tithes and the Individual* (Manchester and New York, 1998).

I wondered at the richnesse, but am lost,
To see the workmanship so exceed the cost!
To mark the excellent seas'ning of your Stile!
And manly elocution.[39]

This eulogy was printed in a prefatory epistle to Selden's *Titles of Honour* and invites its reader to contemplate the inextricable links between the heroism of Selden's 'unwearyed paine' in gathering prodigious quantities of source material and the 'manly elocution' of his plain, uncluttered prose style. Jonson is keen to construct a peculiar kind of heroism here though. Selden's 'paine' is distinctly different from that we might expect of the internationally renowned textual scholar. With the poet's emphasis on 'skill' and 'will' rather than 'wealth', the humanist finds himself instead in an artisanal community where 'workmanship' rather than intellect is the ennobling, masculinizing force. To put it in nineteenth-century terms, Jonson's Selden is more Adam Bede than Edward Casaubon. Some three hundred years later F. Smith Fussner also remembered the laborious nature of Selden's 'workmanship', presenting him as an archetypal scholar-mason who:

> built his historical works in an almost Cyclopean fashion, with quotations piled upon quotations, most of them still in the languages in which he found them. History was the study of problems; and historical method was as scientific as Selden could make his procedures of verification and proof ... the very virtues of his scholarship worked against any fluency of style.[40]

Selden once again emerges the humanist-as-craftsman, or draughtsman, who speaks as he finds and whose discipline is as much physical as it is mental.

Selden himself baulked at such imaginative comparisons in the *Historie*. He fashioned his masculinity in a different style, preferring to see himself as an impartial, copiously documenting, even-handed common lawyer removed from the partisanship of the tithes controversy. His *Historie*:

> is not written to proue that Tithes are not due by the Law of God; not written to proue that the Laity may detaine them, not to proue that Lay hands may still enioy Appropriations; in some, not at all against the Maintenance of the Clergie. Neither is it any thing else but it self, that is a meer Narration, and the *Historie of Tithes*.[41]

Numerous critics have highlighted that such claims for the *Historie*'s pure narrativity or the 'scientific' neutrality of historical empiricism, are riddled with

---

[39] Ben Jonson, 'An Epistle to Master Selden' in C. H. Herford and Percy and Evelyn Simpson (eds.), *Ben Jonson*, 10 vols (Oxford, 1925–50), vol. 8, pp. 159–60.

[40] F. Smith Fussner, *The Historical Revolution*, p. 276.

[41] John Selden, *The Historie of Tithes: That is the Practice of Payment of them. The Positive Laws Made for them. The Opinions Touching the Right of Them. A Review of It is also annext, which both Confirmes it and directs the use of it* (London, 1618), sig. a3v–a4r.

ideological investment.[42] Nevertheless, few commentators have attended to the masculinist imperative behind Selden's exhaustive, humanistic historical approach. Whereas other writers attributed heroic, artisanal qualities to his work, Selden conceived of his endeavours as conforming to entirely different, class-based paradigms of male behaviour. This was something alluded to in a lecture given to the Selden society in 1969, when Sir Eric Fletcher praised the historical method of the *Historie* and reminded his audience that:

> John Selden's contribution was his complete mastery of legal authorities and his vast unrivalled knowledge of constitutional precedent. He supplied the munitions of attack from a peerless armoury of learning. He was not a Rupert, but an Ajax of debate, always ready to overwhelm an opponent with a mass of facts.[43]

It is not the supposed neutrality of Selden's copia that is lauded so much as the virility of the act. Writing and amassing legal and historical evidence become as much the valorous, martial deeds of a seventeenth-century soldier as the day-to-day practice of the common lawyer, whilst erudition *per se* features as the necessary 'armoury' of that warrior-lawyer. This was exactly the sense that Selden himself was keen to foster in the readers of his *Historie*:

> To supply therefore the want of a full and faithfull collection of the Historicall part, was the end and purpose why this was composed which might remaine as a furnisht Armorie for such as inquire about Ecclesiastique Reuenue, and preferring Truth before what dulling custom hath too deeply rooted in them.[44]

If this quest for 'Truth' in the matter of 'Ecclesiastique Reuenue' was a battle in which only the 'Armorie' of learning could adequately defend the warring readers and writers, it is also clear that the participants in this arena were seen as exclusively male. As Selden's own dedicatory Epistle makes clear, there was no room for any Britomarts in the polemical cut and thrust of the tithes controversy. Instead, the scholarly methodology and image-stocks of juristic humanism conscripted its advocates as chivalric men. It is telling, then, that Selden should dedicate his work on tithes to his close friend the humanist, politician and antiquary Sir Robert Cotton at the same time as he reveals the processes by (and environment in) which it was possible to steel oneself in the 'armourie' of learning.[45] Selden had:

---

[42]   Hitherto, however, criticism of Selden's historical method has been restricted to an exposure of its complicity in promoting the cause of common law against the jurisdictions of canon and civil law or in tactics of suppressing the force and originality of Hebraic thought. The most thorough treatment of this material to date is to be found in Glaser, '"Uncircumcised Pens"'.

[43]   Eric Fletcher, *John Selden*, p. 7

[44]   Selden, *Historie,* sig. b2v.

[45]   The best full-length study of Cotton to date is still Kevin Sharpe, *Sir Robert Cotton 1586–1631: History and Politics in Early Modern England* (Oxford, 1979).

Used that your inestimable Library (which lives in you) [which] assures a curious Diligence in search after the inmost, least known and most vsefull parts of Historical Truth both of Past and Present Ages. For such is that Truth which your Humanitie liberally dispenses; and such is that whereby conference is learned by you. Such indeed as it were, by your example, more sought after; so much head-long Error, so many ridiculous impostures would not be thrust upon the too credulous by those which stumble on in the Rode, but never with any care looke on each side or behind them that is those which keep their Vnderstandings alwaies in a weake Minoritie that euer wants the Autoritie and Admonition of a Tutor.[46]

The preparation for tithe debate is unmistakably paternalistic and aristocratic; it is Cotton himself who metes out 'Autoritie and Admonition', and in whose sole power it lies to correct the 'head-long Error' and 'ridiculous impostures' of the 'too credulous'. More significant, however, is the manner in which Selden's prime humanistic learning resource, Cotton's 'inestimable library', is not only delimited by masculine parameters, but furthermore actually assumes male corporeality as it is transformed into and relocated 'in' Cotton himself.[47]

Given the oft-cited egalitarianism of the Quaker movement, it is surprising to discover that the juristic humanism of Selden's *Historie* is the prime influence on the most significant and extensive Quaker contribution to the tithes controversy. Anthony Pearson (1628–1670), close friend of George Fox and Margaret Fell, was one of the most influential Quakers in the north of England whose main concern was the unjustness and illegality of the extreme punitive measures taken against Quakers who refused to pay tithes.[48] He was both well educated and had legal training and in 1655 began a systematic visitation of all law courts and prisons to gather information about tithe payment and Quaker punishment. As a result of his extensive research he was granted an interview with Cromwell where he pressed for greater religious toleration, a less draconian governmental approach to ministerial maintenance and the release of those Quakers who had been imprisoned for non-payment of tithes. When this met with little success, he widened his scope to deliberate, like Selden, on tithe payment throughout history, eventually publishing *The Great Case of Tythes truly stated, clearly opened, and fully resolved* in 1657. This proved to be extremely popular amongst Quakers and non-

---

[46]   Selden, *Historie*, sig. a2r–a2v.

[47]   Selden was appointed custodian of the Cottonian library during the 1640s. On the importance of the library as a resource for scholars, courtiers and politicians from across Europe see C. J. Wright (ed.), *Sir Robert Cotton as Collector: Essays on an Early Stuart Courtier and his Legacy* (British Library, 1997); C. G. C. Tite, *The Panizzi Lectures: The Manuscript Library of Sir Robert Cotton* (British Library, 1994); Sharpe, *Sir Robert Cotton*, pp. 48–83. For further discussion of the masculinist nature of Selden's writing on tithes see my 'John Selden Among the Quakers: Antifeminism and Seventeenth-Century Tithes Controversy', in L. Hutson and E. Sheen (eds.), *Literature, Politics and Law in Renaissance England* (London, 2004), pp. 189–208.

[48]   For biography of Pearson see the entry in *DNB* 44, pp. 161–2; Amy E. Wallis, 'Anthony Pearson (1626–1666)' *Journal of the Friends Historical Society* 51:2 (1966), pp. 77–95.

Quakers alike and new editions of the work were published every year until the Restoration, after which Pearson renounced Quakerism and was employed by Charles II's government in Scotland as an adviser on tithes and other agricultural 'customs'.[49]

The first edition of the pamphlet, which is replete with Latin, Greek and Hebraic references, opens with an epistle dedicatory which aims to provide a context of even-handed neutrality in the ensuing discussion, and lays claim to the impartiality of historical empiricism. It begins in florid, frank mood:

> Country-men, Farmers, and Husbandmen of England ... it is for your sake that this small Treatise is sent abroad, that in a matter wherein you are so much concerned, you might be truly informed: And because there are many differing opinions, and of late years have been great disputes concerning the right of Tythes, which makes the case seem difficult to be resolved, I have given you the substance of all that ever I could find written, or hear discoursed touching that point ... for more than two yeers last past I have made much enquiry into it.[50]

As Pearson strives to match the grandiloquence of Marc Anthony's funeral oration in Shakespeare's *Julius Caesar*, the homosociality of his address becomes unmistakable. The claim to exhaustive reading, research and unwearied gathering here is equally significant and places the pamphlet firmly in a humanistic tradition of tithe debate. It seems wholly implausible, however, that such a copiously referenced, meticulously compiled treatise on the history of tithes, one based on 'the substance of all that ever I could find written ... touching that point', should not make one reference to Selden or the *Historie* at any point in its 40 pages. It seems even stranger that Pearson should ignore the work when it was being referred to by all sides in the tithes controversy throughout the 1650s. Prynne could, after all, cite Selden as an authority, despite his Presbyterian pro-tithe perspective, and Milton is known to have used the *Historie* as one of the main sources for his anti-tithe *Considerations*.[51] The question is even more provocative once one realizes that it is not so much a case of Pearson not reading Selden but of wilfully neglecting to cite him. Isaac Jackson, the Quaker editor of the 1756 edition of Pearson's tract, noted this when he mentioned that Pearson's 'short History of Tithes ... [is] taken chiefly from the History of Tithes by the learned

---

[49] *CSPD* (1663–64), p. 191. Further editions of *The Great Case of Tythes Truly Stated* appeared after the Restoration. The work was especially popular among eighteenth-century Quakers keen to stress the reasoned and rational aspects of their religion. By 1850 around ten editions were in print.
[50] Anthony Pearson, *The Great Case of Tythes Truly Stated* (London, 1657), sig. a2r.
[51] William Prynne, *Ten Considerable Quaeries*, p. 3; J. P. Rosenblatt makes an overstated case for Milton's use of Selden in *Considerations* in *Torah and Law in Paradise Lost*, p. 86.

Antiquary *John Selden*'.[52] What the hagiographical introduction to this edition fails to mention, however, is that large sections of Pearson's treatise are merely wholesale verbatim reproductions of Selden's *Historie*.[53] It is my argument that Pearson, the Quaker who offered the most acute, extended and influential critique of the tithing system in the period, is not only culpable of plagiarism but furthermore of complicity in the marginalization of women in the public arena of tithe debate. He deliberately, if silently, uses the influence of Selden's juristic humanism as applied to the tithe debate earlier in the century (which is, as we have seen, inextricably linked to its masculinist force) to nullify the effects of *jure divino* appeals by his own opponents in the later 1650s. Accordingly, Pearson's appeals to 'Countrymen, Farmers and Husbandmen of England', whilst certainly not invoking Selden's privileged pan-European humanistic community, is less the inclusive rallying cry that it initially appears, and is instead a call sounded along segregated gender lines.

'Here are our names who are the witnesses of Jesus Christ': Petitioning, Signatures, Agency

At one level, the stark fact that few Quaker women wrote about tithes at a time when (in a wider cultural context) public resistance to them had almost become as clear a sign of Quakerism as the physiological state from which the movement got its name, points towards the relative efficacy of this segregation process. If such segregation was a prevalent patriarchal mechanism, however, it was neither completely successful nor submitted to meekly. Thus was it on the 20th July 1659 that two nameless women presented a petition to the House of Commons. Despite the fact that the Commons would not accept the petition, it was published later that year by Mary Westwood as a 72-page pamphlet entitled *These Several Papers Was*

---

[52]   Isaac Jackson (ed.), *The Great Case of Tithes Truly Stated, Clearly Opened and Fully Resolved. By Anthony Pearson, Formerly A Justice of the Peace in Westmoreland* (London, 1756), sig. A3v.

[53]   For instance, Selden writes: 'Agreeing with him [Ambrose, Bishop of Milan] is Augustine in a whole Homily for the right of them; About Harvest hee made it. Then exorts them *Decimae tribut a sunt egentium animarum redde ergo tribut a pauperibus; offer libamina sacerdotibus*; and admonishes, that, if they have no fruits of the earth, they should pay the Tithe of whatsoever they liue by ... And then vrging more Texts out of the old Testament touching Tithes and first fruits, and telling them, that the neglect of payment is the cause of sterility and blasting ... These two great Bishops agree; and from the Law giuen to the Israelites', *Historie*, pp. 54–5. Whilst Pearson cites the same Augustinian sermon as a source text for the corresponding section of his own treatise however, it is clear from the simple replication of certain phrases that he is working from Selden's account of the Augustinan sermon rather than the primary text itself. Thus, for example, Selden's translation and interpretation 'if they haue no fruits of the earth, they should pay the Tithe of whatsoever they liue by' and 'the neglect of payment is the cause of sterility and blasting' feature unreferenced in *The Great Case* as Pearson's own words.

sent to the Parliament The twentieth day of the fifth Moneth 1659 Being above seven thousand of the Names of the Handmaids and Daughters of the Lord.[54] The text bearing this unwieldy, ungrammatical title was actually a densely printed collection of petitions by different groups of Quaker women from various parts of the country collated together as a single female response to 'the oppression of Tithes, in the names of many more of the said Handmaids and Daughters of the Lord, who witness against the oppression of Tithes'.[55] The tenor of *These Several Papers* differs from petition to petition, but all are characterized by a shared concern to expose the material depredations and economic hardships (including imprisonment and property distraint) that all Quaker, but particularly Quaker women, suffered as a result of the institution of tithe payment. The women of Lancashire, Northumberland and Cumberland, for instance, verbalize their resistance by invoking Old Testament modes of address and gender solidarity simultaneously:

> We ... are the Seed of the Woman, which bruiseth the Serpent's head, to which the Promise is, Christ Jesus in the Male and the Female, which is the Everlasting Priest, not after the Order of Aaron, which took Tithes ... but of the Tribe of Judah ... who is a Priest for ever ... And therefore can we set our hearts and hands against *Aaron's Order*, which is disannulled, and the Law changed.[56]

The women of Gloucestershire, by contrast, organize their protest by replacing biblical register with materialist critique as they address 'the Parliament of England' with arresting directness:

> How do you who are the heads of the Nation expect we should pay your taxes, when you suffer the Priests to take away our goods, that do no worke for us, and they come and claime through a pretence Tythe from ... us for their preaching, that to us does not preach and will not suffer us to try their doctrine ... and if we do question it, six moneths in the house of correction, or five pounds fine: And if the Priest come and pretend 15 *l* Tythes they will take a hundred pounds.[57]

---

[54] Ronald Hutton contends that the petition was not accepted because it was not presented. Our readings of the treatment of Elizabeth Poole and Elizabeth Alkin ought to remind us that 'official' records often have more than a purely empirical agenda. George Fox himself refers to the fact that 'two women did present ye testimonies of {above} 7000 women's hands against tyths & ye reasons why they coulde not holde uppe the preists yt did take tyths now & how yt Christ had ended Jewish presthoode that did take tythes & sent foorth his messengers & ministers & Apostles freely & commanded ym yt as they had received freely soe they shoulde give freely againe' in Norman Penney (ed.), *The Journal of George Fox*, vol. 1 (London, 1911), p. 385. See also Hutton, *The Restoration*, p. 47.

[55] The pamphlet has been catalogued in Wing under Mary Forster, *These Several Papers* (1659) due to an appended epistle to the reader which bears her name. As this significantly ignores the act of collective authorship which the pamphlet represents and the patterns of agency which propelled the work into the public sphere, it will be referred to here as *These Several Papers*.

[56] Ibid., p. 7.

[57] Ibid., p. 51.

The signatories of Southwark sound a similar note, but they locate their boldly interrogative appeal in a revolutionary historical context. When comparing the ravages of civil war with those experienced under prelacy, they remind their readers of 'our friends who have been for the Parliament ever since the beginning of the late Wars, [who]have suffered more by these plundering Priests, then by the plundering Cavaliers'.[58]

This remarkable, rhetorically diverse pamphlet is perhaps best viewed among those renewed appeals by sectarian groups for religious toleration following the restoration of the Rump parliament on 5th May 1659. Before it was expelled by Cromwell in 1653, this parliament was heavily composed of, and favourably viewed by, sectarians and its restoration at the end of the decade heralded a new optimism in the potential for a tolerationist, anti-tithe lobby to push through legislation, forcing the abolition of tithes. It soon became apparent that this optimism was misplaced. With a deluge of other petitions and issues to contend with, the Rump's idea of debating the issue of tithes was simply to consolidate the former position of forced maintenance of a national ministry.[59] After an inconclusive parliamentary vote on 14 June, a decision was forced with the presentation of an anti-tithe petition signed by some 15,000 Quaker men on the 27th.[60] This eight-page pamphlet, reprinted as *The Copie of A Paper Presented to the Parliament and read the 27th of the fourth Moneth 1659,* desired that Parliament 'with all convenient speed declare a just freedom in thinges pertaining unto God to all the People of this Common-wealth, that tithes, forced maintenances and all other burthens on the conscience may be removed, and Christs Kingdom delivered up to himself'.[61] The petition did not have the desired effect, however, as the House's decision was 'that for the Encouragement of a Godly Preaching Learning Ministry throughout the Nation, the Payment of Tythes shall continue as now they are, until this Parliament shall find out some other more equal and comfortable Maintenance, both for the Ministry and the Satisfaction of the People'.[62] This decision was especially contentious because this final version of the proclamation contained the substitution of 'until' for the draft's 'unless' – a rather brusque attempt to put an end to tithe discussion at the parliamentary level. The author of that week's pro-government *The Weekly Post* noted the furore surrounding the alteration of the proclamation and lamented:

---

[58]   Ibid., p. 54.
[59]   The best narrative of these events is Hutton, *The Restoration,* pp. 42–8, but see also Godfrey Davies, *The Restoration of Charles II, 1658–1660* (San Marino, 1955), pp. 101–22.
[60]   Davies, *The Restoration of Charles II,* p. 120; Hutton, *The Restoration,* p. 47; Braithwaite, *Beginnings,* p. 458.
[61]   *The Copie of A Paper Presented to the Parliament: And Read the 27th of the fourth Moneth, 1659* (London, 1659), p. 7.
[62]   *Commons Journals* 7 (1651–1659), p. 694.

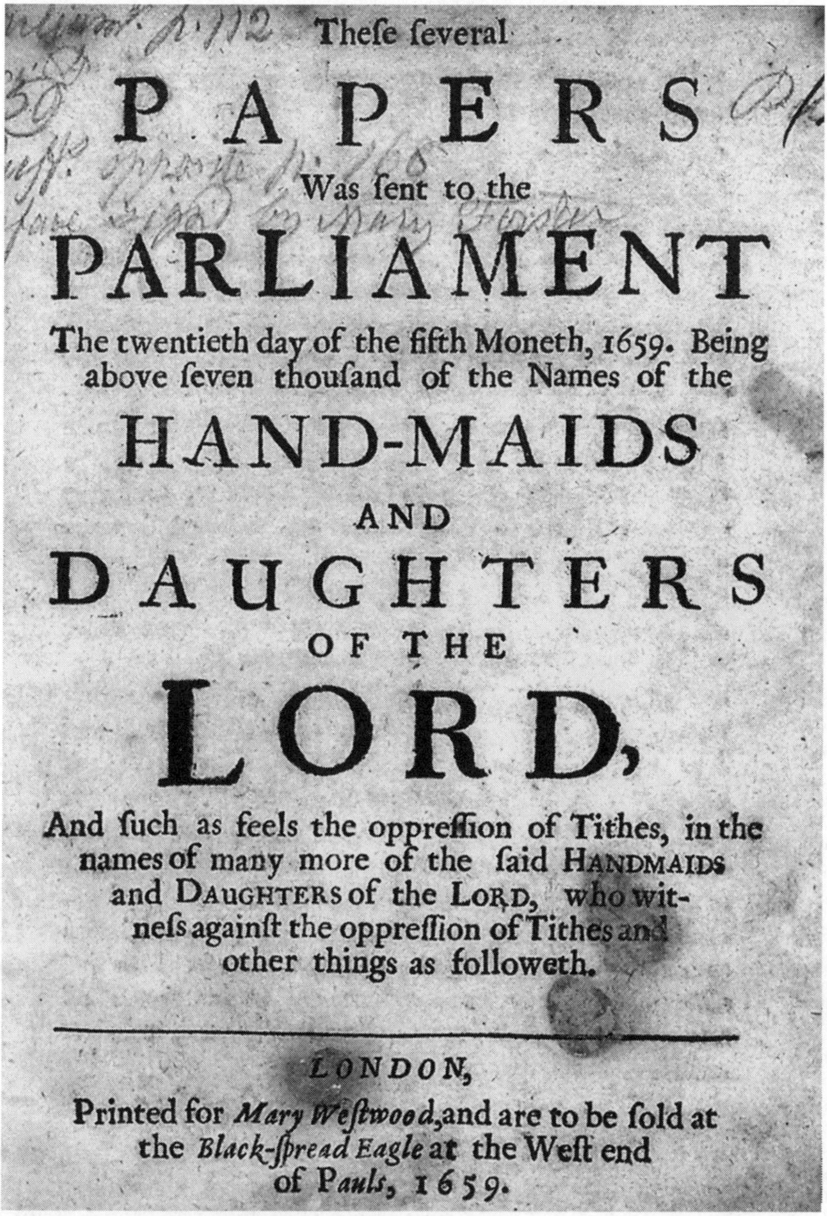

These several

PAPERS

Was sent to the

PARLIAMENT

The twentieth day of the fifth Moneth, 1659. Being
above seven thousand of the Names of the

HAND-MAIDS

AND

DAUGHTERS

OF THE

LORD,

And such as feels the oppression of Tithes, in the
names of many more of the said HANDMAIDS
and DAUGHTERS of the LORD, who witness against the oppression of Tithes and
other things as followeth.

_____

LONDON,

Printed for *Mary Westwood*, and are to be sold at
the *Black-spread Eagle* at the West end
of *Pauls,* 1659.

Figure 12: *These Several Papers* (1659), title page
A collection of anti-tithe petitions by Quaker women from all areas of England.

Lord! What an Age do we live in? *Did ever English-men appear against Magistracy with such Heretical and Bloudy Vizards?* Surely no: But certainly their Opticks are much eclipsed with a new forged Blasphemy against the Truth; and I question not, but their God-father will one day congratulate their Licentious Reproaches with a meritorious Reward.[63]

Therefore, if sectarian men were vilified and threatened with eternal damnation for daring to question governmental policy by interrogating the institution of tithes, the value of the Quaker women's petition of the following month (representing nothing short of an attempt to re-open a public, political debate in the masculinist world of tithe dispute) ought not to be underestimated.

The pamphlet accordingly opens with an acknowledgement of the strangeness of its appearance in the public sphere:

Friends,
It may seem strange to some that women should appear in so publick a manner, in a matter of so great concernment as this of Tithes, *and that we also should bring in our testimony even as our brethren against that Anti-christian law and oppression of* Tithes, *by which many of the Servants of the Lords have suffered in filthy holes and dungeons until death; But let such know, that this is the work of the Lord at this day, even by weak means to bring to pass his mighty work in the earth, that all flesh may be silent, and the Lord alone may be exalted in them who can truly say,* Now I live, yet not I, but Christ liveth in me, and the life that I now live is by the faith of the Son of God.[64]

The reasons why this text should 'seem strange to some' are manifold. Even as the Quaker women address the presumably sympathetic, fellow members of the Society of 'Friends', they still feel the need to stress the peculiarity of petitioning in a 'publick ... manner', and draw attention to the problematic status that women's printed petitions had attained by the late 1650s. Whereas the private petitions of Elizabeth Alkin, which we read earlier, manipulated strategies of private petitioning developed by countless women throughout the sixteenth and seventeenth centuries, the printing of mass petitions by women was a much more recent phenomenon.[65] Mass petitioning by women only became commonplace in

[63]   *The Weekly Post*, 28 June–5 July (1659), p. 74; emphasis added.
[64]   *These Several Papers*, 'To the Reader', no sig.
[65]   On women petitioning parliament before Alkin see Barbara J. Harris, 'Women and Politics in Early Tudor England', *Historical Journal* 33:2 (1990), pp. 259–81. For women's petitioning more generally see Raymond, *Pamphlets and Pamphleteering*, pp. 301–7; Mendelson and Crawford, *Women in Early Modern England*, pp. 399–403, 405–9; Andrea Button 'Royalist Women Petitioners in South West England', 1655–1662', *The Seventeenth Century* 15:1 (2000), pp. 53–66; Bell et al., *Biographical Dictionary*, pp. 263–270; Hughes, 'Gender and Leveller Literature'; Ann Marie McEntee, '"The [Un]Civill-Sisterhood of Oranges and Lemons": Female Petitioners and Demonstrators, 1642–1653', in Holstun (ed.), *Pamphlet Wars*, pp. 92–111; Higgins, 'The Reactions of Women'.

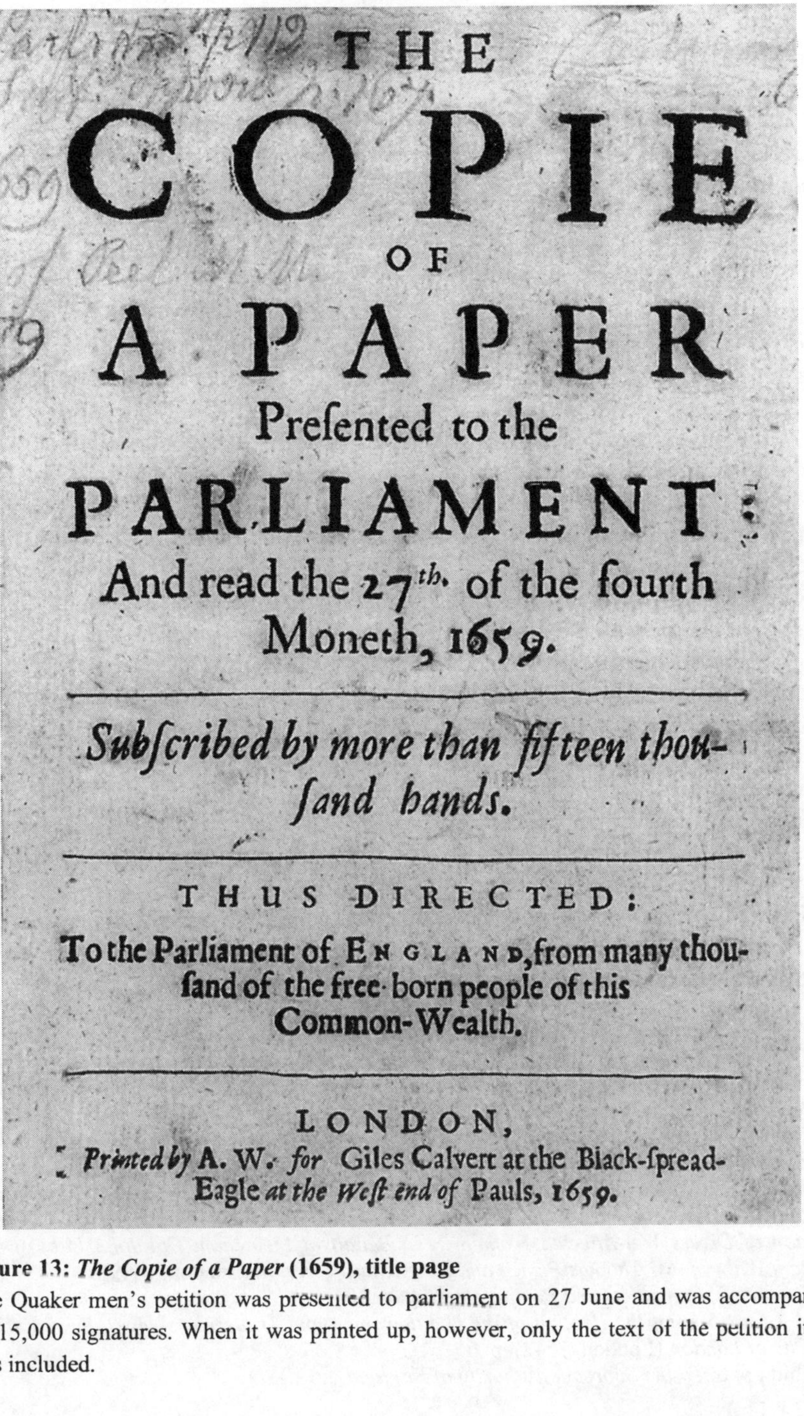

THE
COPIE
OF
A PAPER
Prefented to the
PARLIAMENT:
And read the 27th of the fourth
Moneth, 1659.

Subfcribed by more than fifteen thou-
fand hands.

THUS DIRECTED:

To the Parliament of ENGLAND, from many thou-
fand of the free-born people of this
Common-Wealth.

LONDON,
Printed by A. W. for Giles Calvert at the Black-fpread-
Eagle at the Weft end of Pauls, 1659.

Figure 13: *The Copie of a Paper* (1659), title page
The Quaker men's petition was presented to parliament on 27 June and was accompanied
by 15,000 signatures. When it was printed up, however, only the text of the petition itself
was included.

the 1640s and early 1650s when royalist women and the wives, daughters and friends of Leveller leaders daringly lobbied parliament for the release of loved ones, the preservation of trade, or the fundamental rights of the English people. It was Leveller women (and women with links to the Leveller movement) in particular who made this form their own and proved their 'undoubted Right of Petitioning' in a series of spectacular, politically literate petition pamphlets between 1649 and 1653.[66] The effect of these pamphlets was such that one recent commentator has asserted that by the end of the revolutionary decades 'petitioning had become an acknowledged mode of authorship which women writers could use for polemical purposes'.[67]

However, the precise nature of this acknowledgement was much more fraught than this assessment allows; it does not account, for instance, for the residual sense of 'strange[ness]' that these Quaker women express when petitioning parliament in 1659. This is perhaps related to the fact that male writers continually sought to privilege petitioning as a male speech act throughout the 1640s and 1650s. Thus the leading parliamentarian of the early 1640s, John Pym, accepted a printed petition from a group of 'Gentlewomen and tradesmen's wives' at Westminster in 1642, only to then instruct them to 'repaire to your Houses, and turne your Petition which you have delivered here, into Prayers at home for us'.[68] This authoritative remark strives to reinforce a gendered segregation of social space and discursive activity across class hierarchies and to translate the register of women's political engagement into the (patriarchally oriented and endorsed) language of devotion. It is no accident, therefore, that the vast majority of women's printed petitions from the period spend some considerable time interrogating the assumption that it is 'strange and unbeseeming of our sex to shew our selves by way of Petition'. A group of Leveller women presenting a petition to parliament in 1649, for example, 'grieve that [they] should appear so despicable in your eyes, as to be thought unworthy to Petition'.[69]

Even if women's petitioning was deemed strange, unbeseeming and despicable, it was far from uncommon. Throughout the 1640s and 1650s women repeatedly contested and transgressed exhortations against mass petitioning. However, the

---

[66]   *Unto every Individual Member of Parliament: The Humble Representation of divers afflicted Women-Petitioners to the Parliament on the behalf of Mr John Lilburne* (London, 1653), no sig. For further examples of Leveller women's petitions see *To the Parliament of the Commonwealth of England. The Humble Petition of Diuers Afflicted Women, in Behalf of M:Iohn Lilburn Prisoner in Newgate* (London, 1653); *To the Svpreme Avthority of England ... The Humble Petition of diver well-affected Women of the Cities of London and Westminster* (London, 1649); *To the Supream Authority of this Nation ... The Humble Petition of Divers Wel-Affected Women ... In Behalf of Lieutenant Col John Lilburn, Mr William Walwyn, Mr Thomas Prince and Mr Richard Overton* (London, 1649).

[67]   Raymond, *Pamphlets and Pamphleteering*, p. 304.

[68]   *A True Copie of the Petition of the Gentlewomen and Tradesmens-wives, in and about the City of London* (London, 1642), p. 6.

[69]   Ibid., p. 6; *To the Supream Authority of England*, no sig.

controversial status of women's petitions also prompted the simultaneous development of a widespread and lucrative sub-genre of pamphlet writing, known as mock petitions. The male writers of these fictional texts lampooned real women's mass petitions so that material need is rewritten as sexual appetite and the desire for political agency is transformed into an insatiable and apparently collective libido. In the pacifistic mock petitions of 1643 London's wives, matrons and mid-wives call for an end to the civil strife which endangers their husbands' 'precious and delectable members' in favour of a return to more productive, sexual encounters protesting that they can 'use a weapon as well as men if they get it in their handling'.[70] *The Maid's Petition* of 1647 renders women's solidarity with subordinate apprentice groups as 'hold[ing] out stifly with the Apprentices' for 'days of Recreation'; it bemoans their 'underlying condition (not meaning the naturall posture in reuerence to wedlock which is very tolerable).'[71] Some four months before *These Several Papers* was published, a royalist mock petition sketched the satiric portrait of groups of disaffected London serving women 'grunting under the sad and heavy pressure of a dry and withered Rump, which hath neither moisture to quicken us, or to heat to warm'. If the social standing of this group of women is reminiscent of that of the Leveller women and later Quaker petitioners, their sense of a workable format for religious toleration is decidedly different: 'We declare that we will admit of a tolleration in our Religion that those whose desire is weak and tender may have their choise to lye by a Red man, a Brown man, a Pale man, a Black man, a Flaxen-haired man, a Fat man, a Lean man, a Tall man, a short man, an Old Man or a Young Man; provided that they be not too superstitious or rigid'.[72]

One aspect of the strangeness of the Quaker women's petition of the same year, therefore, is that it probes the issue of tithes at the same time as it reinvigorates an originally transgressive mode of women's civil war protest, which had gone into decline through endless male parody towards the end of the revolutionary decades. Another peculiarity resides in the manner in which the women choose to open the printed edition of their petition by signalling the generic and intertextual links between their pamphlet and the male Quaker petition from the previous month

---

[70] *The Mid-wives just Petition* (London, 1643), sig., A4v; *The Humble Petition of Many Thousands of Wives and Matrons of the City of London, and other parts of this Kingdom* (London, 1643), p. 6.

[71] *The Maid's Petition* (London, 1647), title page, sig. A3r. See figure 14. For other examples of mock petitions see *The City-Dames Petition in behalfe of the long afflicted but well-affected Cavaliers* (London, 1647); *A Remonstrance of the Shee-Citizens of London* (London, 1647); *The Mid-wives Just Complaint* (London, 1646); *The Widowes Lamentation for the Absence of their deare Children, and Suitors* (London, 1643).

[72] *The Ladies Remonstrance or a Declaration of the Waiting Gentlewomen, Chambermaid, and Servant Maids of the City of London* (London, 1659), pp. 1, 3.

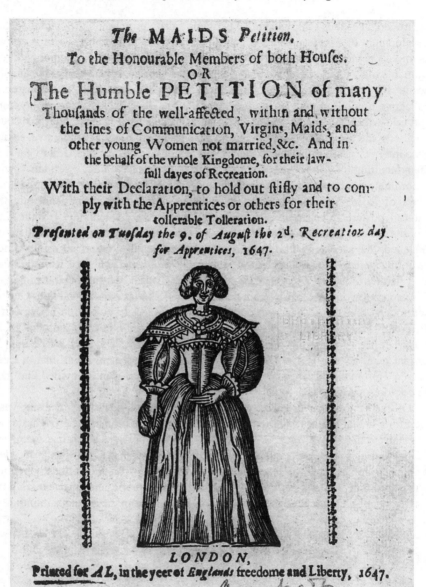

Figure 14: *The Maid's Petition* (1647), title page

The mock petition had become a lucrative sub-genre of pamphlet writing by the late 1640s. Expansive borders and (relatively) expensive woodcuts were rarely seen in genuine petitions from the period.

rather than other women's mass petitions.[73] 'We ... also bring in our testimony even as our brethren' styles the Quaker men's petitionary act as imitable at the same time as it intimates at an almost exact similitude between two texts which appeared within a month of each other. However, the briefest analysis of both petitions indicates that *These Several Papers* is nowhere influenced by *The Copie Of A Paper*; the former is much more innovative and ambitious in its scope and is some nine times the length of its male-authored predecessor. The reasons for this expansiveness will be considered in due course, but positing male, rather than female, petitioning as imitable was a well-established humility *topos* in female-authored mass petitions. Thus, as early as 1641, women from the City and Suburbs of London concluded a petition which extensively and innovatively asserts women's petitionary rights by alerting readers to the primacy of male petitioning. They are merely 'following herein the example of ... Men, which have gone in this duty before us'.[74] By refusing to signal explicit links with earlier groups of women petitioners, the Quaker women of 1659 also reduce the likelihood of becoming the satirical targets for a mock petition.

Instead, they reinvigorate the importance of women's petitioning in strikingly different ways. Primarily, this is a matter of rhetoric and exegesis. Thus the epistle to the reader proceeds by acknowledging varieties of imitable female behaviour necessary for godly reformation. For instance:

> Behold our God is appearing for us, and they that be in the light may see him, choosing the foolish things of the world to confound the wise, weak things to confound the Mighty, vile things, and things that are despised hath God chosen, ye and things which are not, to bring to nought the things which are; Surely the Lord is risen, he is risen indeed and hath appeared unto many, he is also ascended and is taking to himself great power, he is owning and will own his spouse, his Church which hath long lain desolate and afflicted. But now arise and shine O daughter of Sion, shake thy self from thy dust, put on thy beautifull garments, for thy maker is thy husband, the holy One of Israel, and he will plead thy cause.[75]

The rhetoric of the true church figured female, as 'a spouse', was a well-worn trope (it is used elsewhere in the petition) which acquires a peculiar force in this particular illocutionary context.[76] The women are modifying an original Isaiac text which begins 'Awake, awake; put on thy strength O Zion; put on thy beautiful garments, O Jerusalem, the holy city'.[77] By gendering Zion at the start of a verse that early modern exegetes interpreted in terms of the 'Reformation in the Church',

---

[73] This is a strategy which, albeit for different ends, Quaker historians have replicated. Thus, W. C. Braithwaite refers to *These Several Papers* as 'a supplemental paper' to the men's petition; *Beginnings of Quakerism*, p. 458.

[74] *A True Copie of the Petition of the Gentlewomen*, p. 6.

[75] *These Several Papers*, 'To the Reader', no sig.

[76] The Quaker women from Cheshire refer to 'the true Church' as 'preparing herself for her Husband and coming out in her glory'; ibid., p. 21.

[77] Isaiah 52 v.1–2.

the women thereby manipulate the original Isaiac injunction to give national politico-religious concerns a specifically feminine appeal.[78] However, the 'desolate and afflicted' state of the true church only becomes apparent with the recognition that it is the 'oppression' of tithes, which is desolating and afflicting both that church, imaginatively figured female, and those very real women who were petitioning for relief in 1659. This gendered, empathetic alliance through suffering enables the petitioners to relocate the imminent glory of the church not merely in a symbolic companionate marriage with Christ, where both parties are recognized or 'owned', but also in the actual moment of female petitioning. The act simultaneously becomes a Christ-like plea for the 'cause' of tithe abolition and a feminine costuming performance. Thus the transfigurative 'beautifull garments' are both the ceremonial public appearance of the ideally reformed church and the material of the petition itself. Hence, just as the church is transformed from 'dust' to glorious beauty, so, too, the women rework the rhetoric of the Pauline Epistle to the Corinthians to propel themselves from weakness, 'foolish' ignorance and non-existence to a position of collective authorship and authority in Christ.[79]

The protestation that 'foolish things of the World' were to 'confound the Wise' is a significant rallying cry in what we have seen to be the culture of erudition which dominated tithe discussion. However, the appeal and daring originality of this printed petition is not simply due to the innovativeness of its patterns of rhetoric and exegesis. The pamphlet deserves a prominent place in the histories of early modern women's writing, revolutionary pamphlet culture and popular protest because of the way in which it foregrounds the combined material traces of associative agency. The printed petition eschews individualistic modes of authorship, preferring instead to stress the communality and collectivity of female deliberation on the institution of tithes. In the process it re-routes the masculinist logic of juristic humanism's 'unwearyed pain / Of gathering' in an entirely new direction. Therefore each one of the seven thousand women's signatures, which were collected in support of the Quaker anti-tithe position in 1659, are actually reprinted at sporadic intervals on 59 of the pamphlet's 72 pages. This is testament not only to the efficiency of the networks through which the Quakers could organize protest, but it also gives a new immediacy and palpability to the authorial 'we' which structures the petition genre. All petitions stress the communality of their endeavour by deploying collective pronouns in abundance, but the women

---

[78]   In the original biblical text, the gendered image of the Church as 'daughter of Zion' only occurs later in the following verse. Early modern exegetes glossed the text reformation of the Church 'Whereby he intimates, that there should be a greater purity and Reformation in the Church than formerly there had been, which was eminently accomplished in the Church and Kingdom of Christ', Matthew Poole, *Annotations Upon the Holy Bible Wherein the Sacred Text is Inserted and Various Readings Annex'd, Together With Parallel Scriptures*, vol. 1 (London, 1700), sig. 6F3v.

[79]   The biblical text is 1 Cor 1 v. 27–8.

petitioners from Norfolk, Suffolk, Cambridge and Huntington demonstrate the subtlest awareness of the generic form they are operating within:

> Now Friends ... is not petitioning often for exalting such that will not do justice without flattering petitions, and then but have thanks and seldom the thing done? and [have] not flattering petitions and addresses exalted such as God has overthrown, that hath not done justice, nor will do justice to the just, when oppressions and grievances have been laid before them? the cry hath been, It hath not been a petition, it hath not been an address, because it hath not been in the World's method and form; therefore the oppressed shall not have justice done to them ... according to justice and equity, when the thing is made known unto you in simplicity and innocency, without flattering petitions and addresses, you ought to do them justice ... if the grievance be made to you known ... *for here are our Names who are the witnesses of Jesus Christ, that he hath disannulled the Commandment that gave Tithes, and hath ended the priesthood that took them.*[80]

Whereas the names at the bottom of petitions tend at best to be used as biographical footnotes by the historian or ignored completely by the literary critic, the signatories of *These Several Papers* assert the absolute centrality of the slavish reproduction of all of their names to the material form and rhetoric of the pamphlet. As they proclaim 'Here are our names' and list each one of them in all of their seemingly orderless detail, they spectacularly transgress the typographic decorum and material restrictions of the traditional printed mass petition which normally ran from a single folio sheet to a handful of quarto pages at most. Neither the Quaker men's petitions of the previous month, nor the women's printed mass petitions from the 1640s and 1650s, reproduce a single name in support of their messages in accordance with the overwhelming majority of other printed petitions from the period. This is not to say that collections of petitioners' names and signatures were deemed unimportant before *These Several Papers*; in fact petitioners to parliament from all points on the socio-political scale agreed with the assessment of one anonymous pamphleteer that 'if multitude of hands be not got, it will not answer expectation'.[81] It is rather the case that whilst names and signatories were valued at the point of collection in the community that compiled the original petition in manuscript, a final, printed version (if it included anything other than the stock concluding flourish of 'And your petitioners shall ever pray &c.') rarely printed anything other than a severely edited and ranked list of the

---

[80] *These Several Papers*, p. 33; emphasis added.
[81] *A New Birth of the City-Remonstrance* (London, 1646), p. 5. The relatively small number of 'Well-affected' petitioners from Southampton confirm this when they account for the paucity of names affixed to their petition by claiming that 'your Petitioners glorie not in ... an innumerable traine of names, yet if we had hoped thereby to have obtained the more favor in your Honors eyes, we might have had many thousands to have subscribed it'; *The Humble Petition of the Well-affected of the County of Southampton* (London, 1653), p. 3.

most respectable or significant names.[82] For instance, the names of those army officers included at the bottom of a 1647 petition to Sir Thomas Fairfax at Saffron Walden observe strict rank and degree; as we read from Colonel Sir Robert Pye down to more junior officers such as 'Quartermaster Colingwood', we are finally asked to remember 'many more Officers who concurre herein ... but could not subscribe ... for want of time' and, presumably, sufficient status. Similarly, a printed petition from 1659 originally subscribed by 150 London printers only includes the names of the ten most eminent members of the profession in that year.[83]

The 7,000 names at the heart of *These Several Papers* are multiply transgressive, then. In their apparently random, haphazard arrangement, they defy the hierarchizing principles of alphabet, age, marital status, seniority and perhaps even sectarian affiliation itself.[84] Only county boundaries appear to hold any distinguishing force for these anti-tithe protestors, a fact which attests to the vital importance of local (rather than national) affiliation and networks of parochial association during the revolutionary decades. Our understanding of the central, disorderly place of these women's signatory marks is sharpened most, however, by Nancy Miller who, in a different context, has written about 'women who have lost and still routinely lose their proper name in marriage, and whose signature – not merely their voice – has not been worth the paper it was written on; women for whom the signature – by virtue of its power in the world of circulation – is *not* immaterial.'[85] The Quaker women's insistence on the material importance of the printed ciphers representing every one of their names therefore gives the work an innovative substantiality (this was by far the longest work presented to parliament on this subject and the largest that Mary Westwood ever published) and impels it as far away from individualistic, competitive models of authorship as is conceivably possible. Moreover, it privileges an altogether different principle of copia from that traditionally favoured in the rarefied, humanistic atmosphere of tithe debate. 'Gathering' or 'collecting' on the subject of tithes no longer merely signifies the heroic ability of male communities to master resources with artisanal skill or 'manly elocution'; it now pleads for a vital, anti-hierarchical recognition of

---

[82] The best discussion of collections of names in petitions is in Zaret, *Origins of Democratic Culture, passim.*

[83] *A Petition of Divers Officers of the Army Presented to Sir Thomas Fairfax* (London, 1647), no sig.; *To the Right Honourable Knights, Citizens and Burgesses assembled in Parliament, The Humble Petition of the Workmen Printers, Freemen of the City of London* (London, 1659), no sig.

[84] Amid the signatories for London and Southwark we find the name of Elizabeth Poole who, as we have seen in chapter 3, was a Baptist, *These Several Papers*, p. 55. Maureen Bell has suggested, following Barry Reay, that 'the petition was signed by women opposed to tithes regardless of their religious adherences', 'Mary Westwood: Quaker Publisher', p. 25.

[85] Nancy K. Miller, *Subject to Change: Reading Feminist Writing* (New York, 1988), p. 75.

(27)

Margret Winne	Margret Hodges	Aime Freayre	Mary milles
Mary Robbinson	Margret Stonas	Margret Leming	Eliz. Smith
Sufanna Tyreman	Jane Parrit	Dorothy Leming	Dorothy Godd
Ifabel Fample	Elizabeth Spark	Katherin Bowch	Hellen Barwick
Barbarah Hildreth	Margeret Ruddock	Eliz. Horfman	Mary Roundiree
Mary Dunning	Margret Purfglove	Jennet meafin	Ifabel Fardin
Margret Sample	Margery Coulthcift	Mary Hardcaftle	Elizabeth Jackfon
Anne mannings	Ifabel Outhwait	Jane Simpfon	Eliz. Raw
Margret Wood	Elizabeth Thorp	Gennet Graing	Ifabel Simpfon
Urfula Rimer	Elizabeth Larneft	Mary Grang	Lucy Prat
Elizabeth Johnfon	Mary Radcliff	Mary Bridgwaters	Alice Kirton
Margret Parving	Effam Word	Agnes Atkinfon	Elizabeth Cherry
Katherin Rimer	Elizabeth Hodyfoe	Efter Bridgwaters	Agnes Cherry
Margret Pate	Margret Hoddyfoe	Ellen Umpelly	Alice Typlady
Rofamond Snowdon	Dorothy Hoddyfoe	Eliz. Grime	Eliz. Cherry
Elizabeth Fofter	Ifabel Burdftead	Iabel Lapington	Phillice Thompfon
Ellen Tyreman	Anne White fenior	Kathe. Kirkby	Dorothy Thompfon
Anne Smith	Anne White junior	Eliz. Stevenfon	Iabel Clarkfon
Elizabeth Tutin	Efter Chapman	Eliz. Sadman	Agnes Langftaff
Amey Waid	Anne Cockeril	Mirtha Coward	Katherin Wilfon
Margery Whitehead	Jane Cockeril	Frances Befwick	Elizabeth Langftaff
Jane Robbinfon	Magdalen Slightbolm	Ellinor Cresby	Margret Carter
Elizabeth Bell	Ifabel Knowles	Ellinor Hodgfon	Margret Robbinfon
Margret Heddon	Ellen Smalwood	Elizabeth Star	Mary Robbinfon
Mary Todd	Margery Cockeril	Elizabeth magdfon	Eliz. Raw
Katherin Rimer	Ellen Smalwood	Margret Hodgfon	Elizabeth Robbifon
Mary Linfey	Ifabel Smalwood	Katherin Dickfon	Eliz. Spenclay
Ellen Rowland	Mary Pearfon	Alice Hopper	Agnes allenby
Hellen John'on	Anne Pearfon	Eliz. meggifon	Eliz. Hawxwel
Margret Tomlinfon	Anne Greenbank	Katherin Allefon	Ifabel Clark
Rachel Garbut	Ellis Green	Elizabeth Thomlinfon	Agnes Langsdale
Margret Simpfon	Elizabeth Hart	Ellen Leak	Anne Prat
Mary mafon	Jane Bimftil	Elizabeth Stevenfon	Alice VValter
Ifabel Orton	Ellen Hay	Frances Write	Alice Tompfon
Ifabel Ray	Katherin Stockley	Martha mainckiun	Eliz. Honfdail
Sufan Wim	Jane Rider	Anne Caylew	Grace Smith
Margery Braderig	Sufanna Lotherington	Frances Kyther	Alice maw
Anne marwood	Jane Fafton	Ifabel Arluck	Anne Parkin
Jane Furbank	Jane Rogers	Eliz. Wats	Anne Dawfon
Jane Hohn	Sarah Jones	Jane Hunter	Anne Taylor
Ifabel Story	Alice Pickering	Anne Hunter	Sufan mainforth
Elizabeth Tiplady	Dorothy Smalls	Ifabel Barker	Barbarah Kirk
Ifabel Barher	Dorothy Heflam	Eliz. Pelch	Barbarah Tindal
Anne Barher	Ifabel Sulon	Anne Northen	Katherin milner
Margret Stonas	Margery Grange	Barbarah Jowfey	Jane Goodman
Anne Grayftorck	Eliz. Pennet	Margret Chafman	Ifabel applyurd
Bettriffe Tenting	Eliz. Blenkhorn	Alice Sowly	Clare marfton
Alice Nelliff	Katherin Clark	Anne Fardin	Hannah Ceplaygh
Ifabel Tompfoe	Dorothy Roodds	Eliz. Jackfon	Eliz. Goodbarn

Figure 15: *These Several Papers* (1659), p. 27
Women tithe protestors from Yorkshire defying the hierarchical principles of alphabet, age, marital status and seniority.

the subjectivities of others as revealed through the sufferings and signatures of communities of women. A cheaply printed, prosaic list of proper nouns has rarely seemed so poetic.

Awareness of the assertion 'here are our Names' is thus crucial to understanding the creative agency of the pamphlet. The very act of signing one's name represents the most basic performance of rhetoricized self-assertion, wherein the signature becomes a meta-inscription which can only ever participate in the conferral and renewal of authorship and authority. Yet when this is transported to the context of mass public protest, the nature of that authority is fundamentally ambiguous. In this context, every signatory mark is riven by the competing forces of individuation and collectivisation, presence and absence. Jacques Derrida would perhaps have traced this moment of conflict back to the 'enigmatic originality of every paraph', but it is more precisely a moment of radical irresolution, a complicated negotiation of self and other which, for these Quaker women at least, witnesses the potentialities of Jesus Christ, religious faith and collective action.[86]

The Material Culture of Suffering

The possibilities for this kind of agency were undoubtedly promoted by the fact that the Quaker movement itself enabled women to develop and explore the limits of a material culture of collectivity. Much recent work has examined the importance of the establishment of Quaker women's meetings in this context.[87] These sprang up in the wake of the men's business meetings and despite much confusion as to their origins they were actually implemented in London between 1656 and 1657.[88] In the earliest stages, their basic business was the issue of poor relief, but as the century progressed, the certification of marriages and disciplining of unruly Friends or the public condemnation of backsliders also came under their jurisdiction. However, it was not until 1697 that such separate women's meetings were recognized by the Quaker polity, such separation perhaps representing too

---

[86]   'By definition, a written signature implies the actual or empirical nonpresence of the signer. But, it will be said, it also marks and retains his having-been-present in a past now, which will remain a future now, and therefore a now in general, in the transcendental form of nowness (maintenance). This general maintenance is somehow inscribed, stapled to present punctuality, always evident and always singular, in the form of the signature. This is the enigmatic originality of every paraph.'; Jacques Derrida, 'Signature Event Context', in Peggy Kamuf (ed.), *A Derrida Reader: Between the Blinds* (Hemel Hempstead, 1991), p. 107.

[87]   On Quaker women's meetings see W. Beck and T. F. Ball, *The London Friends Meetings* (London, 1896), pp. 343–54; Braithwaite, *Beginnings of Quakerism*, pp. 340–42; idem., *The Second Period of Quakerism*, pp. 272–4, 286–8; Beatrice Carré, 'Early Quaker Women', pp. 45–7; Bonnelyn Young Kunze, *Margaret Fell and the Rise of Quakerism*, pp. 143–57.

[88]   See Kunze, *Margaret Fell*, pp. 144–5.

radical an incursion into the privileged authority of male Friends.[89] Notwithstanding the separateness of such women's meetings, a sense of collective identity was undoubtedly fostered by their participation in a crucial communal and collative activity which was characteristic of Quaker culture more generally; they, too, collected and published testimonies of Quaker sufferings. This practice was essential to the movement's campaign against tithes in the late 1650s and involved the meticulous recording (in manuscript and printed broadside) of written testimonies against the governmental or ministerial persecution of Friends. Thus each monthly meeting kept, or was supposed to keep, records for every arrest, distraint, and imprisonment of its members, principally for offences such as non-payment of tithes, the interruption of church services and refusal to take oaths. These were then passed on to a quarterly meeting where they were transcribed and bound, from whence they were submitted as an annual account of sufferings to the annual Meeting for Sufferings in London.[90] They were used to ensure both conformity amongst Friends on matters of public Quaker policy and as a means of confronting a given administration with extensive material evidence of their religious persecution.

These accounts still survive in the manuscript Great Book of Sufferings in the Friends House Library in London, and in Joseph Besse's retrospective printed *Collection of the Sufferings of the People Called Quakers* (1753), and even cursory attention to them demonstrates that Quaker women were willing testifiers. Thus, for example, in the same year that *These Several Papers* was presented we come across one Jane Vickers, 'a poore antient widdow' in the county of Berkshire who:

> labours hard for a living having only half an acre of ground on which she planted some hemp — for refusing to pay tithe 4 men took away 6s 8d worth of hemp, when all the poore woman had then grown was worth 26s 8d — taking away a 4th of what she had grown — 2s 6d was formerly demanded.[91]

The Great Book of Sufferings is littered with hundreds more instances of such women having property distrained or being imprisoned for not paying tithes. This may imply something about the status and perception of Quaker women (especially widows and those left behind by missionary husbands) as property-

---

[89]　The issue of women's meetings was one of the principle sources of the factional conflict which characterized the movement in the early 1670s, a conflict that saw John Wilkinson and John Story disputing the leadership of Fox for his advocacy of separate women's meetings. They viewed the separation as 'monstrous and ridiculous'. Similarly, the earliest sensationalistic drawings of the London Quakers tend to recycle a scene of Quaker women meeting together. See Braithwaite, *Second Period of Quakerism*, pp. 290–323; Beck and Ball, *London Friends Meetings*, p. 344.

[90]　On the Quaker culture of suffering see J. R. Knott, 'Joseph Besse and the Quaker Culture of Suffering' in Lowenstein and Corns (eds.), *The Emergence of Quaker Writing*, pp. 126–41; R. T. Vann, 'Friends' Sufferings Collected and Recollected', *Quaker History* 61:1 (1972), pp. 24–35.

[91]　'Great Book of Sufferings', vol. 1, Berkshire, p. 77.

holding subjects in the seventeenth century, but the nature of the manuscript record and the manner of data collection prevents easy theorization on the subject.[92] However, instead of reading the Great Book of Sufferings as a historical document capable of providing the historian or literary critic with simple 'evidence' of how individual Quaker women lived and endured hardships under the early modern tithing system, it is perhaps more useful to consider it as a collectively written text produced by multiple agencies which informed and drew upon the collative culture which produced the women's petition of 1659.

This is certainly a link that *These Several Papers* itself is keen to forge. Referring to the 'unjust oppression of tithes' 'which hath taken away many of our friends lives', the first petition of the pamphlet continues:

> Therefore what havock, what spoiling of Goods, and peoples estates taken away by the Priests impropriators, worse then ever the plundering Cavilliers? and what prisoning, what haling into Courts and Sessions people all about the Nation there is, and chiefly about these Tithes? and how many of their lives have been a testimony against it, and ended their lives in nasty holes and dungeons, for their Testimony against Tithes? therefore for us to be clear of your blood, we lay these things upon you.[93]

Whilst reconfiguring the stock image of conspicuously consuming royalists to represent established clerical abuse, the passage also draws attention to religious persecution by developing the idea of Quaker testimony against suffering. It could almost be the post-structuralist's dream as the extra-textual dimension is recuperated by the textual. 'Lives in nasty holes and dungeons' seem to become signifiers in some kind of archi-textual scheme wherein all experience is mediated and defined by an endless series of testimonial inscriptions. However, to embrace such ludic theorizations is surely also to lose sight of the material culture of suffering through which so many Quakers lived, wrote and died, and erases the ultimate referent of those countless pages of the Great Book of Sufferings. What the pamphlet's development of testimony achieves therefore is less fulfilment of post-structuralist fantasy than the consolidation of communal sectarian bonds, and the promotion of the multiply-authored text. The creative process involved in the production of this 'Testimony for tithes' is less creation of the illusion of seamless intertextuality than the conflation of author and text, facilitated by the fact that the act of testifying (as both actual suffering and inscription) and the testimony itself are accorded an equivalence amongst the faithful.

The petition continues and draws the parallelism more distinctly:

---

[92] This is because statistical analysis of the women in the Great Book of Sufferings proves difficult as a result of the inaccurate way in which the sufferings are dated and the technical problem of recording women's sufferings for tithes at a time when all distraints would have been recorded in the husband's name, even if he were absent when the distraint was made. See Carré, 'Early Quaker Women', p. 45.

[93] *These Several Papers*, p. 3.

Therefore keep it clear from off your own heads, we warn you which to you is the word of the Lord God; there are many in the Prison at this day in nasty Gaols, bearing their testimony for the Lord Jesus Christ (that disannulled the command that gave Tithes) ... So here are our hands and Testimony to you now, not that we are weary of suffering and of Imprisonment, nor cry to you for help, but because the blood of our brethren has been spilt and also many thousands have had their goods spoyled and taken away, and many of them Imprisoned to death, whose blood lies upon the heads of their persecutors, but it is that you may keep yourselves from blood, and stop the oppressors that causeth it.[94]

At one level, this culture of collectivity is revealed when persecution is appropriated as one of the defining characteristics of the minority group, but furthermore it suggests the complex interrelationship between agency and text. The public sphere of tithe debate is entered with the premise that authorship is not, in any sense, a solitary, singular act, nor need it be, more radically, simply a matter of the pen. Heads of state can be warned and advised by the Quaker women at the same moment that fellow Friends are embraced and the marks of their sufferings are simultaneously inscribed for the first time and remembered again.

With such a culture of collective suffering behind them, the petitioners were confident that the providential resolution to the current crisis would be in their favour; that there was joy for the persecuted was, after all, the daily example of Christ. Thus the women of Berkshire, Hampshire and Wiltshire could rejoice that:

The Lamb, the Saints shall have the victory, the Lamb, the Bride is known again, preparing for her husband's coming out of the Wilderness, and the daughters of Abraham are meeting her, who gives in their Testimony against this oppressive Church, Ministry and maintenance, and their Testimony of the Lord Jesus Christ to reign.[95]

The women's public testimony against 'the oppressive Church, Ministry and maintenance' of tithes is justified because it is utterly self-less and collective. This can be seen in a subtle moment of exegesis which reworks a biblical text which in the early modern period was mobilized for a variety of antifeminist ends. Amid the references to 'husbands' and 'Brides', the inclusion of 'the daughters of Abraham' would have conjured up a biblical text (the first letter of Peter) into the minds of the petition's readers. Invoking this particular epistle might initially seem appropriate as it constitutes an encouragement and exhortation to an oppressed minority of Christian communities to endure suffering at the hands of civil powers in anticipation of the spiritual joy to follow.[96] In this case, however, it becomes less apposite a text for female petitioners to be citing as soon as one recalls that this is

---

94 Ibid., p. 4
95 Ibid., p. 39.
96 For instance: 'Christ also suffered for us, leaving us an example, that ye should follow in his steps ... Who, when he was reviled, he reviled not again; when he suffered, he threatened not; but committed himself to him that judgeth righteously' 1 Peter 2 v. 21–3.

one of the most cited and recycled moments of biblical antifeminism. However problematically, these women (as daughters of Abraham) are asked to behave:

> Even as Sara obeyed Abraham, calling him Lord: whose daughters ye are, as long as ye do well, and are not afraid with any amazement.
> Likewise, ye husbands, dwell with them according to knowledge, giving honour unto the wife, as unto the weaker vessel, and as being heirs together of the grace of life.[97]

The deleterious effects that the label 'the weaker vessel' has had for women throughout history is, of course, well documented; more significant here, however, is the manner in which Quaker women try to rehabilitate and shift the emphasis of traditional exegesis of the epistle text.[98] By drawing attention away from Peter's singular (in every sense) and derogatory epithet and focusing it instead on their contextual status as multiple 'daughters of Abraham', the women assert their collectivity and demonstrate the concomitant ability to survive and thrive in the patriarchal culture that enveloped seventeenth-century tithe dispute.

---

[97] 1 Peter 3, v. 6–7.

[98] See, for example, Matthew Poole's gloss on the phrase: 'weaker than the Husbands, and that both in Body and Mind, as Women usually are. In Scripture any Instrument is called a Vessel, and the Wife here is called so, as being not only an Ornament, but an Help to the Husband and Family. This he adds as a reason why the Husband should give honour to the Wife, *viz.* Her being the Weaker Vessel; weak Vessels must be gently handled; the Infirmities of Children bespeak their pardon when they offend ... it is a part of that prudence according to which Men should dwell with their wives, to have more regard for them because of their infirmities', *Annotations Upon the Holy Bible*, vol. II (1685), sig. 5Lr. For further exploration of the phrase see Antonia Fraser, *The Weaker Vessel: Woman's Lot in the Seventeenth Century* (London, 1984).

Conclusion

We began with a woman talking in bed. Through the subsequent analyses of the ways in which women's agency manifested itself within the pamphlet culture of revolutionary England, we have begun to see how one of the most inclusive social phenomena of the early modern period was potentially more exclusive and divisive than has generally been acknowledged. There can be no doubt that pamphlets were crucial in extending the boundaries of political literacy and participatory politics further down the social scale; this book simply asks that we explore the concealed agencies within (and gendered nature of) such narratives of expansion and extension in greater detail. It is, of course, well known that revolutionary pamphlet writing flourished in contexts of political and epistemological crisis, but it has been less frequently acknowledged that it also took root in a culture which nurtured male agency at the same time as it censured or concealed women's praxis.

The preceding case studies have all demonstrated that non-aristocratic women's agency can be traced in both material and rhetorical strategies which are simultaneously the necessary results of and productive responses to patriarchal assumptions which held sway over English culture of the 1640s and 1650s. Situating agency in those locations and negotiations which are absolutely dependent upon the careful effacement of self rather than in more instantly recognizable or strident assertions of autonomous individuality allows us to begin recovering movement and noise from the stillness and silences that haunt all historical records. After all, even the most visible, celebrity sectarian woman writer of the 1650s, the Fifth Monarchist Anna Trapnel, presented her public persona as a fascinating mediation between interdependent forces rather than as some kind of stable, self-identical subject position. If, following Trapnel and the other women who have featured in this study, we consider agency as a product of potentially self-effacing negotiations, we can begin to appreciate it in the scarcely conceivable lived experiences of the many as much as in the more radical or enduring transformations of the few. It *can* be that which we apprehend and admire as a prefiguration of our modern selves, but it also always remains in the less discernable actions of others moving towards distant goals not our own.

This, in turn, enables us to conceive of agency as something that is beyond – or at least as something not simply reducible to – text or verbal performance. The agency of non-aristocratic women in the mid-seventeenth century had a material as well as a rhetorical dimension, something that studies have often neglected. Some contemporaries were certainly less reluctant to recognise this. Thus, we end with a quotation from a prominent mid-seventeenth-century pamphleteer surveying the pamphlet culture of this period all too aware, as we now are, of the troubling (if frequently silent) fact that women *did* assume active positions therein. John Crouch was the editor of the sensational royalist serial *The Man in the Moon* whose high-flown, flamboyant journalistic style represents the polar opposite of the unspectacular, self-effacing journalism of Elizabeth Alkin. As noted earlier, Crouch had made a career of writing misogynistic and satirical newsbooks whose bawdy, scatological style was extravagantly deployed against all things puritan.[1] Here, in the final extant edition of this serial, he scrutinizes the landscape of politics and cheap print in the wake of the hanging and quartering of the royalist hero James Graham, Marquis of Montrose at the Grassmarket in Edinburgh on 21 May 1650:

> *Montrosse* is executed over and over in the Rebells *Libels*, *Walker* has hang'd him three or four times and *Peck* the *Perfect Liurnall* [sic] maker, hath hang'd him no less than thrice in his last *Sundays work*, quarter'd him as handsomly as a hang man need to doe, jerk'd him up by degrees, (as he doth his *Shee-Intelligencers*) till they lie for dead in a Trance half an hour together, and wake with a Vision, to help patch up his two sheets of *Bum-fodder*, that would make a man have need to be – himselfe to read to the last Page.[2]

His political dismay in the weeks immediately following this event is mediated through a reflection upon what he perceives to be the deplorable state of the revolutionary culture of cheap print. Characteristically for Crouch, if the times have become execrable then pamphlets have become excremental; they are the '*Bum-fodder*' that can only be read through the apparently contiguous acts of interpretation and defecation; being and beshitting are, he reminds us, only a dash away from each other. More specifically, though, Crouch's invective is directed at the rhetorical and material methods of pamphlet production deployed by two parliamentarian newsmen, Samuel Pecke and Henry Walker. Firstly, he lambastes the ways in which they have circulated and reprinted the gruesome image of the dead Marquis in the previous issue of their newsbooks. Whilst Pecke's *Perfect Diurnall* compiled four different manuscript accounts of the execution, Walker chose to offer three, including one extremely detailed transcript of the trial.[3] Crouch derides such reportage as tortuously repetitive, and condemns it as the stylistic correlate of the spectacular repeated violence done to an aristocratic body.

However, it is Crouch's vilification of another aspect of Pecke's methods of pamphlet publication that demands our attention here. Moving on from his vision of the related sins of aristocratic execution and repetitive narrative, he pauses to

---

[1] See pp. 88–9.

[2] *The Man in the Moon* 57, 29 May–5 June 1650, pp. 426–7. For biographical details of Montrose see *DNB*, vol. 22, pp. 316–19; Barbara Hutton, *The Fiery Cross; or the Vow of Montrose* (London and Edinburgh, 1875).

[3] See *The Perfect Diurnall* 25, 27 May–5 June 1650, sig. Bbr, B2r, p. 273; *Severall Proceedings in Parliament* 35, 23 May–30 May 1650, pp. 497–502.

pour scorn on the fact that '*Shee-Intelligencers*' are apparently involved in the production of *The Perfect Diurnall*. This is not necessarily surprising since we saw in chapter 3 how Henry Walker collaborated with Elizabeth Alkin on single issues of *The Moderne Intelligencer, Mercurius Anglicus,* and *The Modern Intelligencer.* Yet whereas that chapter was keen to tease out the implications of multiple and effaced female agencies, the final issue of *The Man in the Moon* reflects upon the horror of such possibilities. As Montrose's condemned body is 'Jerked ... by degrees' up the gallows, the image begins to mutate and we are invited to behold instead a terrifying or titillative vision of female participation in the material production of pamphlets. Pecke's collaborative work with 'Shee-Intelligencers' is complexly rendered as a graphic 'jerk[ing]' up of the female body, so that women's creative agency is reduced either to the operations of male desire or to the results of one man's necrophilic impulses. The terms, though, in which Crouch depicts multiple female agencies are particularly instructive. As women 'help patch up [the] two sheets' of pamphlet text, that is, as they engage in those material forms of associative, collaborative and self-effacing agency upon which the newstrade was so dependent, they are transformed into prophetesses like Anna Trapnel or Elizabeth Poole who deploy 'Vision[s]' and 'Trance[s]' to communicate politico-religious messages to audiences. Such royalist, misogynistic remarks work on two levels. At one, they elide the differences between the parliamentarian and the sectarian to make oppositional political capital; at another they conflate women's material engagement in pamphlet production with the more rhetorically complex and spectacular varieties of the visionary's work.

This study obviously recoils from the heightened misogyny of Crouch's antifeminist, anti-Puritan invective, yet it does seek to embrace one aspect of his reading of seventeenth-century women's involvement in the pamphlet culture of revolutionary England. In yoking together the activities of more famous female visionaries and those of other less visible, non-aristocratic women who were making and shaping the pamphlets and petitions of the times, he does at least (albeit unwittingly) open up a discursive framework which subsequent writers might exploit to discuss female agency as something that was both textual and extra-textual. However this is an opportunity that critics who have written upon the relationship between women's agency in seventeenth-century pamphlet literature have failed, largely, to avail themselves of. A number of modern literary scholars have written upon the *rhetoric* of self-effacement in sectarian women's prophecy and polemic, but, clearly, attention to rhetorical strategies alone does little to assess or engage with the work and struggle of those countless women whose every day lives were the most material expressions of self-effacement. As daughters, wives and mothers, women were daily reminded that their being actually meant being for others, relinquishing their names, transferring rights and property from one generation of men to the next. This is the point at which this book has aimed to make its intervention. It has been the business of the previous pages to begin to uncover or recover the agency of women who have been largely (or until recently) effaced from official historical records because of their 'inferior' status as women. Such recovery asks that we attend to the different ways in which silences might be resonant, apparent absences might be productive, and self-effacing negotiations might be recuperated as necessary and complex sites of agency.

Bibliography

Manuscript Sources

British Library

Sir James Harrington's Diary	Add. MS. 10114
Correspondance of Archbishop William Sancroft	Harl. MS. 3784 Harl. MS. 4931 f. 9

Brotherton Library, University of Leeds

Poems Breathed Forth by the Noble Hadassas	MS Lt q. 32

Guildhall Library

Minutes of the Court of Governors of Bridewell and Bethlem Hospitals	MS. 33011/9

Public Record Office

State Papers	SP 18/66/74
	SP 19/4/72
	SP 19/4/77
	SP 19/5/284
	SP 19/98/80
	SP 23/8/151
	SP 23/62/228
	SP 23/62/232
	SP 23/62/233
	SP 23/62/235
	SP 25/24/68
	SP 25/24/71
	SP 25/63/16
	SP 25/65/238
	SP 25/72/174
	SP 25/75/258
	SP 25/75/545
	SP 25/76/73
	SP 25/87/61

Friends House Library

The Great Book of Sufferings

Printed Sources

Anonymous Primary Works

A Brief Narrative of the Mysteries of State Carried on by the Spanish Factions in England (London, 1651).

A Declaration of the Parliament of England Expressing the Grounds for their Late Proceedings and Setting of the Present Government in the Way of a Free State (London, 1649).

An Hue-And-Cry After Vox Populi. Or An Answer to Vox Diaboli, or a Libellous Pamphlet falsly styled Vox Populi (London, 1646).

A Letter to A Letter to Mr Tho Edwards. The Dedication of the Letter To our much suspected friend, Mr T. Edwards, Scavenger Generall, throughout Great Britaine, New England, and the united Provinces (London, 1646).

A Parliament of Ladies: With their Lawes Newly Enacted (London, 1647).

A Perfect Narrative of the Whole High Court of Justice (London, 1649).

A Remonstrance of the Shee-Citizens of London And of many thousands of other the free-borne Women of England (London, 1647).

A Shrill Cry in the Eares of Cavaliers, Apostates and Presbyters for the Resolve (London, 1649).

A Treatise of Tithes Written By a Wel-Wisher to Religion and Proprietie, As they have been established by the Law of the Land, and as they have been continued, and confirmed throughout divers Ages by Several Acts of Parliament (London, 1653).

A True Narrative of the Title, Government and Causes of the Death of the Late Charles Stuart (London, 1649).

A New Bull-Bayting (London, 1649).

Eikon Alethine: The Portraiture of Truths Most Sacred Majesty (London, 1649).

Eye Salve (London, 1649).

Faces About. Or A Recrimination charged Upon Mr John Goodwin, In the Point of Fighting against God, and opposing the way of Christ. And A Justification of the Presbyterian way in the Particulars by him unjustly charged upon it. With other short Animadversions upon his late Book called Oeomaxia or, The Grand Impudence of Men running the hazard of fighting against God, &c (London, 1644).

Goliah's Head Cut Off With His Own Sword (London, 1655).

King Charls His Speech Made Upon the Scaffold at Whitehall-Gate (London, 1649).

King Charls His Tryall: Or a Perfect Narrative of the Whole Proceedings of the High Court of Justice (London, 1649).

Manus Testium Movens: Or a Presbyteriall Glosse Upon many of those obscure prophetick texts (London, 1651).

More Light Shining in Buckinghamshire (London, 1649).

Newes from the New Exchange, or the Commonwealth of Ladies (London, 1650).

Rump: Or An Exact Collection of the Choycest Poems and Songs Relating to the Late Times (London, 1662).

The Account Audited (London, 1649).

The Banner of Truth Displayed: Or a Testimony for Christ and Against Anti-Christ (London, 1656).

The Character of a Rebellion (Oxford, 1681).

The City-Dames Petition, In the behalfe of the long afflicted but well affected Cavaliers (London, 1647).

The Copie of A Paper Presented to the Parliament and read the 27th of the fourth Moneth 1659. Subscribed by more than fifteen thousand hands. Thus Directed To the Parliament of England, from many thousand of the free born people of this Commonwealth (London, 1659).

The Execution of the Late King Justified and the Parliament and the Army therein Vindicated (London, 1649).

The Great Assises Holden in Parnassus (London, 1644).

The Humble Petition of Many Thousands of Wives and Matrons of the City of London, and other parts of this Kingdome (London, 1643).

The Ladies, A Second Time Assembled in Parliament (London, 1647).

The Ladies Parliament (London, 1647).

The Life and Death of King Charles the Martyr (London, 1649).

The Maid's Petition, To the Honourable Members of both Houses. Or The Humble Petition of many Thousands of the well-affected within and without the lines of Communication, Virgins, Maids and other young Women not married, &c. And in the behalf of the whole Kingdome, for their lawfull dayes of Recreation. With their Declaration to hold out stifly and to comply with the Apprentices or others for their tollerable Tolleration. Presented on Tuesday the 9 of August the 2d Recreation day for Apprentices, 1647 (London, 1647).

The Manner of the Deposition of Charles Stuart (London, 1649).

The Mid-wives Just Complaint (London, 1646).

The Mid-wives Just Petition: Or. A Complaint of divers good Gentlewomen of that Faculty (London, 1643).

The Parliament of Women With the Merrie Lawes by them Newly Enacted (London, 1656).

The Quakers Fiery Beacon, or the Shaking Ranters Ghost (London, 1655).

The Ranters Recantation: And their Sermon Delivered at a Meeting on Tuesday last, in WhiteChappel (London, 1650).

The Resolver Continued, Or Satisfaction to Some Scruples About the Putting of the Late King to Death (London, 1649).

The Sense of the Covenant (London, 1649).

The Widowes Lamentation for the Absence of their deare Children and Suitors. And for Divers of their Deaths in these fatall Civill Wars (London, 1643).

The Women's Petition, to the Right Honourable, his Excellency, the most Noble and Victorious Lord General Cromwell (London, 1651).

To the High Court of Parliament. A Dilemma from a Parallel Humbly Presented (London, 1646).

To the Honourable Knights, Citizens and Burgesses of the Commons House of Parliament (London, 1641).

To the Honourable the Knights, Citizens and Burgesses; in the Commons House of Parliament Now Assembled. The Humble Petition of 15000 poore labouring men, known by the name of Porters, and the lowest Members of the Citie of London (London, 1641).

To The Honourable the House of Commons Assembled in Parliament. The Humble Petition of many thousand poore people, in and about the Citie of London (London, 1641).

To the Parliament of the Commonwealth of England The Humble Petition of Diuvers Afflicted Women in behalf of Mr John Lilburne Prisoner in Newgate (London, 1653).

To the Parliament of the Commonwealth of England, The Humble Petition of many of the well-affected of the County of Kent (London, 1653).

To the Right Honourable, the High Court of Parliament; The Humble Petition of many hundreds of distressed Women, Trades-mens Wives, and Widdowes (London, 1641).

To the Right Honourable the House of Peeres Now Assembled in Parliament. The Humble Petition of man thousands of Courtiers, Citizens, Gentlemens and Trades-mens wives (London, 1641).

To the Supream Authority of this Nation, the Commons Assembled in Parliament: The humble Petition of Divers Well Affected Women Inhabiting the Cities of London, Westminster, the Borough of Southwark, Hamblets and Places Adjacent (Affecters and Approvers of the late Large Petition of the Eleventh of September 1648) (London, 1649).

To the Supreme Authority of England, The Commons Assembled in Parliament. The Humble Petition of Diverse well-affected Women of the Citis of London and Westminster (London, 1649).

Two Conferences Between Some of those that are called Separatistsand Independents Concerning their Different Tenets (London, 1650).

Unto every individual Member of Parliament: The humble Representation of divers afflicted Women-Petitioners to the Parliament, on behalf of Mr John Lilburne (London, 1653).

Other Printed Works

Abbot, Margaret, *A Testimony Against the False Teachers of this Generation* (London, 1659).

Abbott, W. C., *The Writings and Speeches of Oliver Cromwell*, 4 vols (Cambridge MA, 1937–47).

Adams, Mary, *The Ranters Monster* (London, 1652).

Alle, Thomas, *A Brief Narration of the Truth of Some Particulars in Mr Edwards His Booke Called Gangraena* (London, 1646).

Audland, Ann, *A True Declaration of the Suffering of the Innocent, who is hated and prosecuted without a cause. Wherein is discovered the zeale of the Magistrates and people of Banbury, persecuting and imprisoning them that are sent of the Lord in love to their Sould to warn the of the evill of their wayes* (London, 1655).

Bairn, Robert, *The Labyrinth the Kingdom's In* (London, 1649).

Banaster, John, *An Alarm to the World of the Appearing of Zion's King* (London, 1649).

Barbaro, Francesco, *Directions for Love and Marriage In Two Books Written Originally by Franciscus Barbarus a Venetian Senator. And Now Translated into English By a Person of Quality* (London, 1677).

Barclay, Robert, *The Anarchy of the Ranters* (London, 1676).

Barwick, Grace, *To all Present Rulers, whether Parliament, or Whomsoever of England* (London, 1659).

Bastwick, John, *Independency Not God's Ordinance* (London 1645).

Becon, Thomas, *The Worckes of Thomas Becon, which he hath hytherto made and published with diuerse other newe Bookes*, 3 vols (London, 1560–64).

Benson, Gervaise, *The Cry of the Oppressed from Under Their Oppressions* (London, 1656).

Beynon, Michael, *The Antitythe-Monger Confuted; or Ministers Maintenance Defended and Vindicated* (London, 1662).

Bishop, George, *New-England Judged, By the Spirit of the Lord* (3rd edn London, 1703).

Blackborow, Sarah, *Herein is held forth the Gift and Good-will of God* (London, 1659).

Blount, Thomas, *Glossographia* (London, 1656).

Boulbie, Judith, *A Testimony for Truth Against All Hireling Priests* (London, 1665).

Bourne, Immanuel, *A Defence and Justification of Ministers Maintenance By Tythes* (London, 1659).

Braithwait, Richard, *The English Gentlewoman* (London, 1631).

Bray, Thomas, *A New Sect of Religion Descryed* (London, 1641).

Brown, David, *The Naked Woman,or a rare epistle sent to Mr Peter Sterry Minister at Whitehall* (London, 1652).

Brown, David, *To the Supream Authority of England, the Parliament Assembled, the Scope of the humble RemembranceOf that Prodigious Conspiracy Called the Bloody Petition* (London, 1652).

Brown, David, *The True Understanding of the Whole Arte of Expedition in Teaching to Write. Intermixed with rare discourses of other matters, to shew the possibilitie of skill in teaching, and probabilitie of successe in learning, to write in 6 hours* (London, 1638).

Bryan, John, *A Public Disputation sundry dayes at Killingworth in Warwickshire between John Bryan and John Onley ... upon this Question, Whether the Parishes of this nation generally be true Churches* (London, 1655).

Canne, John, *The Golden Rule, or Justice Advanced* (London,1649).

Cary, Mary, *The Resurrection of the Witnesses* (2nd edn London, 1653).

Cary, Mary, *Twelve Humble Proposals* (London, 1653).

Cary, Mary, *The Little Horns Doom and Downfall* (London, 1651).

Cary, Mary, *A New and More Exact Mappe or Description of New Jerusalems Glory* (London, 1651).

Cary, Mary, *The Resurrection of the Witnesses* (London, 1648).

Cary, Mary, *A Word in Season to the Kingdom of England* (London, 1647).

Cary, Mary, *The Glorious Excellencie of the Spirit of Adoption* (London, 1645).

Case, Thomas, *Spirituall Whordome* (London, 1647).

Channel, Elinor, *A Message from God [By a Dumb Woman]* (London, 1654).

Chidley, Katherine, *Good Counsel to the Petitioners for Presbyterian Government That They May Declare Their Faith Before They Build Their Church* (London, 1645).

Chidley, Katherine, *A New-Yeares Gift, or a Brief Exhortation to Mr Thomas Edwards* (London, 1645).

Chidley, Katherine, *The Justification of the Independent Churches of Christ* (London, 1641).

Chidley, Samuel, *A Vindication of Lieu Col John Lilburn and Others. From those Aspersions cast upon them by David Brown in his idle pamphlet directed to the Supream Authority of England the Parliament assembled, and presented to curry favour with them* (London, 1652).

Chidley, Samuel, *Cloathing for the Naked Woman, Or the Second Part of the Dissembling Scot* (London, 1652).

Clarke, Frances, *A Brief Reply to the Narration of Don Pantaleon Sa* (London, 1653).

Clarke, Samuel, *A Caution Against Sacriledge: Or Sundrie Queries Concerning Tithes* (London, 1659).

Clarkson, Lawrence, *A Single Eye: All Light, no Darkness; or Light and Darkness One* (London, 1650).

Crawford, Patricia and Gowing Laura (eds.), *Women's Worlds in Seventeenth-Century England: A Sourcebook* (London and New York, 2000).

Collins, J. G., *Strange News from Newgate* (London, 1651).

Cook, John, *King Charls his Case; or an Appeal to all Rationall Men Concerning His Tryal* (London, 1649).

Cope, Esther S. (ed.), *The Prophetic Writings of Lady Eleanor Davies* (Oxford, 1995).

Crofton Croker, T. (ed.), *Autobiography of Lady Warwick* (London, 1848).

Crook, John, *Tythes No Property to, nor lawful maintenance for a Powerful Gospel Preaching Ministry* (London, 1659).

Culmer, Richard, *The Ministers Hue and Cry* (London, 1651).

Davies, Lady Eleanor, *Strange and Wonderfull Prophesies By the Lady Eleanor Audley; who is yet alive, and lodgeth in Whitehall* (London, 1649).

Davies, Lady Eleanor, *Given to the Elector Prince Charles of the Rhyne* (Amsterdam, 1633).

Davies, Lady Eleanor, *The Blasphemous Charge Against Her* (London, 1649).

Dent, Arthur, *The Plaine Man's Path-way to Heaven*, 2nd edn (London, 1640).

Donaldson, Ian (ed.), *Ben Jonson: Poems* (Oxford, 1975).

Drapes, Edward, *A Plain and Faithfvll Discovery of A Beame in Master Edwards his Eye* (London, 1646).

Dunn Macray W. and Coxe, H. O. (eds.), *Calendar of the Clarendon State Papers Preserved in the Bodleian Library,* 5 vols (Oxford, 1872–1970).

Eccles, Solomon, *Signes are from the Lord to a People or Nation* (London, 1663).

Eden, Adam, *A Vindication of the Reformation on foot, among the Ladies, To Abolish Modesty and Chastity, and Restore the Native Simplicity of going Naked. And An Attempt to reconcile all Opposers to it, And Make them join in a speedy Completion of this Glorious Design* (London, 1755).

Edwards, Thomas, *Gangraeana, or a Catalogue and Discovery of Many of the Errours, Heresies, Blasphemies and Pernicious Practices of the Sectaries of this Time, Vented and Acted in England in these Four Last Years*, ed. M. M. Goldsmith and I. Roots (Ilkley, 1977).

Edwards, Thomas, *Antapologia: Or a Full Answer to the Apologeticall Narration* (London, 1644).

Edwards, Thomas, *Reasons Against the Independent Government of Particular Congregations* (London, 1641).

Ellwood, Thomas, *The History of the Life of Thomas Ellwood, Written By his Own Hand*, ed. S. Grayson (London, 1906).

Elson, Mary, *A True Information of our Blessed Women's Meeting* (London, 1680).

Evans, Arise, *The Bloudy Vision of John Farly* (London, 1653).

Evans, Arise, *The Great and Bloody Visions* (London, 1653).

F. J., *A New Proclamation* (London, 1653).

Farnworth, Richard, *The Ranters Principles and Deceits Discovered and Declared Against* (London, 1655).

Farnworth, Richard, *A Woman Forbidden to Speak in the Church* (London, 1653).

Feake, Christopher, *The Oppressed Close Prisoner in Windsor Castle His Defiance* (London, 1654).

Fell, Margaret, *A Testimonie of the Touchstone for al Professions and all Forms ... And a Tryal by the Scriptures, who the False Prophets Are..... Also some of the Ranters Principles Answered* (London, 1656).

Fidoes, J., *The Parliament Justified in their late Proceedings Against Charles Stuart* (London, 1649).

Forbes, Alexander, *The Anatomy of Independencie Or a Briefe Commentary and Moderate Discourse Upon the Apologeticall Narration* (London, 1644).

Forster, Mary, *These Several Papers* (1659).

Fox, George, *An Answer to Doctor Burgess His Book, entitules, A Case Concerning of Buying Bishops Lands Which he Spread Before the Parliament* (London, 1659).

Gilpin, John, *The Quakers Shaken: Or a Fire-brand snach'd out of the fire* (London, 1653).

Goodwin, John, *The Obstructours of Justice, Or a Defense of the Honourable Sentence Passed Upon the Late King* (London, 1649).

Goodwin, John, *Cretensis: Or A Brief Answer to an Ulcerous Treatise lately Published by Mr Thomas Edwards intituled Gangraena* (London, 1646).

Goodwin, John, *A Defence of the True Sence and Meaning of the Words of the Holy Apostle Rom 4 vv.3–9* (London, 1649).

Goodwin, John, *Anapologesiates Antapologias. Or the Inexcusableness of that Grand Accusation of Brethren, called Antapologia. Complaining as well of the want of Truth, as of Christianity, in many of the Reports and Assertions made in the said Discourse* (London, 1646).

Goodwin, John, *Innocencies Triumph: Or an Answer to the Backpart of A Discourse Lately Published by Wiliam Prynne, Esquire, intituled, A Full Reply, &c* (London, 1644).

Goodwin, Thomas et al., *An Apologeticall Narration, Humbly Submitted to the Honourable House of Parliament* (London, 1644).

Graham, Elspeth, Hinds, Hilary, Hobby, Elaine, Wilcox, Helen (eds.), *Her Own Life: Autobiographical writings by seventeenth-century Englishwomen* (London and New York, 1996).

Hall, Joseph, *A Defence of the Humble Remonstrance Against the Frivolous and False Exceptionsof Smectymnvvs* (London 1641).

Hall, Thomas, *The Pulpit Guarded* (London, 1651).

Harrison, Edward, *Plain Dealing: or the Countrymans Doleful Complaint to the Statesmen of the Times* (London, 1649).

Hartlib, Samuel, *The Hartlib Papers* (Sheffield, 1996).

Herford, C. H. and Simpson, Percy and Evelyn, *Ben Jonson*, 10 vols (Oxford, 1925–50).

Herrick, Robert, *Hesperides: Or the Works Both Human and Divine of Robert Herrick Esq* (London, 1648).

Higginson, Francis, *A Brief Relation of the Irreligion of the Northern Quakers* (London, 1653).

Hobbes, Thomas, *Behemoth Or the Long Parliament* (ed.), Ferdinand Tönnies (Chicago and London, 1990).

Holmes, Nathaniel, *A Sermon [on Psal. Cxlix. 9] preached before the ... Lord Maior... and severall companies of the city of London upon the generall day of thanksgiving, Oct. 8. 1650* (London, 1650).

Hooker, Richard, *Of the Lawes of Ecclesiastical Politie* (London, 1617).

Huehns, G. (ed.), *Clarendon: Selections from The History of the Rebellion and The Life of Himself* (Oxford, 1978).

Hutchinson, Lucy, *Memoirs of the Life of Colonel Hutchinson*, ed. N. H. Keeble, (London, 1995).

Hyde, Edward, *History of the Rebellion and Civil Wars in England* ed. W. Dunn Macray, 6 vols (Oxford, 1888).

Jackson, Isaac (ed.), *The Great Case of Tithes Truly Stated, Clearly Opened and Fully Resolved. By Anthony Pearson, Formerly A Justice of the Peace in Westmoreland* (London, 1756).

Jessey, Henry, *The Exceeding Riches of Grace Advanced By the Spirit of Grace, In an Empty Nothing Creature, (viz) Mrs Sarah Wight, Lately Hopeless and Restless* (London, 1647).

Keith, George, *The Woman Preacher of Samaria* (London, 1674).

Kiffin, William, *To Mr Thomas Edwards* (London, 1644).

Laing, D (ed.), *The letters and journals of Robert Baillie AM*, 3 vols (Edinburgh, 1841).

Lanseter, John, *Lanseters Lance, for Edwards'es Gagrene: or A ripping up and laying open of some rotten, putrified, corrupt, stinking Matter in Mr Thomas Edwards his Gangren* (London, 1646).

Latham, Robert and Matthews, William (eds.),*The Diary of Samuel Pepys*, 11 vols (London, 1974).

Leinsula, Franciscus, *The Kingdoms Divisions Anatomised* (London, 1649).

Leslie, Henry, *The Martyrdom of King Charles* (London, 1649).

Lewis, Thomas Taylor (ed.), *The Letters of Lady Brilliana Harley, Wife of Sir Robert Harley* (London, 1854).

Ley, John, *A Discourse of Disputations Chiefly Concerning Matters of Religion with Animadversions on two printed Books* (London, 1653).

Lightfoot, John, *The Harmony, Chronicle and Order of the Old Testament* (London, 1647).

Lilburne, John, *Regall Tyrannie Dicovered* (London, 1647).

Lilburne, John, *The Oppressed Mans Oppressions Declared* (London, 1646).

Lilly, William, *Monarchy or No Monarchy* (London, 1651).

Maddocks, John and Pinnell, Henry, *Gangraenachrestum, or A Plaister to Allay the Tumor, and prevent the spreading of a pernicious Ulcer, like to have grown upon, and putrefied the good report of Jo, Maddocks, & Henry Pinell* (London, 1646).

Marten, Henry, *A Corrector of the Answerer* (London, 1646).

May, Thomas, *The History of the Parliament of England: Which began November the third, M. DC. XL. With a short and necessary view of some precedent years* (London, 1647).

Milbourne, Thomas, *The Court and Kitchen of Elizabeth* (London, 1664).

Molineux, Mary, *Fruits of Retirement: Or Miscellaneous Poems, Moral and Divine, Being Some Contemplations, Letters, &c. Written on a Variety of Subjects and Occasions* (London, 1702).

Montague, Richard, *A Diatribe Upon the First Part of the Late History of Tithes* (London, 1621).

Moore Smith, G. C. (ed.), *The Letters of Dorothy Osborne to William Temple* (Oxford, 1928).

Munda, Constantia, *The Worming of a mad Dogge: Or, A Soppe for Cerberus The Iaylor of Hell* (London, 1617).

Nalson, John, *The Character of a Rebellion* (London, 1681).

Nalson, John, *The Trial of Charles the First, King of England, Before the High court of Justice for High Treason* (Oxford, 1753).

Nedham, Marchamont, *The Case of the Commonwealth of England Stated* (London, 1650).

Nedham, Marchamont, *Independencie No Schisme* (London, 1646).

Nettles, Stephen, *An Answer to the Jewish Part of Mr Selden's History of Tithes* (Oxford, 1625).

Osborne, John, *An Indictment Against Tythes: Or Tythes no Wages for Gospel-Ministers* (London, 1659).

Overton, Henry, *To the High Court of Parliament. A Dilemma from a Parallel Humbly Presented* (London, 1646).

Overton, Richard, *Overton's Defyance of the Act of Pardon* (London, 1649).

Overton, Richard, *The Bayting of the Great Bull of Bashan* (London, 1648).

Overton, Richard, *The Arraignement of Mr. Persecution* (London, 1645).

P. H., *Tumulus Decimarum: or, the history of tythes from their nativity to this present day of their expected ruine and downfal* (London, 1659).

Pearman, W. D. (ed.), *Cicero: De Legibus Libri Tres* (Cambridge, 1881).

Pearson, Anthony, *The Great Case of Tythes Truly Stated* (London, 1659).

Penney, Norman (ed.), *The Journal of George Fox*, 2 vols (London, 1911).

Penney, Norman, (ed.), *The First Publishers of Truth, Being the Early Records ... Of the Introduction of Quakerism Into The Counties of England and Wales* (London, 1907).

Pollock, F. (ed.), *Table Talk of John Selden* (London, 1927).

Poole, Elizabeth, *A Prophesie Touching the Death of Charles I* (London, 1649).

Poole, Elizabeth, *A Vision* (London, 1649).

Poole, Elizabeth, *An Alarum of War* (2nd edn London, 1649).

Poole, Elizabeth, *An Alarum of War* (London, 1649).

Poole, Matthew, *Annotations Upon the Holy Bible Wherein the Sacred Text is Inserted and Various Readings Annex'd, Together With Parallel Scriptures* (London, 1700).

Prynne, William, *Ten Considerable Quaeries Concerning Tithes, The Present Petitioners and Petitions for their total abolition, as Antichristian, Jewish, burdensome, oppressive to the godly, conscientious People of the Nations* (London, 1659).

Prynne, William, *The Quakers Unmasked, And clearly detected to be but the Spawn of Romish Frogs, Jesuites and Franciscan Freers; sent from Rome to seduce the intoxicated Giddy-headed English Nation* (London, 1654).

Prynne, William, *A Gospel Plea (Interwoven with a Rational and Legal) For the Lawfulness & Continuance of the Ancient Setled Maintenance and Tenthes of the Ministers of the Gospel* (London, 1653).

Prynne, William, *Histrio-Mastix. The Players Scourge; or Actors Tragaedie, divided into 2 parts* (London, 1633).

Prynne, William, *The Church of Englands old antithesis to new Arminianism* (London, 1629).

Reynolds, S. H. (ed.), *The Table Talk of John Selden* (Oxford, 1892).

Ricraft, Josiah, *A Nosegay of Rank Smelling Flowers, Such as Grow in Mr John Goodwin's Garden Gathered Upon Occasion of his Late Lying Libell Against M. Thomas Edwards, which he himself fitly stiled Cretensis, for the foule lies therein contained, with sundry others, exactly gathered and published* (London, 1646).

Robbins, Rob., *Reasons to Resolve the Unresolved People of the Legality of the Kings Tryal and Judgement* (London, 1649).

Robinson, John, *A Justification of Separation from the Church of England. Against Mr Richard Bernard his invective Intitvled The Separatists Schisme* (London, 1610, 1639).

Rogers, John, *Jegar-Sahadutha: An Oiled Pillart ... From Carisbrook Castle in the third Year of My Captivity* (London, 1657).

Rogers, John, *Mene, Tekel, Perez, Or A little Appearance of the Handwriting (In a Glance of Light) Against the Powers and Apostates of the Times. By a letter Written To and lamenting over Oliver Lord Cromwell* (London, 1654).

Rutherford, Samuel, *A Free Disputation Against Pretended Liberty of Conscience* (London, 1649).

Rutherford, Samuel, *The Divine Right of Church Government and Excommunication; or a peaceable dispute for the perfection of holy Scripture in point of ceremonies and Church Government* (London, 1646).

Rutherford, Samuel, *The Due Right of Presbyteries: Or a Peacable Plea for the Government of the Church of Scotland* (London, 1644).

Rutherford, Samuel, *A Peaceable and Temperate Plea or Pavls Presbyterie in Scotland* (London, 1642).

Sa, Don Pantaleon, *A Narration of the Late Accident at the New Exchange* (London, 1653).

Sanderson, William., *A Compleat History of the Life and Reign of King Charles From His Cradle to his Grave* (1658).

Schofield, Bertram (ed.), *The Knyvett Letters, 1620–1644* (Norwich, 1949).

Schurman, Anne Maria à, *The Learned Maid; Or Whether a Maid may be a Scholar* (London, 1659).

Sclater, William, *The Quaestion of Tithes Revised* (London, 1623).

Selden, John, *The Historie of Tithes: That is the Practice of Payment of them. The Positive Laws Made for them. The Opinions Touching the Right of Them. A Review of It is also annext, which both Confirmes it and directs the use of it* (London, 1618).

Sempill, Sir James, *Sacrilege Sacredly Handled* (London, 1619).

Simpson, Sidrach, *The Anatomist Anatomized or A Short Answer to some things in the Book Intituled An Anatomy of Independencie* (London, 1644).

Simpson, William, *Going Naked, A Signe* (London, 1666).

Simpson, William, *A Discovery of the Priests and Professors and their Nakedness and Shame, which is coming upon them* (London, 1660).

Smith, Humphrey, *Concerning Tithes* (London 1659).

Sowernam, Ester, *Ester hath hang'd Haman: Or An Answere to a lewd Pamphlet, entituled The Arraignment of Women* (London, 1617).

Spedding, James et. al., *The Works of Francis Bacon*, 14 vols (London, 1857–1874).

Speght, Rachel, *A Mouzell for Melastomus, The Cynical Bayter Of, and foule mouthed Barker against Evahs Sex* (London, 1617).

Spinoza, Benedict de, *Ethics*, ed. James Gutman (New York, 1949).

Sterry, Peter, *A Discourse of the Freedom of the Will* (London, 1675).

Sterry, Peter, *The Commings Forth of Christ* (London, 1649).

Studley, Peter, *The Looking- Glasse of Schisme* (London, 1635).

Swetnam, Joseph, *The Arraignment of Lewd, Idle, Froward and Unconstant Women* (London, 1615).

T. R., *A Testimony for God's Everlasting Truth, As it hath been learned of and in Jesus* (London, 1669).

Tatham, John, *The Rump* (London, 1660).

Taylor, Christopher, *Certain Papers Which is the Word of the Lord as was moved from the Lord by his servants to several places, and persons, that they may be left without excuse, and God may be cleared when he judges and justified in his judgements* (London, 1654).

Tillesley, Richard, *Animadversions upon M. Seldens History of Tithes* (London, 1619).

Tillinghast, John, *Mr Tillinghast's Last Eight Sermons* (London, 1656).

Townsend, Theophilia, *A Word of Counsel in the Love of God* (London, 1687).

Trapnel, Anna, *Poetical Addresses* (London, 1659).

Trapnel, Anna, *A Voice for the King of the Saints and Nations* (London, 1658).

Trapnel, Anna, *A Legacy for Saints* (London, 1654).

Trapnel, Anna, *The Cry of a Stone: Or a Relation of Something Spoken in Whitehall, by Anna Trapnel, being in the Visions of God* (London, 1654).

Trapnel, Anna, *Strange and Wonderful Newes from Whitehall* (London, 1654).

Trapnel, Anna, *Anna Trapnel's Report and Plea, Or a Narrative Of her Journey from London into Cornwal, the occasion of it, the Lord's encouragements to it, and signal presence with her in it* (London, 1654).

Travers, Rebecca, *Testimony Concerning the Light and Life of Jesus* (London, 1663).

Treleinie, Philip, *The Undeceiving of the People in the point of Tithes* (London, 1651).

Verney, Frances Pathernope, *Memoirs of the Verney Family During the Civil War: Compiled from the Letters and Illustrated By the Portraits at Claydon House*, 2 vols (London, 1892).

Vives, Johannes Ludovicus, *A very frutefull and pleasant boke called the instruction of a Christian women [sic], made fyrst in Laten and dedicated unto the quenes good grace, by the right famous clerke mayster Lewes Vives, and turned out of Laten into Englysshe by Richard Hyrd* (London, 1592).

Walker, Henry, *Collections of Notes taken at the Kings Tryall at Westminster Hall* (London, 1649).

Walwyn, William, *An Antidote Against Master Edwards his Old and New Poyson* (London, 1646).

Walwyn, William, *A Prediction of Mr Edwards his Conversion and Recantation* (London, 1646).

Walwyn, William, *A Word More to Mr Edwards Minister* (London, 1646).

Walwyn, William, *A Whisper in the Eare of Mr Thomas Edwards Minister* (London, 1646).

Warren, John, *The Potent Potter* (London, 1649).

Webbe, Thomas, *Mr Edwards Pen No Slander* (London, 1646).

Webster, John, *The Duchess of Malfi and Other Plays*, ed. by René Weiss (Oxford, 1998).

Wharton, Robert, *A Declaration to Great Briton and Ireland, Shewing the Downfall of their Princes* (London, 1649).

White, Dorothy, *Friends You that are the Parliament, hear the Word of the Lord* (London, 1662).

Whiting, John, *Catalogues of Friends Books* (London, 1708).

Winstanley, Gerard, *The Law of Freedom in a Platform* (London, 1652).

Winstanley, Gerard, *An Appeale to all Englishmen, to judge between bondage and freedom* (London, 1650).

Winstanley, Gerard, *Fire in the Bush. The Spirit burning, not consuming, but purging mankind* (London, 1650).

Winter, Robert, *The Plea and Protest of Robert Winter of Elmston in the County of Kent, for his Non Payment of Tithes* (London, 1656).

Wolfe, Don M. (gen. ed.), *Complete Prose Works of John Milton*, 8 vols (New Haven, 1953–82).

Woodward, Hezekiah, *Soft Answers, Unto Hard Censures* (London, 1645).

Woodward, Hezekiah, *A Short Letter Modestly Intreating A Friends Judgement upon Mr Edwards His Booke, he calleth a Anti-Apologie: With a Large But Modest Answer Thereunto. Framed (in desire) with such eveness of hand, and uprightness of heart, as that no godly man might be offended at it: And with a soule-desire also, That they who are contrary minded, not be offended neither, but instructed* (London, 1644).

Newsbook Sources

A Diary or Exact Journal,	20, 19–26 Sept. 1644.
A Perfect Account of the Daily Intelligence from the Armies of England, Scotland and Ireland,	82, 21–28 July 1652.
A Perfect Diurnall,	287, 22–29 Jan. 1648. 310, 2–9 July 1649.
England's Moderate Messenger,	1, 23–30 April 1649.
French Occurrences,	26 July–27 Aug. 1652.
Mercurius Anglicus,	1, 31 Jan.–7 Feb. 1644.
Mercurius Anglicus,	1, 27 July–3 Aug. 1648.
Mercurius Anglicus,	1, 24 Sept.–1 Oct. 1650.
Mercurius Aulicus,	2, 7–13 Jan. 1644.
Mercurius Britanicus,	92, 28 July–4 Aug. 1645.
Mercurius Britannicus,	1, 19–26 July 1652.
Mercurius Civicus,	4, 25 May–1 June 1643. 26, 26 June–3 July 1645. 79, 21–28 Nov. 1644.
Mercurius Democritus,	17, 21–28 July 1652.
Mercurius Elencticus,	69, 21–28 Feb. 1649.
Mercurius Militaris,	1, 17–24 April 1649.
Mercurius Politicus,	17, 26 Sept.–3 Oct. 1650. 201, 13–20 April 1654. 245, 15–22 Feb. 1655.
Mercurius Pragmaticus,	43, 20–27 Feb. 1649.
Mercurius Scoticus,	23–30 Sept. 1651.
Packets of Letters,	4, 11 April 1648. 5, 17 April 1648.
Perfect Diurnall,	42, 23–30 Sept. 1650.

Perfect Occurences of Every Daies journal in Parliament,	121, 20–27 April 1649.
Perfect Occurences of Parliament,	63, 10–17 March 1648. 26 Jan–2 Feb. 1649. 129, 15–22 June 1649.
Perfect Passages of Every Daies Intelligence from the Parliaments Army,	10, 9–13 Sept. 1650. 57, 16–23 July 1652.
Severall Proceedings in Parliament,	35, 23 May–30 May 1650.
Severall Proceedings of Parliament,	53, 23 Sept.–3 Oct. 1650.
Severall Proceedings of State Affaires,	225, 12–19 Jan. 1654.
The Faithful Scout,	80, 23–30 July 1652. 139, 18–25 Nov. 1653.
The Impartial Scout,	2 (54), 28 June–5 July 1650. 53, 21–28 June 1650. 4 (56), 12–19 July 1650. 5 (57), 19–25 July 1650.
The Kingdomes Faithfull and Impartiall Scout,	19, 1–8 June 1649. 20, 8–15 June 1649. 36, 28 Sept.–5 Oct. 1649.
The Man in the Moon,	2, 16–23 April 1649. 21, 5–12 Sept. 1649. 43, 13–20 Feb. 1650. 57, 29 May–5 June 1650.
The Moderate Intelligencer,	1, 6–13 March 1645.
The Moderate Publisher,	6, 19 Nov.–2 Dec. 1653
The Modern Intelligencer,	V, 26 Aug.–3 Sept. 1651.
The Moderne Intelligencer,	1, 11–18 Sept. 1650. 2, 18–25 Sept. 1650.
The Parliament Scout,	5, 20–27 July 1643.

The Perfect Diurnall,	25, 27 May–5 June 1650.
The True and Perfect Dutch-Diurnall,	2, 19–26 July 1653.
The Weekly Account,	46, 28 Oct.–4 Nov. 1646. 8, 17–24 Feb. 1647. 13, 24–30 March 1647.
The Weekly Intelligencer,	129, 19–29 July 1653.
The Weekly Post,	28 Jun–5 July 1649.
Severall Proceedings of State Affairs,	217, 17–Nov.–24 Nov. 1653. 218, 24 Nov.–1 Dec. 1653.

Unpublished Theses

Bell, Maureen, 'Women Publishers of Puritan Literature in the Mid-Seventeenth Century: Three Case Studies' (unpublished Ph.D. thesis, Loughborough University, 1987).

Bershadsky, Edith, 'Politics, Erudition and Ecclesiology: John Selden's *Historie of Tithes* (unpublished Ph.D. thesis, John Hopkins University, 1994).

Boorman, Catherine F., 'Royalism and Female Authorship in the English Civil War Period: Contexts, Literary Strategies and Rewards' (unpublished Ph.D. thesis, University of Sheffield, 2004).

Cotton, Anthony, 'London Newsbooks in the Civil War: Their Political Attitudes and Sources of Information' (unpublished D.Phil. thesis, Oxford University, 1971).

Davies, Kate, 'Women and Republicanism in Britain and America 1760–1785' (unpublished D.Phil. thesis, University of York, 1999).

Filloy, Richard A., 'The Religious and Political Views of John Selden: A Study in Early Stuart Humanism' (unpublished Ph.D. thesis, University of California at Berkeley, 1977).

Gillespie, Katharine, 'Table Talk: Seventeenth-Century English and American Women Writers and the Rhetoric of Radical Domesticity' (unpublished Ph.D. dissertation, SUNY Buffalo, 1996).

Glaser, Eliane, '"Uncircumcised Pens": Judaizing in Print Controversies of the Long Reformation' (unpublished Ph.D. thesis, University of London, 2000).

Hubbard, D. G. B., 'Early Quaker Education, c. 1650–1780' (unpublished M.A. thesis, University of London, 1939).

Ward Lowery, Nicholas, 'Patriarchal Negotiations: Women, Writing and Religion in the English Civil War, 1640–1660' (unpublished Ph.D. thesis, University of London, 1993).

Secondary Works

Achinstein, Sharon, *Milton and the Revolutionary Reader* (Princeton, 1994).

Achinstein, Sharon, 'Women on Top in the Pamphlet Literature of the English Revolution', *Women's Studies* 24 (1994), pp. 131–63.

Adair, John, *Puritans, Religion and Politics in Seventeenth-Century England and America* (Stroud, 1998).

Adburgham, Alice, *Women in Print: Writing and Women's Magazines From the Restoration to the Accession of Victoria* (London, 1972).

Aers, David, 'A Whisper in the Ears of Early Modernists; or, Reflections on Literary Critics Writing the History of the Subject', in David Aers (ed.), *Culture and History, 1350–1600: Essays on English Communities, Identities and Writing* (Detroit, 1992), pp. 177–202.

Amussen, S. D., '"Being Stirred to Much Unquietness": Violence and Domestic Violence in Early Modern England', *Journal of Women's History* 6:2 (1994), pp. 70–89.

Amussen, S. D., *An Ordered Society: Gender and Class in Early Modern England* (New York and Oxford, 1988).

Amussen, S. D. and Kishlansky, M.A. (eds.), *Political Culture and Cultural Politics in Early Modern England: Essays Presented to David Underdown* (London, 1995).

Andersen, Jennifer and Sauer, Elizabeth (eds.), *Books and Readers in Early Modern England: Material Studies* (Philadelphia, 2002).

Andressen-Thom, M., 'Shrew Taming and other Rituals of Aggression: Baiting and Bonding on the Stage and in the Wild', *Women's Studies* 9 (1982), pp. 121–43.

Anselment, Raymond A., *'Betwixt Jest and Earnest': Marprelate, Milton, Marvell, Swift and the Decorum of Religious Ridicule* (Toronto, 1979).

Aram Veeser, H. (ed.), *The New Historicism* (London, 1989).

Armitage, David et al. (eds.), *Milton and Republicanism* (Cambridge, 1995).

Armstrong, Isobel (ed.), *New Feminist Discourses: Essays in Literature, Criticism and Theory* (London, 1992).

Auski, Peter, 'Milton's "Sanctifi'd Bitternesse": Polemical Technique in the Early Prose', *Texas Studies in Literature and Language* 19 (1977), pp. 363–81.

Bakhtin, Mikhail, *Speech Genres and Other Late Essays*, trans. by V. W. McGee (Austin, 1986).

Bakhtin, Mikhail, *Problems of Dostoevsky's Poetics*, trans. by Caryl Emerson (Manchester, 1984).

Bakhtin, Mikhail, *The Dialogic Imagination: Four Essays*, trans. by Caryl Emerson and Michael Holquist (Austin, 1981).

Bal, Mieke, *Murder and Difference: Gender, Genre, and Scholarship on Sisera's Death*, trans. Matthew Gumpert (Indiana, 1988).

Barber, Sarah, *Regicide and Republicanism: Politics and Ethics in the English Revolution* (Edinburgh, 1998).

Bauman, Richard, *Let Your Words Be Few: Symbolic Speaking and Silence Among Seventeenth-Century Quakers* (London, 1983).

Beck, W. and Ball, T. F., *The London Friends Meetings* (London, 1896).

Beier, A. L., *Masterless Men: The Vagrancy Problem in England, 1560–1640* (London and New York, 1985).

Bell, Maureen, 'Hannah Allen and the Development of a Puritan Publishing Business, 1641–1651', *Publishing History* 26 (1989), pp. 5–66.

Bell, Maureen, 'Mary Westwood, Quaker Publisher', *Publishing History* 23 (1988), pp. 5–66.

Berg, Christine, and Berry, Phillipa, 'Spiritual Whoredom: An Essay on Female Prophets in the Seventeenth Century', in Francis Barker, Jay Bernstein, John Coombes, Peter

Hulme, Jennifer Stone and John Stratton (eds.), *1642: Literature and Power in the Seventeenth Century. Proceedings of the Essex Conference on the Sociology of Literature* (Colchester, 1981), pp. 37–54.

Berry, Phillipa, *Of Chastity and Power: Elizabethan Literature and the Unmarried Queen* (London and New York, 1994).

Bershadsky, Edith, 'Controlling the Terms of the Debate: John Selden and the Tithes Controversy', in G. J. Schochet, P. E. Tatspaugh and C. Brobeck (eds.), *Law, Literature and the Settlement of Regimes* (Washington, DC, 1990), pp. 187–220.

Beveridge, W., *A Short History of the Westminster Assembly* (Edinburgh, 1904).

Bevington, D. and Holbrook, P. (eds.), *The Politics of the Stuart Court Masque* (Cambridge, 1998).

Birch, Una, *Anna Van Schurman: Artist, Scholar, Saint* (London, 1909).

Boose, Lynda E., 'Scolding Bridles and Bridling Scolds: Taming the Woman's Unruly Member', in Ivo Kamps (ed.), *Materialist Shakespeare: A History* (London, 1993), pp. 239–79.

Bourne, H. R. Fox, *English Newspapers: Chapters in the History of Journalism*, 2 vols (London, 1887).

Boyarin, Daniel, *Carnal Israel: Reading Sex in Talmudic Culture* (Berkeley; Oxford, 1993).

Brace, Laura, *The Idea of Property in Seventeenth-Century England: Tithes and the Individual* (Manchester and New York, 1998).

Braddick, Michael J. and Walter, John (eds.), *Negotiating Power in Early Modern Society: Order, Hierarchy and Subordination in Britain and Ireland* (Cambridge, 2002).

Brailsford, H. N., *The Levellers and the English Revolution*, ed. by Christopher Hill, (Nottingham, 1983).

Brailsford, Mabel, *Quaker Women, 1650–1760* (London, 1915).

Braithwaite, Alfred W., 'Early Tithe Prosecutions: Friends as Outlaws', *Journal of the Friends Historical Society* 49 (1959/1961), pp. 148–56.

Braithwaite, W. C., *The Second Period of Quakerism* (Cambridge, 1961).

Braithwaite, W. C., *The Beginnings of Quakerism* (Cambridge, 1955).

Brant Clare, and Purkis, Diane (eds.), *Women, Texts and Histories 1575–1760* (London, 1992).

Bridenthal, Renate, and Koonz, Claudia (eds.), *Becoming Visible: Women in European History* (London, 1987).

Brod, Manfred, 'Politics and Prophecy in Seventeenth-Century England: The Case of Elizabeth Poole', *Albion* 31:3 (1999), pp. 395–412.

Burckhardt, Jacob, *The Civilisation of Renaissance Italy* (London, 1890).

Burgess, Glenn, *The Politics of the Ancient Constitution* (Basingstoke, 1992).

Burke, Peter, *The Art of Conversation* (Cambridge, 1993).

Burke, Peter, and Porter, Roy (eds.), *The Social History of Language* (Cambridge, 1987).

Burke, Seán, *The Death and Return of the Author: Criticism and Subjectivity in Bathes, Foucault and Derrida* (Edinburgh, 1992).

Burns, J. H., and Goldie, M. (eds.), *The Cambridge History of Political Thought 1450–1700* (Cambridge, 1991).

Burns, N. T., 'From Seeker to Finder: The Singular Experiences of Mary Pennington', in Corns and Loewenstein, *Emergence of Quaker Writing*, pp. 70–87.

Burrage, Champlin, 'Anna Trapnel's Prophecies', *English Historical Review*, 26 (1911), pp. 526–35.

Burrage, Champlin, 'The Fifth Monarchy Insurrections', *English Historical Review*, 5 (1910), pp. 722–47.

Butler, Judith, *The Psychic Life of Power: Essays in Subjection* (Stanford, 1997).

Butler, Judith, 'Contingent Foundations: Feminism and the Question of Postmodernism', in Seyla Benhabib et al., *Feminist Contentions: A Philosophical Exchange* (New York and London, 1995), pp. 35–57.

Butler, Judith, 'For a Careful Reading', in Benhabib et al., *Feminist Contentions*, pp. 127–44.

Butler, Judith, *Gender Trouble: Feminism and the Subversion of Identity* (London and New York, 1990).

Calhoun, Craig (ed.), *Habermas and the Public Sphere* (London, 1992).

Capp, Bernard, *The Fifth Monarchy Men: A Study in Seventeenth-Century Millenarianism*, (London, 1972).

Carey, John, 'Seventeenth-Century Prose', in Christopher Ricks (ed.), *History of Literature in the English Language*, vol. 2 (London, 1970).

Carré, Beatrice, 'Early Quaker Women in Lancaster and Lancashire', in Michael Mullet (ed.), *Early Lancaster Friends* (Leeds, 1978), pp. 43–53.

Carroll, Kenneth, 'Early Quakers and "Going Naked as a Sign"', *Quaker History* 67 (1978), pp. 69–87.

Cesario, S. P., and Wynne-Davies, Marion (eds.), *Gloriana's Face: Women, Public and Private in the English Renaissance* (Hemel Hempstead, 1992).

Chedgzoy, Kate, Hansen, Melanie, and Trill, Susan (eds.), *Voicing Women: Gender and Sexuality in Early Modern Writing* (Edinburgh, 1998).

Christianson, Paul, *Discourses on History, Law and Governance in the Public Career of John Selden 1610–1635* (Toronto, 1996).

Clark, Stuart, *Thinking With Demons, The Idea of Witchcraft in Early Modern Europe* (Oxford, 1997).

Clyde, William M., *The Struggle for Freedom of the Press from Caxton to Cromwell* (London, 1934).

Cohen, Alfred, 'The Fifth Monarchy Mind: Mary Cary and the Origins of Totalitarianism', *Social Research* 31 (1964), pp. 195–213.

Cohn, Norman, *The Pursuit of the Millennium* (London, 1970).

Cope, Esther S., *Handmaid of the Holy Spirit: Dame Eleanor Douglas, "Never So Mad a Ladie"* (Michigan, 1992).

Corns, Thomas N., *The Royal Image: Representations of Charles I* (Cambridge, 1999).

Corns, Thomas N., *John Milton: The Prose Works* (New York, 1998).

Corns, Thomas N., *Uncloistered Virtue: English Political Literature, 1640–1660* (Oxford, 1992).

Corns, T. N., and Loewenstein, D. (eds.), *The Emergence of Quaker Writing: Dissenting Literature in Seventeenth-Century England* (London, 1995).

Crawford, Patricia, *Women and Religion in England 1500–1720* (London, 1993).

Crawford, Patricia, 'The Challenges to Patriarchalism: How Did the Revolution Affect Women?', in John Morrill (ed.), *Revolution and Restoration: England in the 1650s* (London, 1992), pp. 112–28.

Crawford, Patricia, 'Attitudes to Menstruation in Seventeenth-Century England', *Past & Present* 91 (1981), pp. 47–74.

Crawford, Patricia, '"Charles Stuart, That Man of Blood"', *The Journal of British Studies* 16 (1974), pp. 41–61.

Creasey, M. A., '"Inward" and "Outward"': A Study of Early Quaker Language', *Journal of the Friends Historical Society* Supplement 30 (1962).

Cressy, David, *Agnes Bowker's Cat: Travesties and Transgressions in Tudor and Stuart England* (Oxford, 2000).

Cross, Claire, '"He-Goats Before the Flocks": A Note on the Part Played by Women in the Founding of Some Civil War Churches', *Studies in Church History* 8 (1972), pp. 195–202.

Cust, Richard and Hughes, Ann (eds.), *The English Civil War* (London, 1997).

Davies, Godfrey, *The Restoration of Charles II 1658–1660* (San Marino, 1955).

Davis, J. C., 'Fear, Myth and Furore: Reappraising the Ranters', *Past and Present* 129 (1990), pp. 79–103.

Davis, J. C., *Fear, Myth and History: The Ranters and the Historians* (Cambridge, 1986).

Dawson, W. H., *Cromwell's Understudy: The Life and Times of General John Lambert and the Rise and Fall of the Protectorate* (London, 1938).

Derrida, Jacques, 'Signature Event Context', in Peggy Kamuf (ed.), *A Derrida Reader: Between the Blinds* (Hemel Hempstead, 1991), pp. 80–111.

Di Cesare, Mario A., *Reconsidering the Renaissance: Papers from the Twenty-First Annual Conference* (New York, 1992).

Diethe, Jürgen, '*The Moderate*: The Politics and Allegiances of a Revolutionary Newspaper', *History of Political Thought* 4.2 (Summer 1983), pp. 247–279.

Dobin, Howard, *Merlin's Disciples: Prophecy, Poetry and Power in Renaissance England* (Stanford, 1990).

Dooley, Brendan, and Baron, Sabrina A. (eds.), *The Politics of Information in Early Modern Europe* (London and New York, 2001).

Duke, A. C. and Tamse C. A. (eds.), *Too Mighty to Be Free: Censorship and the Press in Britain and the Netherlands* (Zutphen, 1987).

Easterby, W., *The History of the Law of Tithes in England* (Cambridge, 1888).

Edwards, Karen L. '*Suzanna's Apologie* and the Politics of Privity', *Literature and History* 6.1 (Spring, 1997), pp. 1–17.

Egan, James, 'Milton and the Marprelate Tradition', *Milton Studies* 8 (1975), pp. 103–22.

Eley, Geoff, and Hunt, William (eds.), *Reviving the English Revolution: Reflections and Elaborations on the Work of Christopher Hill* (London and New York, 1988).

Erickson, Amy Louise, *Women and Property in Early Modern England* (London and New York, 1993).

Esterby, William, *The History of the Law of Tithes in England. Being the Yorke Prize Essay of the University of Cambridge for 1887* (Cambridge, 1888).

Ferguson, Moira (ed.), *First Feminists: British Women Writers 1578–1799* (Bloomington, 1985).

Fincham, Kenneth (ed.), *The Early Stuart Church* (London, 1993).

Finkler, Noam, 'Ranter Sexual Politics: Canticles in the England of 1650', in M. H. Gelber (ed.), *Identity and Ethos: A Festschrift for Sol Liptzin* (New York, 1986), pp. 325–42.

Fish, Stanley, 'Standing Only: Christian Heroism in *Paradise Lost*', *Critical Quarterly* 9:2 (1967), pp. 162–78.

Fletcher, Eric, *John Selden 1584–1654: Selden Society Lecture Delivered in the Old Hall of Lincoln's Inn* (London, 1969).

Fletcher, Joseph, *The History of Independency*, 4 vols (London, 1847).

Foucault, Michel, 'What Is an Author?', in *Textual Strategies: Perspectives in Post-Structuralist Criticism* (Ithaca, 1979), pp. 141–60.

Fowler, Elizabeth and Greene, Roland (eds.), *The Project of Prose in Early Modern Europe and the New World* (Cambridge, 1997).

Foxton, Rosemary, *Hear the Word of the Lord: A Critical Bibliographical Study of Quaker Women's Writing* (Melbourne, 1994).

Frank, Joseph, *Cromwell's Press Agent: A Critical Biography of Marchamont Nedham, 1620–1678* (Lanham, MD, 1980).

Frank, Joseph, *The Beginnings of the English Newspaper, 1620–1660* (Cambridge, MA, 1961).

Fraser, Antonia, *The Weaker Vessel: Woman's Lot in the Seventeenth Century* (London, 1984).

Fraser, Nancy, 'Rethinking the Public Sphere: A Contribution to the Critique of Actually Existing Democracy', in Craig Calhoun (ed.), *Habermas and the Public Sphere*, (Cambridge, MA, and London, 1992), pp. 109–42.

Fraser, Nancy, *Unruly Practices: Power, Discourse and Gender in Contemporary Social Theory* (Cambridge, 1988).

Freist, Dagmar, *Governed by Opinion: Politics, Religion and the Dynamics of Communication in Stuart London, 1637–1645* (London, 1997).

Fussner, F. Smith, *The Historical Revolution: English Historical Writing and Thought 1580–1640* (London, 1962).

Gardiner, J. K., 'Margaret Fell Fox and Feminist Literary History: A "Mother in Israel" Calls to the Jews'in Corns and Loewenstein (eds.), *The Emergence of Quaker Writing*, pp. 42–56.

Gardiner, S .R., *History of the Great Civil War 1642–1649*, 4 vols (London, 1987).

Gentles, Ian, *The New Model Army in England, Ireland and Scotland, 1645–1683* (Oxford and Cambridge, MA, 1992).

Gentles, Ian, 'London Levellers and the English Revolution: The Chidleys and their Circle', *Journal of English History* 29.3 (1978), pp. 281–309.

Gill, Catie, *Women in the Seventeenth-Century Quaker Community: A Literary Study of Political Identities, 1650–1700* (Aldershot, 2005).

Gill, Catie, 'Identities in Quaker Women's Writing', *Women's Writing* 9:2 (2002), pp. 267–84.

Gillespie, Katharine, *Domesticity and Dissent in the Seventeenth Century* (Cambridge, 2004).

Gillespie, Katharine,'Elizabeth Cromwell's Kitchen Court: Republicanism and the Consort', *Genders* 33 (2001), <http://www.genders.org/g33/g33_gillespie.html>.

Gillespie, Katharine, 'A Hammer in her Hand: The Separation of Church from State and the Early Feminist Writings of Katherine Chidley', *Tulsa Studies in Women's Literature* 17:2 (1998), pp. 213–33.

Greaves, Richard, and Zaller, Robert (eds.), *A Biographical Dictionary of Radicals in the Seventeenth Century*, 3 vols (Brighton, 1982).

Green, Ian, *Print and Protestantism in Early Modern England* (Oxford and New York, 2000).

Greenblatt, Stephen, *Renaissance Self-Fashioning From More to Shakespeare* (Chicago and London, 1984).

Greengrass, M., Leslie, M. and Raylor, T. (eds.), *Samuel Hartlib and Universal Reformation: Studies in Intellectual Communication* (Cambridge, 1994).

Gregg, Pauline, *Free-born John: A Biography of John Lilburne* (London, 1961).

Grell, O. P., Israel J. I., and Tyacke N. (eds.), *From Persecution to Toleration: The Glorious Revolution and Religion in England* (Oxford, 1991).

Grundy, Isobel and Wiseman, Susan (eds.), *Women, Writing, History, 1640–1740* (London, 1992).

Habermas, Jurgen, *The Structural Transformation of the Public Sphere: A Inquiry into a Category of Bourgeois Society*, trans. by Thomas Burger (Cambridge, MA, 1989).

Halasz, Alexandra, *The Marketplace of Print: Pamphlets and the Public Sphere in Early Modern England* (Cambridge, 1997).

Haller, William, *Libery and Reformation in the Puritan Revolution* (New York, 1955).

Haller, William, *The Rise of Puritanism* (New York, 1938).

Haller, William, *Tracts on Liberty in the Puritan Revolution, 1638–1647*, 3 vols (New York, 1934).

Hamilton, D. B., and Strier, R. (eds.), *Religion, Literature and Politics in Post-Reformation England* (London, 1997).

Hanbury, Benjamin, *Historical Memorials Relating to the Independents or Congregationalists: From their Rise to the Restoration of the Monarchy*, 3 vols (London, 1841).

Harris, Barbara J., 'Women and Politics in Early Tudor England', *The Historical Journal* 33:2 (1990), pp. 259–81.

Hawes, Clement, *Mania and Literary Style: The Rhetoric of Enthusiasm from the Ranters to Christopher Smart* (Cambridge, 1996).

Healy, Thomas, and Sawday, Jonathan (eds.), *Literature and the English Civil War* (Cambridge, 1990).

Henderson, Katherine Usher, and McManus, Barbara F. (eds.), *Half Humankind: Contexts and Texts of the Controversy about Women in England* (Urbana and Chicago, 1985).

Higgins, Patricia, 'The Reactions of Women', *Politics, Religion and the English Civil War*, ed. by Brian Manning (New York, 1973).

Hill, Christopher, *A Nation of Change and Novelty: Radical Politics, Religion and Literature in Seventeenth-Century England* (London, 1993).

Hill, Christopher, *The English Bible and the Seventeenth-Century Revolution* (London, 1993).

Hill, Christopher, *The World Turned Upside Down: Radical Ideas During the English Revolution* (London, 1991).

Hill, Christopher, *Milton and the English Revolution* (London, 1977).

Hill, Christopher, *Puritanism and Revolution* (London, 1968).

Hill, Christopher, *Economic Problems of the Church: From Archbishop Whitgift to the Long Parliament* (Oxford, 1956).

Hill, Christopher, Reay, Barry, and Lamont, William (eds.), *The World of the Muggletonians* (London, 1983).

Hinds, Hilary, *God's Englishwomen: Seventeenth-Century Radical Sectarian Writing and Feminist Criticism* (Manchester and New York, 1996).

Hinds, Hilary, *Writing and Reaction: Seventeenth-Century Englishwomen's Struggle for Authorship,* Occasional Paper No. 7 (University of Birmingham Institute for Advanced Research in the Humanities, 1993).

Hinds, Hilary, 'Sectarian Women's Writing in the Second Half of the Seventeenth-Century', in S. P. Cerasano and Marion Wynne-Davies (eds.), *Gloriana's Face*, pp. 205–27.

Hirschkop, Ken, 'Is Dialogism for Real?', *Social Text* 30 (1987), pp. 102–13.

Hirschkop, Ken, 'Bakhtin, Discourse and Democracy', *New Left Review* 160 (1986), pp. 92–113.

Hobby, Elaine, 'Handmaids of the Lord and Mothers of Israel: Early Vindications of Quaker Women's Prophecy', in T. N. Corns and D. Loewenstein (eds.), *The Emergence of Quaker Writing: Dissenting Literature in Seventeenth-Century England* (London, 1995), pp. 88–98.

Hobby, Elaine, 'O Oxford Thou Art Full of Filfth: The Prophetical Writings of Hester Biddle, 1629[?]–1696', in Susan Sellers (ed.), *Feminist Criticism Theory and Practice* (London and New York, 1991), pp. 157–70.

Hobby, Elaine, *Virtue of Necessity: English Women's Writing, 1649–1688* (London, 1988).

Hobman, D. L., *Cromwell's Master Spy: A Study of John Thurloe* (London, 1961).

Holquist, Michael, *Dialogism: Mikhail Bakhtin and his World* (London and New York, 1990).

Holstun, James (ed.), *Ehud's Dagger: Class Struggle in the English Revolution* (New York and London, 2000).

Holstun, James, *Pamphlet Wars: Prose in the English Revolution* (London, 1993).

Horle, Craig W., *The Quakers and the English Legal System* (Philadelphia, 1988).

Howell, Roger, Jr., 'Reconsidering the Levellers: The Evidence of *The Moderate*', *Past & Present* 46 (1970), pp. 68–86.

Hufton, Olwen, *The Prospect Before Her: A History of Women in Western Europe 1500–1800* (London, 1995).

Hughes, Ann, '"Popular" Presbyterianism in the 1640s and 1650s: The Case of Thomas Edwards and Thomas Hall', in N. Tyacke (ed.), *England's Long Reformation 1500–1800* (London and Bristol, 1998), pp. 235–59.

Hughes, Ann, 'Gender and Politics in Leveller Literature', in S. D. Asmussen and M. A. Kishlansky (eds.), *Political Culture and Cultural Politics in Early Modern England: Essays Presented to David Underdown* (London, 1995), pp. 162–88.

Hughes, Ann, 'The Meanings of Religious Polemic', F. J. Brenner (ed.), *Puritanism: Transatlantic Perspectives on a Seventeenth-Century Anglo-American Faith* (Boston, 1993), pp. 201–29.

Hughes, Ann, 'The Frustrations of the Godly', J. Morrill (ed.), *Revolution and Restoration* (London, 1993), pp. 70–90.

Hughes, Ann, 'The Pulpit Guarded: Confrontations Between Orthodox and Radicals in Revolutionary England', in Ann Laurence et al. (eds.), *John Bunyan and His England, 1628–1688* (London, 1990), pp. 31–50.

Hughes, P. L., and Larkin, J. F. (eds.), *Tudor Royal Proclamations* (Yale, 1969).

Hull, Suzanne W., *Chaste, Silent and Obedient: English Books for Women 1475–1640* (San Marino, 1983).

Hutson, Lorna, *The Usurer's Daughter: Male Friendship and Fictions of Women in Sixteenth-Century England* (London, 1994).

Hutton, Barbara, *The Fiery Cross; or the Vow of Montrose* (London and Edinburgh, 1875).

Hutton, Ronald, *The Restoration: A Political History of England and Wales, 1658–1667* (Oxford, 1993).

Irigaray, Luce, *Speculum of the Other Woman*, trans. by G. C. Gill (Ithaca, 1985).

Irigaray, Luce, *This Sex Which Is Not One*, trans. by Catherine Porter (Ithaca, 1985).

James, Margaret, 'The Political Importance of the Tithes Controversy in the English Revolution', *History* 26 (1941), pp. 1–18.

James, Margaret, *The Effect of the Religious Changes of the Sixteenth Century and Seventeenth Century on Economic Theory and Development* (London, 1937).

Jaquette, Jane S., 'Contract and Coercion: Power and Gender in Leviathan', in Smith (ed.), *Women Writers and the Early Modern British Political Tradition*, pp. 200–219.

Jones, Ann Rosalind, and Stallybrass, Peter, *Renaissance Clothing and the Materials of Memory* (Cambridge, 2000).

Jones, Ann Rosalind, 'From polemical prose to the Red Bull: The Swetnam controversy in women voiced pamphlets and the public theater', in Elizabeth Fowler and Roland Greene (eds.), *The Project of Prose in Early Modern Europe and the New World* (Cambridge, 1997), pp. 122–37.

Jones, R. M., *The Quakers in the American Colonies*, 2 vols (London 1923).

Jordan, W. K., *The Development of Religious Toleration*, 4 vols (London, 1932–1940).

Kamensky, Jane, *Governing the Tongue: The Politics of Speech in Early New England* (New York and Oxford, 1997).

Kamuf, Peggy (ed.), *A Derrida Reader: Between the Blinds* (Hemel Hempstead, 1991).

Kaplan, E. Ann, *Women and Film: Both Sides of the Camera* (London, 1993).

Katz, David, *The Jews in the History of England 1485–1850* (Oxford, 1994).

Kelsey, Sean, 'Politics and Procedure in the Trial of Charles I', *Law and History Review* 22:1 (2004): 31 pars. 29 Jun. 2004. <http://www.historycooperative.org. journals/lhr/22.1/kelsey.html>.

Kelsey, Sean, 'The Trial of Charles I', *English Historical Review* 118: 447 (2003), pp. 585–616.

Kelsey, Sean, 'The Death of Charles I', *Historical Journal* 45:4 (2002), pp. 727–54.
Kelsey, Sean, *Inventing a Republic: The Political Culture of the English Commonwealth* (Manchester, 1997).
Kelso, Ruth, *Doctrine for the Lady of the Renaissance* (Chicago and London, 1978).
Knoppers, Laura Lunger, *Constructing Cromwell: Ceremony, Portrait and Print, 1645–1661* (Cambridge, 2000).
Knoppers, Laura Lunger, 'Reviving the Martyr King: Charles I as Jacobite Icon', in Corns (ed.), *The Royal Image*, pp. 264–87.
Knoppers, Laura Lunger, *Historicizing Milton: Spectacle, Power and Poetry in Restoration England* (Athens, GA; London, 1994).
Knott, J. R., 'Joseph Besse and the Quaker Culture of Suffering', in Corns and Loewenstein (eds.), *The Emergence of Quaker Writing*, pp. 126–41.
Kranidas, Thomas, 'Style and Rectitude in Seventeenth-Century Prose: Hall, Smectymnuus, and Milton', *Huntingtin Library Quarterly* 46:3 (1983), pp.237–69.
Kronenfeld, Judy, *King Lear and the Naked Truth: Rethinking the Language of Religion and Resistance* (Durham and London, 1998).
Krontiris, Tina, *Oppositional Voices: Women as Writers and Translators of Literature in the English Renaissance* (London and New York, 1992).
Lacey, Andrew, *The Cult of King Charles the Martyr* (London, 2003).
Lamont, William, *Godly Rule: Politics and Religion 1603–1660* (London, 1969).
Lamont, William, *Marginal Prynne* (London, 1963).
Landes, Joan B., *Women and the Public Sphere in the Age of the French Revolution* (New York, 1988).
Lawson, Sarah, 'From Latin Pun to English Puzzle: An Elizabethan Translation Problem', *The Sixteenth Century Journal* 9 (1978), pp. 23–41.
Leverenz, David, *The Language of Puritan Feeling* (New Jersey, 1980).
Lieb, Michael, and Shawcross, John T. (eds.), *Achievements of the Left Hand: Essays on the Prose of John Milton* (Amherst, 1974).
Lieb, Michael, 'Milton's *Of Reformation* and the Dynamics of Controversy', in Lieb and Shawcross (eds.), *Achievements of the Left Hand: Essays on the Prose of John Milton* (Amherst, 1974), pp. 58–83.
Lindley, David (ed.), *The Politics of the Stuart Court Masque* (Manchester, 1984).
Loewenstein, David, 'The Kingdom Within: Radical Religious Culture and the Politics of *Paradise Regained*', *Literature and History* 3:2 (1994), pp. 63–89.
Loewenstein, Jospeh L., 'Legal Proofs and Corrected Readings: Press Agency and the New Bibliography', in D. L. Miller and Harold Weber (eds.), *The Production of English Renaissance Culture* (Ithaca, 1994), pp. 93–122.
Love, Harold, *Scribal Publication in Seventeenth-Century England* (Oxford, 1993).
Lovell, Terry, 'Resisting With Authority: Historical Specificity, Agency and the Performative Self', *Theory, Culture and Society* 20:1 (2003), pp. 1–17.
Luckyj, Christina, '"*A Moving Rhetoricke*": Gender and Silence in Early Modern England' (Manchester and New York, 2002).
Ludlow, Dorothy P., 'Shaking Patriarchy's Foundations: Sectarian Women in England, 1641–1700', in R. L. Greaves (ed.), *Triumph Over Silence: Women in Protestant History* (Westport, CT, 1985), pp. 93–123.
MacDonald, Isabel, *Elizabeth Alkin: A Florence Nightingale of the Commonwealth* (Keighley, 1935).
Mack, Phyllis, *Visionary Women: Ecstatic Prophecy in Seventeenth-Century England* (Berkeley and Los Angeles, 1992).
MacLeod, Arlene Elowe, 'Hegemonic Relations and Gender Resistance: The New Veiling as Accommodating Protest in Cairo', *Signs* 17:3 (1992), pp. 533–57.

Maguire, Nancy Klein, 'The Theatrical Mask/Masque of Politics: The Case of Charles I', *Journal of British Studies* 28 (1989), pp. 1–22.

Mahoney, M., 'Presbyterianism in the City of London, 1645–1647', *Historical Journal* 22 (1979), pp. 93–114.

Manwaring, G. E., 'Parliament Joan: The Florence Nightingale of the Commonwealth', *The United Service Magazine* 57 (1918), pp. 301–310.

Marotti, Arthur F., *Manuscript, Print, and the English Renaissance Lyric* (Ithaca, 1995).

Marotti, Arthur F. and Bristol, Michael D. (eds.), *Print, Manuscript, Performance: The Changing Relations of Media in Early Modern England* (Columbus, 2000).

Marshall, Alan, *Intelligence and Espionage in the Reign of Charles II, 1660–1685* (Cambridge, 1994).

Marshall, Cynthia, *The Shattering of the Self: Violence, Subjectivity and Early Modern Texts* (Baltimore and London, 2002).

Marx, Steven, 'The Prophet Disarmed: Milton and the Quakers', *SEL* 32 (1992), pp. 111–28.

Matar, N. I., *Peter Sterry: Selected Writings* (New York, 1994).

Matar, N. I., '"Oyle of Joy": The Early Prose of Peter Sterry', *Philosophy Quarterly* 71:1 (1992), pp. 31–46.

Matar, N. I., 'Peter Sterry and the Ranters', *Notes and Queries* 29 227: 6 (1982), pp. 504–506.

Matchinske, Megan, *Writing, Gender, and the State in Early Modern England: Identity Formation and the Female Subject* (Cambridge, 1998).

Mayfield, Noel Henning, *Puritans and Regicide: Presbyterian and Independent Differences Over the Trial and Execution of Charles (I) Stuart* (London, 1988).

McArthur, Elen A., 'Women Petitioners and the Long Parliament', *English Historical Review* 24 (1909), pp. 698–709.

McCabe, Richard, 'The Form and Methods of Milton's *Animadversions Upon the Remonstrants Defence Against Smectymnuus*', *English Language Notes* 18:4 (1981), pp. 266–72.

McDowell, Paula, *The Women of Grub Street: Press, Politics, and Gender in the London Literary Marketplace 1678–1730* (Oxford, 1998).

McEntee, Ann Marie, '"The (Un) Civill-Sisterhood of Oranges and Lemons": Female Petitioners and Demonstrators, 1642–1653', in James Holstun (ed.), *Pamphlet Wars: Prose in the English Revolution* (London, 1992), pp. 92–112.

McGregor, J. F. and Reay, B. (eds.), *Radical Religion in the English Revolution* (Oxford, 1986).

Mckenzie, D. F., *Stationer's Company Apprentices, 1605–1640* (Charlottesville, 1961).

McNay, Lois, 'Agency, Anticipation and Indeterminacy in Feminist Theory', *Feminist Theory* 4:2 (2003), pp. 139–48.

McNay, Lois, *Gender and Agency: Reconfiguring the Subject in Feminist and Social Theory* (Cambridge, 2000).

McNay, Lois, 'Subject, Psyche and Agency: The Work of Judith Butler', in V. Bell (ed.), *Performativity and Belonging* (London, 1999), pp. 175–94.

Mendelson, Sara Heller, *The Mental World of Stuart Women* (Brighton, 1987).

Mendelson, Sara, and Crawford, Patricia, *Women in Early Modern England 1550–1720* (Oxford, 1998).

Mendle, Michael, 'News and the Pamphlet Culture of Mid Seventeenth-Century England', in Brendan Dooley and Sabrina A. Baron (eds.), *The Politics of Information in Early Modern Europe* (London and New York, 2001), pp. 57–79.

Mendle, Michael, 'Preserving the Ephemeral: Reading, Collecting, and the Pamphlet Culture of Seventeenth-Century England', in Anderson and Sauer (eds.), *Books and Reading in Early Modern England*, pp. 201–216.

Miles, Margaret R., *Carnal Knowing: Female Nakedness and Religious Meaning in the Christian West* (Boston, 1989).

Miller, Nancy K., *Subject to Change: Reading Feminist Writing* (New York, 1988).

Milton, Anthony, *Catholic and Reformed: The Roman and Protestant Churches in English Protestant Thought 1600–1640* (Cambridge, 1995).

Milton, Anthony, '"The Unchanged Peacemaker"? John Dury and the politics of irenicism in England, 1628–1643', in M. Greengrass, M. Leslie and T. Raylor (eds.), *Samuel Hartlib and Universal Reformation: Studies in Intellectual Communication* (Cambridge, 1994), pp. 95–117.

Montrose, Louis, '"Shaping Fantasies": Configurations of Gender and Power in Elizabethan Culture' *Representations* 1:2 (1983), pp. 61–94.

Morrill, John (ed.), *Revolution and Restoration: England in the 1650s* (London, 1992).

Morrill, John, *The Revolt of the Provinces: Conservatives and Radicals in the English Civil War, 1630–1650* (London and New York, 1976).

Morrill, John and Walter, John, 'Order and disorder in the English Revolution' in Richard Cust and Ann Hughes (eds.), *The English Civil War* (London, 1997), pp. 310–40.

Morson, Gary Saul, and Emerson, Caryl, *Mikhail Bakhtin: Creation of a Prosaics* (Stanford, 1990).

Morton, A. L., *The World of the Ranters: Religious Radicalism in the English Revolution* (London, 1970).

Muddiman, J. G., *The Trial of Charles the First* (Edinburgh and London, 1928).

Muddiman, J. G., 'Henry Walker, Journalist of the Commonwealth', *The Nineteenth Century* (March, 1908), pp. 454–64.

Neill, Michael, *Issues of Death: Mortality and Identity in the English Renaissance* (Oxford, 1997).

Nelson, Carolyn, and Seccombe, Matthew, *British Newspapers and Periodicals: A Short Title Catalogue* (New York, 1987).

Nevitt, Marcus, 'John Selden Among the Quakers', in Erica Sheen and Lorna Hutson (eds.), *Literature, Politics and Law in Renaissance England* (London, 2005), pp. 189–208.

Nevitt, Marcus, 'Elizabeth Poole Writes the Regicide', *Women's Writing* 9:1 (2002), pp. 233–48.

Nevitt, Marcus, 'Women in the Business of Revolutionary News: Elizabeth Alkin, Parliament Joan and the Commonwealth Newsbook', in Joad Raymond (ed.), *News, Newspapers and Society in Early Modern Britain* (London, 1999), pp. 84–108.

Nevitt, Marcus, '"Blessed, Self-Denying, Lamb-Like"? The Fifth Monarchist Women', *Critical Survey* 11:1 (1999), pp. 83–97.

Newman, Jay, *Foundations of Religious Tolerance* (Toronto, 1982).

Ng, Su Fang, 'Marriage and Discipline: The Place of Women in Early Quaker Controversies', *The Seventeenth Century* 18:1 (2003), pp. 113–40.

Norbrook, David, *Poetry and Politics in the English Renaissance*, rev. edn (Oxford, 2003).

Norbrook, David, *Writing the English Republic: Poetry, Rhetoric and Politics, 1627–1660* (Cambridge, 1999).

Norbrook, David, '*Areopagitica*, Censorship, and the Early Modern Public Sphere', in Richard Burt (ed.), *The Administration of Aesthetics: Censorship, Political Criticism and the Public Sphere*, Cultural Politics, vol. 7 (Minneapolis and London, 1994), pp. 3–33.

Nuttall, Geoffrey F., *Visible Saints: The Congregational Way 1640–1660* (Oxford, 1957).

Nutall, Geoffrey F., *The Holy Spirit in Puritan Faith and Experience* (Oxford, 1946).

Okin, Susan Moller, *Women in Western Political Thought* (Princeton, 1979).

Orgel, Stephen, *Impersonations: The performance of gender in Shakespeare's England* (Cambridge, 1996).

Partridge, Robert B., *'O Horrable Murder': The Trial, Execution and Burial of Charles I* (London, 1998).

Pateman, Carol, *The Sexual Contract* (Cambridge, 1989).

Patrides, C. A., *Premises and Motifs in Renaissance Thought and Literature* (Princeton, 1982).

Patton, Brian, 'The women are revolting? Women's activism and popular satire in the English Revolution', *Journal of Medieval and Renaissance Studies* 23:1 (1993), pp. 69–88.

Paul, Robert S., *The Assembly of the Lord: Politics and Religion in the Westminster Assembly and the 'Grand Debate'* (Edinburgh, 1985).

Peacey, Jason, *The Regicides and the Execution of Charles I* (London, 2001).

Pearl, V., 'London's counter-revolution', in G. E. Aylmer (ed.), *The Interregnum: The Quest for Settlement* (London, 1972), pp. 29–56.

Pincus, Stephen, '"Coffee Politicians Does Create": Coffeehouses and Restoration Political Culture", *Journal of Modern History* 67 (1995), pp. 807–34.

Pinto, Vivian de Sola, *Peter Sterry: Platonist and Puritan, 1613–1672* (Cambridge, 1934).

Plomer, H. R., *A Dictionary of the Booksellers and Printers Who Were at Work in England, Scotland and Ireland from 1641–1667* (London, 1907).

Plowden, Alison, *Women All on Fire: The Women of the English Civil War* (Stroud, 1998).

Pocock, J. G. A., *The Ancient Constitution and the Feudal Law* (Cambridge and New York, 1987).

Poole, Kristen, *Radical Religion From Shakespeare to Milton* (Cambridge, 2000).

Pooley, Roger, *English Prose of the Seventeenth Century, 1590–1700* (London, 1992).

Popkin, Jeremy D., *Media and Revolution: Comparative Perspectives* (Kentucky, 1995).

Potter, Lois, 'The royal martyr in the Restoration', in T. N. Corns (ed.), *The Royal Image*, pp. 264–87.

Potter, Lois, *Secret Rites and Secret Writing: Royalist Literature, 1641–1660* (Cambridge, 1989).

Potts Brown, E. and Mosher Stuard, S. (eds.), *Witnesses for Change: Quaker Women Over Three Centuries* (New Brunswick and London, 1989).

Prosser, Jay, *Second Skins: The Body Narratives of Transexuality* (New York, 1998).

Purkiss, Diane, 'Material Girls: The Seventeenth-Century Woman Debate', in Brant and Purkiss (eds.), *Women, Texts and Histories 1575–1760* (London and New York, 1992), pp. 69–101.

Questier, Michael C., *Coversion, Politics and Religion in England, 1580–1625* (Cambridge, 1996).

Raymond, Joad, *Pamphlets and Pamphleteering in Early Modern Britain* (Cambridge, 2003).

Raymond, Joad (ed.), *News, Newspapers and Society in Early Modern Britain* (London, 1999).

Raymond, Joad, *The Invention of the Newspaper: English Newsbooks 1641–1649* (Oxford, 1996).

Raymond, Joad, 'The Daily Muse; or, Seventeenth-Century Poets Read the News', *The Seventeenth Century* (Spring, 1996) pp. 189–218.

Raymond, Joad, (ed.), *Making the News: An Anthology of the Newsbooks of Revolutionary England 1641–1660* (Moreton-in-Marsh, 1993).

Reay, Barry, *Popular Cultures in England, 1550–1750* (London, 1998).

Reay, Barry, *Popular Culture in Seventeenth-Century England* (London, 1985).

Reay, Barry, 'Quaker Opposition to Tithes 1652–1660', *Past & Present* 83 (1980), pp. 98–120.

Rice, Colin, *Ungodly Delights: Puritan Opposition to the Theatre, 1576–1633* (Alessandria, 1997).

Roots, I. (ed.), *Cromwell: A Profile* (London, 1973).

Rosenblatt, Jason P., *Torah and Law in Paradise Lost* (Princeton, 1994).

Rowse, A. L., *Four Caroline Portraits: Thomas Hobbes, Henry Marten, Hugh Peters, John Selden* (London, 1993).

Rupp, Gordon et al., *Luther and Erasmus: Free Will and Salvation* (London, 1969).

Saussure, Ferdinand de, *Course de linguistique générale* (London, 1983).

Sawday, Jonathan, 'Self and Selfhood in the Seventeenth Century', in Roy Porter (ed.), *Rewriting the Self: Histories from the Renaissance to the Present* (London and New York, 1997), pp. 29–48.

Sawyer, J. K., *Printed Poison: Pamphlet Propaganda, Faction Politics and the Public Sphere in Early Seventeenth-Century France* (Los Angeles and Oxford, 1990).

Scarisbrick, Jack, *Henry VIII* (London, 1997).

Schochet, Gordon J., *Rights in Context: The Historical and Political Construction of Moral and Legal Entitlements* (Lawrence, KS, 1998).

Schochet, Gordon J., *Patriarchalism in Political Thought* (Oxford, 1975).

Schochet, G. J., Tatspaugh, P. E. and Brobeck, C. (eds.), *Law, Literature and the Settlement of Regimes* (Washington, DC, 1990).

Scott–Luckens, Carola, 'Propaganda or Marks of Grace? The Impact of the Reported Ordeals of Sarah Wight in Revolutionary London, 1647–52', *Women's Writing* 9:2 (2002), pp. 215–52.

Sellers, Susan (ed.), *Feminist Criticism Theory and Practice* (London and New York, 1991).

Shapiro, James, *Shakespeare and the Jews* (New York, 1996).

Sharpe, Kevin, *The Personal Rule of Charles I* (New Haven, 1992).

Sharpe, Kevin, *Sir Robert Cotton 1586–1631: History and Politics in Early Modern England* (Oxford, 1979).

Sharpe, Kevin and Lake, Peter (eds.), *Culture and Politics in Early Stuart England* (London, 1994).

Sharpe, Kevin and Zwicker, Steven N. (eds.), *Refiguring Revolutions: Aesthetics and Politics from the English Revolution to the Romantic Revolution* (Berkeley and London, 1998).

Sharpe Kevin and Zwicker, Steven N. (eds.), *Politics of Discourse: The Literature and History of Seventeenth-Century England* (Berkeley, 1987).

Shaw, W. A., *A history of the English church during the civil wars* Shaw, *and under the commonwealth* (London, 1890).

Sheils, W. J. (ed.), *Persecution and Toleration: Papers Read at the Twenty-Second Summer Meeting and the Twenty-Third Winter Meeting of the Ecclesiastical History Society* (Oxford, 1984).

Shevelow, Kathryn, *Women and Print Culture: The Construction of Femininity in the Early Periodical* (London and New York, 1989).

Shoemaker, Robert S., *Gender in English Society, 1650–1850* (London and New York, 1998).

Shuger, Debora Kuller, *Habits of Thought in the English Renaissance: Religion, Politics and the Dominant Culture* (Berkeley and Oxford, 1990).

Sirluck, Ernest, '*To Your Tents, O Israel*: A Lost Pamphlet', *Huntingdon Library Quarterly*, 19 (1955–56), pp. 301–305.

Skerpan, Elizabeth, *The Rhetoric of Politics in the English Revolution 1642–1660* (Columbia, MO, 1992).

Skerpan, Elizabeth, 'Writers-Languages-Communities: Radical Pamphleteers and Legal Discourse in the English Revolution', *Explorations in Renaissance Culture* (Fall 1990), pp. 37–56.

Smith, Hilda L., *All Men and Both Sexes: Gender, Politics, and the False Universal in England 1640–1832* (Philadelphia, 2002).

Smith, Hilda L. (ed.), *Women Writers and the Early Modern British Political Tradition* (Cambridge, 1998).

Smith, Hilda L., 'Women, intellect and politics: their intersection in seventeenth-century England', in idem., (ed.), *Women Writers and the Early Modern British Political Tradition*, pp. 1–14.

Smith, Hilda L. and Cardinabe, Susan (eds.), *Women and the Literature of the Seventeenth Century: An Annotated Bibliography Based on Wing's Short Title Catalogue* (New York, 1990).

Smith, Joseph, *A Descriptive Catalogue of Friends Books, or Books Written by Members of the Society of Friends, commonly called Quakers*, 3 vols (London, 1867–1893).

Smith, Nigel, *Literature and Revolution in England 1640–1660* (London and New Haven, 1994).

Smith, Nigel, *Perfection Proclaimed: Language and Literature in English Radical Religion 1640–1660* (Oxford, 1989).

Smith, Nigel, 'Richard Overton's Marpriest Tracts: Towards a History of Leveller Style' *Prose Studies*, 9 (1986), pp. 39–66.

Smith, Nigel, *A Collection of Ranter Writings* (London, 1983).

Staveley, Keith, *The Politics of Milton's Prose Style* (New Haven and London, 1975).

Staves, Susan, *Players' Scepters: Fictions of Authority in the Restoration* (Lincoln and London, 1979).

Sturge, C., *Cuthbert Tunstall* (London, 1938).

Summers, Claude J. and Pebworth, Ted-Larry (eds.), *The English Civil Wars in the English Literary Imagination* (Columbia and London, 1999).

Summers, Claude J. and Pebworth, Ted-Larry (eds.), *Representing Women in Renaissance England* (Columbia and London, 1997).

Taft, Barbara, 'Communications: The Council of Officers' *Agreement of the People*, 1648/9', *The Historical Journal*, 28:1 (1985), pp. 169–85.

Thomas, Keith, *Religion and the Decline of Magic: Studies in Popular Beliefs in Sixteenth-and Seventeenth-Century England* (Harmondsworth, 1971).

Thomas, Keith, *Sir John Berkenhead, 1617–1679: A Royalist Career in Politics and Polemics* (Oxford, 1969).

Thomas, Keith, 'Women and the Civil War Sects', *Past & Present* 13 (1958), pp. 42–62.

Thum, Maureen, 'Milton's Diatribal Voice: The Integration and Transformation of a Generic Paradigm in *Animadversions*', *Milton Studies* 30 (1993), pp. 3–25.

Tillyard, P. D. (ed. and trans.), *Milton: Private Correspondence and Academic Exercises* (Cambridge, 1932).

Tite, C. G. C., *The Panizzi Lectures: The Manuscript Library of Sir Robert Cotton* (London, 1994).

Todd, Margo (ed.), *Reformation to Revolution: Politics and Religion in Early Modern England* (London and New York, 1995).

Trevett, Christine, *Women and Quakerism in the Seventeenth Century* (York, 1991).

Trubowitz, Rachel, 'Female Preachers and Male Wives', in James Holstun (ed.), *Pamphlet Wars*, pp. 112–33.

Tuck, Richard, *Natural Rights Theories: Their Origin and Development* (Cambridge and New York, 1993).

Tuck, Richard, *Philosophy and Government 1572–1651* (Cambridge, 1993).

Tyacke, N. (ed.), *England's Long Reformation 1500–1800* (London and Bristol, 1998).

Underdown, David, *A Freeborn People: Politics and the Nation in Seventeenth-Century England* (Oxford, 1996).

Underdown, David, *Revel, Riot and Rebellion: Popular Politics and Culture in England, 1603–1660* (Oxford, 1985).

Underdown, David, 'The Taming of the Scold: The Enforcement of Patriarchal Authority in Early Modern England', in A. Fletcher and J. Stephenson (eds.), *Order and Disorder in Early Modern England* (Cambridge, 1985), pp. 116–36.

Underdown, David, *Pride's Purge: Politics in the Puritan Revolution* (London, 1971).

Vann, R. T., 'Friends' Sufferings Collected and Recollected', *Quaker History* 61:1 (1972), pp. 24–35.

Vice, Sue, *Introducing Bakhtin* (Manchester and New York, 1997).

Waddington, John, *Congregational History, 1567–1700 In Relation to Contemporaneous Events and the Conflict for Freedom, Purity and Independence* (London, 1874).

Walker, David, 'Thomas Goodwin and the Debate on Church Government', *The Journal of Ecclesiastical History* 34:1 (1983), pp. 85–99.

Wall, Wendy, *The Imprint of Gender: Authorship and Publication in the English Renaissance* (Ithaca and London, 1993).

Wallis, Amy E., 'Anthony Pearson (1626–1666)' *Journal of the Friends Historical Society* 51:2 (1966), pp 77–95.

Walzer, Michael, *The Revolution of the Saints: A Study in the Origins of Radical Politics* (London, 1966).

Watt, Diane, *Secretaries of God: Women Prophets in Late Medieval and Early Modern England* (Woodbridge, 1997).

West, Michael, 'Spenser and the Renaissance Ideal of Christian Heroism', *PMLA* 88:5 (1973), pp. 1013–32.

Wilcox, Catherine M., *Theology and Women's Ministry in Seventeenth-Century English Quakerism* (Lampeter, 1995).

Wilcox, Helen, *Women and Literature in Britain 1500–1700* (Cambridge, 1996).

Wilding, Michael, *Dragon's Teeth: Literature in the English Revolution* (Oxford, 1987).

Williams, E. M., 'Women Preachers in the Civil War', *The Journal of Modern History* 1 (1929), pp. 561–9.

Wilson, John, *Fairfax: A Life of Thomas, Lord Fairfax, Captain-General of All the Parliament's forces in the English Civil War, Creator and Commander of the New Model Army* (London, 1985).

Wiseman, Susan, 'Margaret Cavendish Among the Prophets: Performance Ideologies and Gender in and after the English Civil War', *Women's Writing* 6:1 (1999), pp. 95–112.

Wiseman, Susan, 'Pamphlet Plays in the Civil War News Market: Genre, Politics, and "Context"', in Raymond (ed.), *News, Newspapers and Society*, pp. 66–83.

Wiseman, Susan, *Drama and Politics in the English Civil War* (Cambridge, 1998).

Wiseman, Susan, 'Read Within: Gender, Cultural Difference and Quaker Women's Travel Narratives', in Kate Chedgzoy, Melanie Hansen and Susan Trill (eds.), *Voicing Women*, pp. 153–71.

Wiseman, Susan, 'Unsilent Instruments and the Devil's Cushions: Authority in Seventeenth-Century Women's Prophetic Discourse', in Isobel Armstrong (ed.), *New Feminist Discourses: Essays in Literature, Criticism and Theory* (London, 1992), pp. 176–96.

Woolrych, Austin, *Britain in Revolution, 1625–1660* (Oxford, 2002).

Woolrych, Austin, *Soldiers and Statesmen: The General Council of the Army and Its Debates 1647/8* (Oxford, 1987).

Woolrych, Austin, *Commonwealth to Protectorate* (Oxford, 1982).

Wootton, David, *Republicanism, Liberty and Commercial Society, 1649–1776* (Stanford, 1994).

Wootton, David, 'Leveller Democracy and the Puritan Revolution' in J. H. Burns and M. Goldie (eds.), *The Cambridge History of Political Thought 1450–1700* (Cambridge, 1991), pp. 412–42.

Wootton, David, *Divine Right and Democracy: An Anthology of Poltical Writing in Stuart England* (Harmondsworth, 1986).

Worden, A. B., 'Marchamont Nedham and the Beginnings of English Republicanism, 1649–1656', in David Wooton (ed.), *Republicanism, Liberty and Commercial Society, 1649–1776* (Stanford, 1994), pp. 45–81.

Worden, A. B., 'Literature and Political Censorship in Early Modern England', in A. C. Duke and C. A. Tamse (eds.), *Too Mighty to Be Free: Censorship and the Press in Britain and the Netherlands* (Zutphen, 1987) pp. 45–62.

Worden, A. B., 'Toleration and the Cromwellian Protectorate' in W. J. Sheils (ed.), *Persecution and Toleration: Papers Read at the Twenty-Second Summer Meeting and the Twenty-Third Winter Meeting of the Ecclesiastical History Society* (Oxford, 1984), pp. 199–235.

Wright, C. J. (ed.), *Sir Robert Cotton as Collector: Essays on an Early Stuart Courtier and his Legacy* (London, 1997).

Young Kunze, Bonnelyn, *Margaret Fell and the Rise of Quakerism* (London, 1994).

Zakai, Avihu, 'Religious Toleration and its Enemies: The Independent Divines and the Issue of Toleration during the English Civil War', *Albion* 21:1 (Spring, 1989), pp. 1–33.

Zaret, David, *Origins of Democratic Culture: Printing, Petitions, and the Public Sphere in Early-Modern England* (Princeton, 2000).

Ziskind, Jonathan R. (trans. and ed.), *John Selden on Jewish Marriage Law: The Uxor Hebraica* (London, 1991).

Index